It Pays to Talk

It Pays to Talk

How to Have the Essential Conversations

with Your Family About

Money and Investing

Carrie Schwab-Pomerantz and
Charles R. Schwab

THREE RIVERS PRESS • NEW YORK

Published by Three Rivers Press, New York, New York.
Member of the Crown Publishing Group, a division of Random House, Inc.
www.crownpublishing.com

THREE RIVERS PRESS and the Tugboat design are
registered trademarks of Random House, Inc.

Originally published in hardcover by Crown Business, New York, New York, in 2002.

Printed in the United States of America

Design by Debbie Glasserman

Library of Congress Cataloging-in-Publication Data
Schwab-Pomerantz, Carrie.
It pays to talk: how to have the essential conversations
with your family about money and investing / Carrie Schwab-Pomerantz
and Charles R. Schwab.—1st ed.
Includes bibliographical references and index.
1. Finance, Personal.   2. Investments.   I. Schwab, Charles.   II. Title.
HG179.S3346   2003
332.024'01—dc21   2002005994

ISBN 1-4000-4960-1

10 9 8 7 6 5

First Paperback Edition

To families who already talk about money . . .
and to those who are about to.

Acknowledgments

This book was a true team effort. At the helm, Joanne Cuthbertson guided its creation from start to finish, imparting her special insights and expertise. Linden Gross helped articulate our message and put it on paper. As we worked together month after month, we not only gathered the information you see on these pages, but we also created a personal bond that helped shape the spirit of this book.

Special thanks to the talented Bo Caldwell, who once again captured the essence of our philosophy. We are also indebted to the generous support of the Schwab Center for Investment Research. Thank you Mark Riepe, Darryl Forman, Jim Peterson, Bryan Olson, Rande Spiegelman, Leslie Gent, and Robin Vroom. We also want to thank Schwab employees Rene Kim, Leslie Eggerling, Jim Wilroy, Colita Ellis, Leila Bost, and Stephanie Becker for their wisdom and guidance, as well as Mike Ferguson, our super agent, Gail Ross, and our top-notch editor, Annik La Farge. And thank you to Nicole Young, whose vision inspired us to pursue this topic.

And finally, we could not have written this book without the contributions of the scores of colleagues, clients, friends, and family members who not only shared their personal stories but agreed to allow us to share these experiences with you. We are touched by their candor and generosity.

Carrie Schwab-Pomerantz
Charles R. Schwab

Contents

It Pays to Talk

Prologue

To our readers:

We have a question for you: Does your family talk about money? Think about it. Does money come up in your daily conversations? Do your kids understand your money values? Do you and your mate agree on how you spend and invest your money? Do you know if your parents are financially secure?

All of these are tough issues that you may not have addressed. For if you and your loved ones are at all typical, chances are that while you may read the business section of the newspaper and talk about the stock market, you have a harder time when the topic is personal.

There is no question that *really* talking about money—and by that we mean having candid personal conversations—isn't easy. In fact, we seem to talk about politics and religion more easily than we talk about our money. And that's saying something!

To an extent, there's a reason for this awkwardness: Personal finances are emotionally charged. Money and wealth reflect our value systems and sense of self-worth, so the moment the subject is broached, the stakes rise. Couple that with years of socialization in the financial code of silence, and it's no wonder that the word about money is *mum*.

Most of us have grown up just accepting these money taboos. All that began to change for the two of us in the fall of 2000, when Carrie launched Schwab's Women's Investing Network, an educational program for women. Our mission: to inspire women to increase their financial knowledge and to share that knowledge with others. First, however, we had to find out more about how we Americans feel about those finances we're so reluctant to discuss.

One of Carrie's first steps was to commission a Harris poll to study attitudes about money and investing. Not only did the poll reveal that 44% of women and 27% of men lack confidence in their investing skills, it also showed that most people attribute their discomfort to a lack of education and exposure growing up—in other words, to a lack of meaningful talk. At the same time, our investment consultants across the country began reporting similar findings. Their clients, both men and women, wanted to get their financial affairs in order but simply didn't know where to start. Clearly the need for open communication wasn't restricted to women. The sexes were very similar when it came to avoiding money-related conversations.

What's wrong with this picture? In our view a lot, which is why we wrote the book you are holding. If there is one message you take away from these pages, we want it to be an understanding of how crucial it is to have honest discussions about money and investing with those you care about.

Why? The fact is that if you don't talk to your family about money, chances are that no one else will. Our schools don't teach our kids to manage money, and for the most part neither do we, their parents. Our Harris poll showed that even though most parents think that they, not the schools, should be in charge of their children's financial education, in reality fewer than one-third have regular talks with their children about money.

Further, talking about money with your spouse or partner is one of the most important keys to a healthy, thriving partnership. Actual disagreements and unspoken differences in attitudes about money can damage a relationship in record time. We've seen it happen over and over again.

And if your aging parents can't rely on you, where can they go? If they happen to be at a point in their lives where they could use some financial assistance—whether that means simply a little guidance from you or actual financial support—our feeling is that helping them is not only a duty but a privilege.

The good news is that talking about money with your family doesn't have to be hard. It may feel awkward at first, but with a little effort it gets easier. Because feelings about money are both highly personal and highly individual, no one approach will fit every family. And every situation is different, so the way in which you handle these conversations will be as unique as you are.

But the payoff can be substantial. Talking about money can be very liberating and bring you closer to your family. We also feel that teaching someone to handle money and invest wisely is one of the most important things you can do. It's a skill we all need for our entire lives, and it is, in our experience, central to success. By broaching the subject and encouraging the conversation, you give those you care about, whether older or younger, whether related or not, a wonderful gift. Remember that expression *talk is cheap*? Well, it is our strong belief that when it comes to talking about money with your family, talk is priceless.

We've been in the investment business for over sixty years between the two of us. As a result, we can talk all day about asset allocation and investment strategies—and actually enjoy it. But when it comes to more personal family issues about money, the conversation gets ticklish. Even now we still often fall back on shoptalk—discussions about the market or a new service the company is offering—instead of dealing with more personal issues.

Clearly we don't have all the answers, at least not yet. We wrote this book not because we're experts on family communication but because we believe the topic is essential. We're father and daughter and working parents who have made talking to our spouses, parents, and kids about finances a priority. Our promise to you is that this book will point the way, while introducing you to the facts and figures you'll need to feed the dialogue.

Anyone—including you and your loved ones—can learn how to

manage his or her money effectively. You just have to make it a priority. Our goal is to turn all adults in the country into confident investors who use their money to support their dreams and the dreams of their families.

It is our intent, and our hope, to give you enough in these pages to take on the subject with confidence. The primary text is written by Carrie, with Chuck contributing his "Two Cents" throughout. In addition to getting you up to speed on money-related basics—from investing to retirement planning to estate planning—we'll give you tips and insights that will get your crucial conversations started. And then it's up to you. Remember: This won't happen overnight. It's a process and a journey, not a single event.

One final thought before we begin. In the recent past we have experienced unprecedented world events and extreme stock-market volatility. If there is one lesson that we have learned from these times, it is the value of reaching out to our loved ones. In fact, we believe strongly that during uncertain times we need to talk to each other more than ever. So just take the first step, even if it's a ten-minute conversation over lunch. Once you have that first conversation, which is often the hardest, you're on your way. We applaud your efforts, and we wish you the greatest success.

Carrie Schwab-Pomerantz
Charles R. Schwab

1

Starting the Conversation

When Pete, a longtime colleague of ours, married his wife, Eleanor, in 1973, it would have been safe to assume that she, being a banker, would handle the finances while he, then a schoolteacher, would take a backseat. Then their son was born with a disability, and the couple decided that Eleanor should quit her job and stay home with him. Once Pete, who had returned to graduate school and obtained his MBA, became the only breadwinner, he also inherited the financial-decision-maker role.

At the same time Pete—a generous, jovial, and articulate man—turned into quite the spender, thinking nothing of buying an expensive suit that he'd wear only two or three times. To compensate for his champagne taste in clothes, Eleanor, when she shopped at all, would do so at discount stores (a detail she kept from Pete, who would have been horrified). Sure, her husband's income had shot up, but so had his appetite for luxuries, including high-priced cars.

"We moved to California from New York, and I saw everyone driving around in BMWs," explains Pete with a self-deprecating laugh and the kind of regret that only hindsight can bring. "I thought that must be the state car, so I went out and bought one." Over the next fifteen years he bought another and another and another, just as soon as the mileage on the "old" car passed twenty thousand—or a newer model captured his fancy. Despite hefty sports-car price tags, he never thought to consult his wife about those—or any other—purchases.

That attitude, combined with an overall lack of communication, almost cost Pete his marriage. Since the couple never discussed money, let alone a savings or an investment strategy, Pete never knew how increasingly resentful his highly educated wife, who had spent ten years in the banking industry, was becoming about her lack of participation in the family finances or Pete's spending decisions.

Pete and Eleanor may have avoided facing their issues, but they couldn't escape the downfall of their marriage. After a separation of several months, the couple decided that divorce was inevitable, and together they headed to a financial planner to figure out how to split their assets.

But unlike so many similar stories, this one has a happy ending. "You guys obviously care about and love each other," the financial planner observed one afternoon after numerous joint meetings. "What are you doing getting a divorce?" Thus prompted, Pete and Eleanor asked themselves the same question and subsequently decided to try to work out their differences. After months of marriage counseling and a lot of hard work, Pete and Eleanor learned how to communicate with each other about money and everything else. They identified what was important to them as individuals and as a couple.

The upshot? At forty-seven, Pete quit his job to devote himself full time to the nonprofit international health-related causes about which he's passionate. Investments they've made together now finance their lifestyle, one in which they agree on each and every sizable purchase as a team. "Though I'm ashamed of my past behavior, I'm also proud of our courage to stick it out," says Pete. "It's so much easier to walk away from very difficult issues than to confront them head-on. I am the better—and we are the stronger—for it."

Pete and Eleanor's new financial policies and procedures, along with their ongoing discussions about values and priorities, led to their recently building a dream house in Sun Valley, Idaho. "In almost thirty years of marriage, this is the first major purchasing decision we ever made together," admits Pete.

In short, Pete and Eleanor now make a point of dealing with their life together—and their money—as equal partners. Once every three months they meet with their financial advisor to review their finances and make (or revise) their money decisions for the next six months. Then they go out to a nice restaurant and discuss their decisions and plans.

What better way to reaffirm your love for each other than to talk about the life you're living now and your dreams for the future?

The Emotional Side of Money

As Pete and Eleanor's story so vividly shows, talking about money can allow you to build the life you want. In fact, we believe that financial security begins with a conversation—whether between spouses, between a parent and a child, or between an adult and an aging parent.

But these conversations aren't easy, especially in the beginning. Most of us are used to chatting casually about the stock market or mortgage rates, but when it comes to candid, personal conversations about how much money we'll need for retirement or how we'll possibly be able to pay for our children's college educations, the talk is much tougher. In a wealthy country where millions of investors have money in the stock market, there is still a desperate shortage of honest, candid talk about how we should be planning for the future.

And unfortunately, as Pete and Eleanor's story also points out, not communicating about financial matters, from spending to investing to planning for the future, is an almost surefire way to undermine a relationship. So why, despite the obvious payoff and the equally obvious price of avoidance, do most people neither initiate nor participate in these essential family conversations about money? Because money is never just money, especially in the context of a family.

For starters, money is tied up with our deepest emotional needs (such as security, comfort, success, and confidence) and fears (such as failure, inadequacy, and poverty) as well as with our sense of self-worth and identity. And ultimately, it becomes a reflection of our relationships. "In the first part of our marriage, there were all these inequalities, and money was a huge unspoken one," says Pete. "Now it's more of an equal playing field."

Like it or not, even your parents' attitudes about money have likely influenced yours. If your father or mother always tried to save that little bit, you may have adopted the same fiscally restrained habits. Or like a pendulum, you may do the opposite now that you're an adult, refusing to let those money-saving tactics run your life. Either way, you're reacting to lessons learned at your parents' knees.

For example, I have a friend whose father used to drive her crazy with his penny-pinching habits: He phoned her only after five P.M. (he had one of those old-fashioned phone plans where the rates dropped at night), and he parked his car in a lot a mile away from where he was going if he could save a dollar. In response, as a young girl, my friend would call her dad whenever the urge struck, even if it was a mere ten minutes before the rates changed, partially to prove that her actions weren't being dictated by the chance to save a buck. Valuing time and convenience more than economy, she often took cabs instead of buses and paid a housekeeper for cleaning she could easily have done herself. Figuring that you only go around once, she routinely indulged in expensive wine and top-notch restaurants. Only lately, many years later, has she come to recognize how much all those indulgences compromised her ability to save for her future and the things that mattered more.

My colleague Tom's financial baggage also stems from his upbringing. Despite a steady income, his parents sometimes ran short of cash. Since Tom consistently held jobs as a kid—doing a paper route or umpiring Little League games—he usually had some cash on hand. "As a twelve- or thirteen-year-old, I was proud to always have a few hundred bucks," he recalls. "I remember my dad and mom borrowing from me a few times to buy groceries or go out to a movie. In those pre-ATM days, I was like their bank for short-term credit."

Not surprisingly, this situation made Tom quite resentful in the long run. Thirty years later those emotions continue to affect how he deals with finances and money-related communication, but not in a positive way. Even today Tom never talks to his parents about their financial position since it brings back uneasy memories. He and his wife don't talk very much about their financial decisions or long-term plans either. While Tom attributes a lot of this silence to juggling two careers and raising two children, he also admits that his early negative money associations may play a part in his current attitude.

THE COLOR OF MONEY

What does money represent to you and your loved ones? For some of you it means success. For others it may signify independence, freedom, security, or something else entirely. To find out, Dr. James Gottfurch, principal of Psychology of Money Consultants, a Los Angeles–based company, suggests in his workshops that you try and think of a single symbol that encapsulates how you feel about money. It could be anything from a soft, warm, furry bunny to a runaway train. One of my friends sees money as the sun, because of its ability to make things grow. (Actually, the sun is not a bad metaphor, as it can also burn you if not treated with a certain amount of respect and restraint.) This friend even surrounds herself with sun images, from a decorative tile in her kitchen to a copper and brass sculpture on her desk, to remind her of the positive role that money plays in her life. It's her way of staying focused on what she's trying to achieve and of keeping some of her more negative and self-defeating money attitudes at bay.

What you adopt as your money symbol may surprise you and may reveal attitudes about money that you didn't even know you had. Or not. Either way, comparing notes with those close to you, or even brainstorming about financial symbols together, might prove to be very insightful.

Sidestepping Common Behavioral Traps

Another downside of our silence about money is that we become even more likely to make financial decisions based on emotion rather than on logic or research. In *Why Smart People Make Big Money Mistakes* (Simon & Schuster, 1999), a terrific book that I recommend to all my friends and clients, journalist Gary Belsky and psychologist Thomas Gilovich summarize a new branch of economic research, called behavioral economics, that examines many of the most common traps that lead us to make poor money decisions.

Let me give you just a few examples. If you tend to treat your hard-earned income differently from the way you treat other money—say a tax refund or a lottery winning—you're guilty of what behavioral economists call mental accounting. This concept, developed by Richard Thaler of the University of Chicago, describes our tendency to categorize and value our money according to its source or how we spend it. Mental accounting can be dangerous, because in reality one dollar is worth just as much as the next. One hundred dollars that you get from a windfall will buy you just as much as one hundred dollars you've saved. Likewise, if you feel much freer spending money when you use a credit card than when you pay in hard cash, you are likely practicing a form of mental accounting.

There's also what the behaviorists call the "sunk-cost fallacy." If you're the type who continues to pour money into an old rattletrap, you should train and discipline yourself to think hard before you throw any more good money after bad. If you wouldn't want to buy the car today, knowing that it needs repairs, why would you want to waste money fixing it up just because you already own it?

As an investor, there are two other tendencies you should be aware of, neither of which will help your stock portfolio. If you let your emotions get the best of you, you may be prone to panic selling—or selling when an investment hits a low. As you'll see in Chapters 2 and 3, you are especially vulnerable to this panic if you take on more risk than is appropriate for your investment time frame or personality. At the other extreme, many investors fall victim to what the behaviorists call "loss aversion." This can manifest itself in many ways, including not selling a poor performer to avoid finalizing the loss. Not only can loss aversion cause you to lose even more money, it especially doesn't make sense in light of the fact that you can use your losses to offset your gains, thereby potentially reducing your tax bill.

And finally, you should be aware of what Belsky and Gilovich refer to as "number numbness," or the tendency to tune out when we are faced with numbers and math. Clearly this won't work to your advantage as an investor. Ironically, most of the math you deal with as an investor is simple and straightforward. But if you fail to appreciate the power of compound growth, or avoid evaluating a mutual fund on the basis of its expense ratio, just because numbers are involved, your overall portfolio return could suffer. It's as simple as that.

Once you understand these tendencies, it can be fascinating and instructive to sort through them. A word of caution, however. It can be a lot easier to identify these lapses in someone else than in yourself, so try not to get too critical too fast. We all have our own less-than-desirable financial proclivities. You'll need to be as willing to hear what your family and friends have to say about your habits as you'll want them to be once it's your turn. Though their comments may sound and feel critical, treat this conversation as a growing opportunity and avoid becoming defensive. Remember: Your goal is to open the lines of communication and strengthen your family and friendship ties—not to jeopardize them.

The First Step: What's Important to You?

You work hard for your money. It may seem obvious, but if your money is going to work hard for you and your family, you first have to come to terms with your priorities, then discuss those priorities with the people closest to you.

What we're talking about here are your most cherished values—things like family, love, security, independence, and philanthropy.

Although your values may evolve as you age, they define who you are. Think of values as the prism or filter through which you'll view all your life and money decisions.

Put another way, your values are what make you tick. They're not a reflection of how good or moral you are. They're not a reflection of your personal worth. If you're a homebody or you want to travel the world, that is your decision alone. No one can dictate your values; they're like your emotional DNA.

Can you list your values off the top of your head? Do you know what matters most to your mate, or to your children? In my experience, most people just haven't taken the time to discuss them—at least not on a regular basis.

When I was pregnant with my oldest child, my husband Gary and I would walk through Olmsted Park by our home in Atlanta every Sunday morning, throw the ball for our dog, and discuss our hopes for the future. What kind of life did we want? Where did we want to make that life? What did we aspire to career-wise, and how did those aspirations dovetail? What did we want for our son, and how would we raise him?

Although I tend to be more of a risk-taker than Gary, we've always agreed on our overriding values: that family comes first and that dollars and cents are just a means to an end. As a result, our conversations focused primarily on our long-term goals and the best ways to achieve them. In a way we were drawing our road map, complete with a rough timetable.

With the passage of time and increased demands of both career and family, those walks—and talks—have become less frequent. That's too bad, although probably not uncommon. Like us, I think most families feel they're giving their all just to keep up with every-day demands.

Unfortunately, though, the price we pay for *not* having those talks is a loss of the perspective that is so essential to our long-term happiness. If you value adventure and the most exciting place you've traveled in the last two years is the supermarket, then you may need to reevaluate how you're spending your money (to say nothing of your time). If you value being secure and debt-free yet every month you rack up another $2,500 on your credit cards, that's also a disconnect worth examining.

Without the perspective that your priorities provide, money is likely to slip through your fingers like water through a sieve, getting you no closer to your ultimate goals. That's why talking about money is so crucial: It allows you to restate and reconnect with your values. Any big life event such as marriage, a new child, starting or losing a job, divorce, or death of a spouse presents a natural opportunity to have a money chat with those close to you—whether it's to make sure you're still traveling down your path of choice or to alter your direction.

The Next Step: Identifying and Securing Your Dreams and Goals

Once you've identified your values, there are two more steps to take to build the life you want to lead: identifying your *dreams,* and establishing concrete financial *goals* so you can turn those dreams into reality.

Let me give you an example of how these pieces work together. A close friend of mine would love to own a vacation home in Lake Tahoe (her dream), where she and her family could get away from it all and just be together (one of her strongest values). To make that happen, she'll need a substantial amount of money for a down payment as well as extra money every month to cover the mortgage, taxes, and maintenance (her goal). Last year she took the first step by talking to her family about her dream. At first she wasn't sure that they would agree, but she received unanimous support. Buoyed by their enthusiasm, she then opened up a special investment account and started depositing whatever savings she could scrimp together. She also examined her personal expenses as well as her family's monthly bills to see where she could economize. That meant that she has had to refrain from buying herself a number of things she would have liked. But when she thinks about her family all together in that mountain home, she maintains her resolve. She envisions the hikes and the boat excursions they'll take. She imagines family meals, marathon Monopoly sessions in front of the fire, and golden toasted marshmallows during cookouts. And that's more important to her than just about anything she might covet at the moment.

Although my friend still has a long way to go before she and her family can afford to realize their dream, she's finally working toward it. What made the difference? Actively identifying a vision that supported one of her deepest values—spending time with her family— and then creating a plan of action that would get her there.

Do your spending choices and lifestyle support your values and visions? Far too often we wind up losing sight of the forest for the trees. We run to the store to pick up a single household item and end up walking out with a hundred dollars of impulse purchases, not one of which will help us live the life we really want. Why? Because we haven't made those visions a part of our consciousness.

A Financial Plan

Research reveals that when it comes to finances, most investors focus on their stock portfolios. They enjoy the strategy, the excitement, and the immediate results. Of course this tendency is completely understandable and not necessarily a bad thing—unless it comes at the expense of other important aspects of your financial life, such as your retirement plan, estate plan, tax strategy, college savings, and insurance needs.

I think of fiscal health much as I think of physical health. Like physical well-being, fiscal health depends on the strength of several interrelated parts. Just as you can't afford to ignore the condition of your heart, since that's what pumps the blood through your body, or your spiritual well-being, since that's what keeps you balanced, so too should you have a well-rounded approach to your money. Such an approach takes into account not just your investment portfolio but other aspects of your financial life as well.

One of the goals of this book is to demonstrate how all these pieces work together. Whether you decide to hire a financial planner or choose to work on your own, I encourage you to adopt this type of well-rounded holistic approach to your finances. Discussing your financial plan as a family will encourage you to explore each area. Even better, focusing your thoughts, organizing your paperwork, and then committing your plans to paper will enhance the likelihood that you will achieve the dreams and the financial goals you've articulated.

My goal and my father's is to help make your financial plan come to life so you may actually put it into effect. It's not enough to have a plan—no matter how beautifully detailed and bound—if it just sits on a shelf. You have to put it into action. So as you and your family begin to talk about your financial plan, think about money as a vehicle that can get you where you want to go. It doesn't drive you. You are behind the wheel, and the twists and turns you opt to take both shape and reflect the person you are. The only way to arrive at your destination is to know—and agree on—where you and your family are headed. There's no way around it. Getting where you want to go means talking about your values, your visions for the future, and the detailed plan of action you'll need to get there.

Chuck's Two Cents: Why Talk?

This book is about talking to your family about money, and in a way I think of the book itself as a conversation. It has certainly prompted a fair amount of conversation between Carrie and me, and in these pages we have tried to pass on to you what we've learned about the fine art of talking about money. In that vein, now and then throughout the book I'll add my two cents to the conversation.

I think it would be hard to overemphasize the importance of talking to your family about money. We feel it's essential for every family to be able to communicate about financial matters, and it's our goal to help you develop the tools to do that. That may sound easy enough, but I know from experience that it can be hard. Even in our family, where investing has been my career for more than forty years and Carrie's for more than twenty, we've found that talking about money can be difficult.

But as difficult as it may be, and as uncomfortable as you may feel, the fact is that talking about finances is crucial in close relationships. Talking about finances with your spouse can help lay the foundation for a solid marriage. Teaching your kids about handling money is one of the best things you can do for them, right up there with giving them a good education. And talking to elderly parents about their finances can be the greatest gift you can give them. You may get the valuable opportunity of helping to take care of the people who first took care of you.

So where do you start? Easy: You break the ice, just by bringing up the subject, so that you can get the conversation going. And that's where this book comes in: It will guide you in that conversation, whether you're talking to your parents, your kids, or your partner. We realize that no two families are alike and that, to an extent, each family will have to develop its own approach. But there is some common ground here, and in that spirit we've tried to pass on some guidelines that will help you find your way.

One more thing before you dig in. I'm a big believer in being forthright with people, and because of that I think it's important for you to know what distinguishes the investing philosophy set out in these pages from others. My investing philosophy is based on an unshakable faith in the American economy, specifically in its ability to continue to grow in perpetuity.

What's the basis for my belief? History, and the fact that time and time again we've seen our economy survive and grow. That doesn't mean we won't have bad days or down cycles. It doesn't mean we ignore the consequences of down markets. It means that, recognizing the risks, we endure those not-so-good times with the protection of certain time-tested investing approaches, such as adequate diversification and a sound asset allocation strategy. It means that we go forward with confidence in good times and bad.

Investing isn't about voodoo or luck or gambling. It's about the principles of entrepreneurship and incentives and rewards. It's about human capital and the concept of people working hard to improve their lives. Those very American qualities are the reasons for my confidence in our financial future. I firmly believe that we will absolutely *continue to improve, and I base my investing confidence and my entire investing strategy on the strength of the American economy.*

I've been an investor for more than forty years, and it's a subject I am passionate about, not only because I find it fascinating but because the reward of wise investing is that wonderful thing called freedom. Investing is ultimately about your future and about taking steps now to give you choices later on. And I see that as essential.

Come to Terms with Your Money Style and Money Strengths

There are probably as many money styles as there are fashion styles. Of course, this doesn't come as much of a surprise when you factor in the different influences that shape each of us. The irony, of course, is that when it comes to money-related tendencies, opposites frequently attract. Pete and Eleanor are a perfect example. So don't be surprised if you and your partner find each other diametrically opposed. Instead of sweeping those differences under the rug or fighting about them, try discussing them. Once you and your family have talked about your values—and started to articulate your dreams and goals—your next step is to examine more closely your feelings about money and decide how involved you want to be when managing your finances.

BEGINNERS, TAKE HEART

If the whole idea of dealing with money and making financial decisions makes you or your partner nervous, remember that you've both engaged in a lot of this money-related activity before—every time you've made a budget or comparison-shopped for a big-ticket item. You can do this, no matter how inadequate you're feeling right now.

> It's like learning to swim. Once you get the basics down—and your confidence up—it's really not that hard. And like swimming, knowing how to deal with your money is a critical survival skill—one that you can master. "After my divorce, I was terrified that I wasn't going to be able to take care of myself," says Lauren, a single mom in her forties who had no experience handling her personal finances. Her ex-husband had taken care of everything. It took years for her to get up to speed—but she finally managed. "I started investing for my retirement so late that I felt it would take a miracle for me not to have to work the rest of my life," she adds. "The miracle turned out to be me."

Your money style can be tracked on two continuums. First, you're either a spender or a saver, or you're a bit of both, which means you fall somewhere in between. I admit that I get a charge out of going shopping. Just ask my husband, Gary. "Like a runner's high, Carrie gets a shopper's high," he says with a smile. Still, my commitment to my family dictates that the money I spend never cuts into our budget for other things, our savings, our investments, our vacations, or anything else that's important. We save and invest as much as we can every month. That comes first, no matter what. So I'm definitely both a saver and a spender at heart.

It's necessary to balance those opposing tendencies when you are constantly confronted by the question "to buy or not to buy?" In Chapter 2 we talk more about how to spend your money so you wind up buying what you and your family really need, while not scrimping on investing. For now, whenever you're in doubt, just remember that keeping a long-range perspective about what's important to you and your family will usually steer you clear.

Second, in terms of investing, the continuum goes from being cautious at one end to being a risk-taker at the other end. If your stomach drops at the thought of a bad day in the stock market, then you naturally gravitate toward more cautious or conservative investments—which may or may not work to your best advantage. If, on the other hand, you believe that the opportunity for higher returns is worth the additional risk involved, then you would be classified as a more aggressive investor.

You may not fit exactly where you'd like on either of the saver/spender or cautious/risk-taker continuums. That's okay. Your first step is to simply identify where you are now, and later you can adjust your approach. Once you've read this book and have engaged your loved ones in dialogue, those positions may shift as a result of your newly articulated family priorities and newly acquired knowledge.

Just as we all have our own money style, each of us has strengths and weaknesses. You want to play to your strengths. Of course, most of you aren't starting this process from scratch, so you may have assumed responsibility for a number of financial chores in which you're not particularly interested, or even good at. By identifying your abilities—as well as your loved ones' abilities—and then adjusting who handles what, you can make the most of your strengths and shore up your weaknesses, even if it means enlisting outside help.

Ask yourself and your partner: Are you analytical? Do you love to crunch numbers and dig through corporate reports to figure out if you should invest in a particular company? Are you the sort who will stick with it and be consistent month to month, or do you tend to lose steam after the initial push?

Those answers should help you and your family determine how independent you want to be—or should be—when it comes to financial planning and investing. You may love the idea of doing it all on your own, but if an honest appraisal shows that at this point you lack the necessary knowledge, skill, or perseverance, you'll probably want to seek professional advice until you get up to speed. Of course, maybe you have what it takes but don't want to invest the hours. So you and your partner need to discuss just how much time and energy you've really got to spend on this issue (and whether that fits in with the values you outlined above) and chart out your approach accordingly. If your values include being together as a family as much as possible, that's going to affect a lot of other decisions, including how you choose to handle your finances.

Don't get me wrong. I'm definitely not advocating a hands-off approach. To the contrary—whether or not you choose to work with a financial advisor, you still need to be intimately involved in and fully aware of any and all financial decisions. But don't worry. By the end of this book, you'll have all the tools you need to do just that.

The Game Plan

So what now? It's time to figure out whether your spending and investing lines up with the values, dreams, and financial goals you've just identified. A good way to do this is by tracking your family's expenses for the next month. Save every bill and every receipt, even for a doughnut or a newspaper. At the end of the month, group those receipts and bills into categories and add up the totals so you can see exactly where your money went. (Computer software programs such as Quicken and Microsoft Money can help you track your finances, and if you don't use one of these programs, it might be worth considering.) If the numbers reflect your values and are helping you achieve your dreams and goals, that's great. If they don't, you'll want to make some adjustments. Maybe you can forgo the muffin and cappuccino every morning, thereby saving hundreds of dollars a year (and who knows how many calories). Or maybe you'll want to brown-bag your lunch, cut back on some of those premium cable stations, or buy one less pair of shoes a season.

You'll want to evaluate your investments in the same way. The question to always keep in mind is whether your choices support your values, dreams, and goals—in short, whether they support your current lifestyle as well as the lifestyle you'd like to achieve.

Once you've delineated what's important to you and your family, checked your spending, and started to invest, you'll want to review your progress periodically in light of any life or market changes, to make sure that your plan is still meeting your ever-changing needs. Equally important will be to make sure that those long-term dreams are still viable, as new goals often require a new game plan.

Chuck's Two Cents: On Building Your Financial House

Say you're building a house. Maybe it's your dream house, the home you've been thinking about for years. Because it's so important to you, you're involved in every stage of building. You meet with the architect and then the builder. You oversee everything that goes on, from the foundation and framing to the carpet and tile. You're there, from start to finish.

The same should go for investing. Think of your financial life as a house. It is, in a way, because you're relying on it to provide shelter in the future. By building your house, you're working toward that wonderful state called financial independence. Does it not make sense, then, to pay attention to it? You wouldn't take a hands-off approach if you were building a house—so why do it here? Simply put, in my view it is essential for every modern man and woman to take responsibility for—and to be in control of—his or her financial life. It's just common sense to me, part of being independent individuals who can take care of themselves. It's my belief that financial independence should be a goal for everyone.

There are two parts to taking financial responsibility. First, there's learning about investing and taking the necessary steps to become a savvy investor. If you're reading this book, chances are you're already doing that, and my hat is off to you. But if your attention to financial details has lagged, there's still time. Get involved today; just do something to take the first step. Think of that dream house again: you don't have to be the plumber and the electrician and the landscaper. You just have to know what you want to end up with and to then manage the building of that house.

The second part of taking responsibility is talking about the financial part of your life with your family. It doesn't have to be done all at once, and it doesn't have to be a major ordeal. But it does have to be done. Good communication about your financial situation with your spouse is one of the keys to a solid partnership. And teaching your kids about the value of money is as important as teaching them any other value, like integrity, honesty, and respect.

And the point of taking responsibility for your financial life? That wonderful thing we call financial independence, which simply means having enough to live on when you're no longer receiving a salary. It's all about choice, finally; it's about your future. And that, to me, is a great incentive: Paying attention today can lead to the future you choose—not the one that chooses you.

Chances are that you'll learn even more about yourself when you start exploring these issues. You'll undoubtedly also discover things you never knew about your spouse, your children, and your parents. Of course, old demons like sibling rivalries, former relationships, familial roles, and past behavioral patterns may also arise. On the other hand, who knows? Whether you're exploring your money compatibility or what you each really want in life, you may just find that talking about money is more fun and fulfilling than you think. Indeed, couple after couple has told me that talking about money is the best thing that's ever happened to their relationships.

Including Your Parent

No matter how far you're trying to stray from your old patterns or your parents' ways of handling things, most people find that they still want to talk to their parents about money. This may feel uncomfortable at first, especially since you may experience a bit of role reversal, where you feel more like the parent than the child. Still, this is really the only way to know how your parents are faring. Surprisingly, parents and children think very differently about the need that elderly parents will have for financial assistance. A 1997 study by Elderplan, a Brooklyn-based agency of the Metropolitan Jewish Health System, found that while 31% of the five hundred adult children they surveyed assumed they would eventually provide their parents with significant financial support, only 18% of their parents felt they'd need that support. Similarly, while 53% of those adult children figured that their parents would eventually move in with them, only 22% of the parents assumed the same. Although we don't have the data to settle this difference of opinion, another study conducted in Albany, New York, indicates that not only is help between generations generally reciprocal but in fact more financial and other help is generally given to the child, rather than vice versa, until the parent reaches about seventy-five years of age.

Of course, statistics aside, you'll want to make sure that your parents have enough to live on. You may have to consider how you and your parents will deal with your helping them should that become necessary. You'll also want to see that they've invested wisely, that they're set up for retirement, that they're properly insured, and that their estate is in order.

Even tougher is finding out whether your parents have considered the potential impact of health issues as they age. Although 67% of seniors haven't talked to their children about this, 95% of people polled do want to stipulate the type of life-sustaining care they receive, according to an AARP survey conducted in 2001. The problem? No one brings the subject up.

But that was then, and this book is now. We're going to help you talk to your parents about all of that.

Whether you handle this one-on-one or during a family meeting, you'll want to act in concert with your siblings and their spouses and any other close adult family members. Devising a plan of action together can not only help prevent hard feelings later on, it can potentially broaden your parents' physical, emotional, and financial base of support.

LET'S TALK MONEY . . . BUT HOW?

Financial conversations take practice, lots and lots of practice. Just remember that the more you and your family talk, the more comfortable—and adept—you'll all become. Keep in mind, however, that how you talk can be just as important as the message you're conveying.

The following guidelines will help keep your discussions positive and productive and get you where you want to go. We call them the ten principles of respectful communication:

1. Make an actual date to talk about a specific subject. "Honey, I'd like to talk about _____. Would Saturday at ten A.M. work for you?" By telling your mate what you want to discuss, he or she won't feel blindsided when you bring it up. Choose a time when all parties feel rested, and when you know your time won't be constrained. You want the conversation to be as open-ended as possible, which means giving it as much time as it needs. Mornings are usually best. Steer clear of late nights when you're all tired and preoccupied with the day's events. You'll also want to avoid talking when emotions are running high, even if that means rescheduling. Things that get said in the heat of the moment can never be taken back. Besides, something about anger seems to affect our ability to listen—all we can really hear is ourselves. Once emotions have cooled, you can discuss the issues a lot more clearly.

2. Find a place that's comfortable for all involved and that isn't anyone's particular turf. Sit side by side instead of across from each other in a confrontational position, suggests Patricia Schiff Estess in *Money Advice for Your Successful Remarriage: Handling Delicate Financial Issues with Love and Understanding* (Betterway Books, 1996). Realize that though many women tend to prefer sitting close to intimates they're talking to, as well as touching them and making eye contact, men often prefer the opposite. Being sensitive to these differences and not expecting family members to operate completely out of their comfort zone can take a lot of the potential sting out of your conversations.

3. Start the conversation with a positive subject that the person (or people) you're talking with feels good about. For example: "You've done a great job handling the bill-paying, and I really appreciate it." As money psychologist Olivia Mellan points out in *Money Harmony: Resolving Money Conflicts in*

Your Life and Relationships (Walker & Co., 1995), "People never change when they feel too bad about themselves. Only by validating themselves for their strengths do they have a springboard from which to confront their weaknesses." If one or more parties are participating in the discussion somewhat reluctantly, acknowledge that and voice your gratitude.

4. Once you get started, stick to the subject. Don't let tangential issues—or unrelated topics—sidetrack you. Additionally, be aware of the power of the message behind the message. Whether intended or not, inferences can affect the whole tenor of your present conversation and even all those to come. No matter how innocent, a comment about how high the credit card bill is can instantly put your partner or child on the defensive, especially if spending has been a source of controversy in the past. Since men and women can have different communication patterns, talking about what you hear as well as what's being said is really critical. Only by getting all that out in the open—and airing the underlying message you just sent or think you've received—can you truly get to the bottom of things.

5. Where your children are concerned, consider their age and developmental levels, and gear your conversations accordingly. It's not fair to burden your eight-year-old with your financial concerns. On the other hand, it may be appropriate to rein in your Nike-hungry twelve-year-old with a financial reality check, such as pointing out that the price of a single pair of designer athletic shoes equals one week of groceries for the family.

6. Be aware of your tone. This is especially important when talking to kids, but it applies to all of us. Sarcasm or mocking doesn't help. Treating individuals lightly robs them of confidence, conviction, and dignity.

7. It's okay to disagree, but you need to listen to what someone is saying rather than gather your ammunition for a counterattack. (This can be a tendency even when you're introduced to new people: You're so busy preparing to answer with your

name that you never even hear theirs.) Since there's absolutely no point in arguing about facts—like how much credit card interest you're paying each month, your checkbook or savings account balance, or your retirement account totals—make sure you have the relevant paperwork handy so you can settle any fact-related disagreements and then get back to the important part of your conversation. This is also a great way to make sure you're both (or all) up to speed on the family's finances.

8. No matter how angry you might get, try to stay calm. You want to engage in a fruitful conversation, not a destructive battle. Avoid the blame game. In the end, it really doesn't matter whose fault it was. What matters is fixing the problem and making sure it doesn't happen again. Focus on how something makes you feel, rather than make sweeping pronouncements. "Your buying that without talking to me made me feel invalidated" will get you a lot further than calling someone selfish.

9. Steer clear of hot buttons. When it comes to those close to us, most of us know just which buttons to push when we want to get a reaction. But pushing them will only interfere with achieving your objective, which is to talk about money so you can make it work for you. Throughout this book we'll point out those sore points. Look for the boxes labeled "Don't Touch That!"

10. Acknowledge and encourage any and all efforts and compromises (such as spending less or resolving to get up to speed financially) by letting family members know how much this means to you. And if you don't seem to be working things out? When in doubt, try to put yourself in the other person's shoes long enough to understand his or her perspective. This can be especially important when talking to your children or your parents, since the generations frequently see the world from such radically different perspectives. Remember that everyone is entitled to his or her point of view. If you can't come to terms, you may have to agree to disagree for the moment, but at least you've initiated the discussion. And in the end, the talking will pay off.

No Kidding

You'll also want to make sure that your money decisions for your children or grandchildren dovetail with your values and personal philosophy about money. My parents, for example, have always felt that their kids should have initiative, so they've never simply funneled money to my siblings or me. They believe that giving an endless stream of money would teach us nothing but dependence. Like them, I don't want to hand my children a life. I want them to go out and make their own independent lives.

That means making sure they have the chance to deal with money on their own from a very young age. Telling your children what to do with that money defeats the purpose. Only by making their own decisions—and even their own mistakes—can they develop the money confidence and skills they'll need later on. As a parent or any other concerned or involved adult, your job is to guide them in that process.

An essential part of that guidance entails passing down your values and attitudes about money in a way they can hear and in a way that effectively challenges the powerful influence of both peer pressure and consumerism. In that vein, this book will introduce you to all the money concepts, strategies, and terminology you'll need to raise money-savvy kids, teens, and young adults, as well as gender-based stereotypes to avoid. Of course, you'll also want to make sure that you've adequately planned for your children's future. We'll also give you plenty of advice about that.

Families Come in All Shapes and Sizes

While you may not have living parents, kids, or a spouse, for that matter, you probably have close friends or family who do. Besides, for our purposes, you constitute a family on your own, especially since you're probably surrounded by siblings or peers with children, as well as older relatives, friends, or even surrogate parents. So in almost every chapter—even the one about dealing with money as a couple—you'll find nuggets of information that apply to single people. Throughout this book we'll also address additional considerations for the growing number of nontraditional family structures—such as single parents and same-sex couples. No matter what your family looks like, taking control of your finances means talking about them.

The Key to Financial Fitness

Earlier we compared your fiscal health to your physical health. Nowadays we all know that we have to be a lot more proactive if we're going to stay healthy. We have to talk to our doctors and learn the appropriate questions to ask. We need to get a physical every year so that we can deal with any potential medical problems early on, then have follow-up visits as needed. Our financial lives operate the same way. To manage our money well so that we can live the life we want now and in the future, we need to be able to talk about it and to have smart and open conversations with our family—and our financial advisors.

Notice the *s* on the end of *conversations*. It is not a question of doing it just once. To keep yourself fiscally healthy, you have to schedule regular checkups. Sad to say, but most of us pay more attention to the regular maintenance of our car than to our own financial well-being. So you'll need to do more than simply read this book. You'll need to talk. In fact, you'll need to talk a lot.

There's a frequently quoted theory that we learn from our mistakes. But big decisions—from marriage and kids to career and retirement—don't come around that often. So as much as possible, you want to get those right the first or second time around. Getting yourself up to speed on the basics that affect you and your family, and then engaging in an ongoing dialogue to stay on track, are the only ways to build the life that you really want and deserve.

Remember Pete and the marriage he almost lost? "We handle everything jointly now," he says. So every decision leads to conversation. They talk about their strengths and weaknesses and how those affect their various responsibilities in and out of the family. Together they've created a sound financial plan that reflects who they are, what they value, and what they want from life. "You'd be surprised at the benefits you get not just on the financial front but from a relationship perspective as well," says Pete. "My wife was nineteen when I married her. This is like meeting a whole new person."

Hindsight may be twenty-twenty, but having regrets is no way to live—or end—your life. That's why this book will cover all the basics you'll need to engage those people who are important to you in ongoing discussions that can improve not only how you deal with money but life as you know it. What's our first stop? Building up the finances that will sustain the life you decide you really want.

So let's start talking!

Something to Talk About

Go on! Engage all your loved ones in some preliminary discussions about how money fits into your lives. The following conversation starters should help:

- *What does money represent to you?*
- *What beliefs about money (such as "a penny saved is a penny earned," "money buys happiness," or "money is the root of all evil") do you hold?*
- *What are your money fears?*
- *What kind of financial baggage do you have? How do your parents, siblings, former marriages, or past business experiences affect your current money-related activities?*
- *What is your personal money style? How compatible is it with your partner's style?*
- *Do you occasionally fall victim to mental accounting, treating some of your money differently than other money?*
- *What's important to you? If you were to list your top three or four values, what would they be?*
- *What are your personal dreams? What do your five-, ten-, and twenty-year plans look like?*

• *What are your specific financial goals?*

• *What parts of your financial plan have you neglected, and what do you need to do?*

• *Do you want to handle your financial planning on your own or seek professional help?*

• *Do your actions with money support your values? What do you want to change to better reflect your values and to help you achieve your dreams and goals?*

• *What philanthropic causes do you want to support? Where do you want to make a difference?*

• *Have you engaged your parents and children in open dialogue about money?*

• *How can you make sure you start—and keep—talking about money?*

2

The ABCs of Investing

While growing up, my colleague Kate's father, Eric, never talked about money. The subject was simply off limits, and the household was ruled by an ironclad mantle of financial silence that no one in the family dared to crack. But that didn't mean that Kate's mother or siblings didn't wish things were different. "We'd have done so much better if only your father had invested our savings," Kate overheard her mother lament years after Eric's death. Not that the family was doing poorly. To the contrary, Eric had managed to save a healthy sum, allowing the family to live quite comfortably. But aside from a few perfunctory attempts from time to time, Eric hadn't been an investor. And that cost the family he loved. "We had a very nice lifestyle, but we could have had so much more," says Kate.

Why did an educated man who was successful in so many aspects of his life fail to take control of his finances? "I guarantee you that he was afraid of investing," says Kate. And because he didn't want to reveal his lack of financial acumen, he didn't consult a financial advisor, either. As a result, his hesitancy about money and investing wound up compromising his estate. That unfortunate legacy is now being perpetuated by three of his five children, none of whom invest or even talk about money.

Clearly not everyone is fortunate enough to obtain financial knowledge in a way that he or she can hear and understand. I hope this book will help fill that communication void in your family. For in addition to providing you with information, it's intended to fuel your family's conversations about where you're going, how much money it will take, and which investments might get you there.

This is a chapter for beginners. For those of you who are new to investing, want a refresher, or are introducing a family member or friend to investing, we start at square one and cover the basic concepts. We then launch into a primer on stocks, bonds, and mutual funds: the vocabulary and building blocks you need to talk about to build your financial future. Finally, we discuss professional advice and what you should look for in an advisor.

More experienced investors may want to skip to Chapter 3, where the focus is on putting these basics to work. That's fine, but I urge you to use the information in the following pages to open what I hope will be an ongoing and worthwhile family dialogue about money.

As I hope you'll see in this chapter, investing isn't a sprint to an endless series of finish lines. It's more like a family marathon, with all of you reaching the ends you've identified together, through steady and systematic discussions and planning that allow you to work toward your financial goals.

One more word before we begin: If you are new to investing, you may find that this chapter and the next one are filled with new terminology and concepts. My advice is to simply read through it without worrying too much about remembering everything at once. You may find it useful to flag areas of special interest so that you can easily go back and refer to them later. You may also find it useful to refer to the glossary of investing terms in Appendix C.

Investing to Make Your Dreams Come True

If investing has always seemed like a dry, alien concept that has nothing to do with your life, I have a quick solution for you. Simply put a face on those potential earnings, so they represent a dream instead of a bunch of numbers. Because that's what investing is. It's a tool that enables you to create the life you want for yourself. And that's about as personal as you can get.

But like any tool, it won't do the work by itself. You need to guide it by discussing the vision you want to realize, then setting firm goals. If you don't, you won't be moving toward anything concrete, which will slow you down, if not stop you in your tracks. Let's say you haven't been saving enough money to invest, or you've neglected to invest the money you do have. It is difficult to shift your priorities if you haven't actually defined them.

So think about what you and your family want and why, then challenge yourselves to make it happen. Commit to your vision by making a point to tell family, friends, and even coworkers about your dream and how you plan to achieve it. In addition to clarifying and cementing your vision, making your plans known will make it harder to let them fall by the wayside later on.

Of course, your dreams need to be realistic. It doesn't help to set up a target that you can't possibly reach. If you have several dreams, you'll probably need to prioritize them. You may not be able to buy a boat, acquire a second home, send your three kids to a private college, *and* retire at age fifty. But when done according to a long-term plan, investing can help you realize the important dreams, the ones that reflect your core values.

Although the stock market—traditionally an "old boys' club"—catered to an elite few not so long ago, now more than half of American households own stock. If you've been sitting on the sidelines, now may be your turn. Do you feel nervous about all this? According to our research, so do about one out of every four men and one out of every two women. Sound familiar? Then let me tell you a story.

You may remember Lauren from Chapter 1, who didn't begin saving for her retirement until her mid-forties. Considering her late start, she thought it would take a miracle for her ever to retire. To be honest, after growing up as the seventh of nine siblings in a family that never invested, then being married to a man who handled all the finances, she figured it would take a miracle for her just to learn what to do on the money front.

"I was caught totally unprepared when I divorced," she recalls. "I had gone from my father's house to my husband's house. Nobody ever talked about money in either one. As a married woman, I was given enough money every month to buy the groceries and whatever else we needed—no more, no less. So when I divorced in my early thirties—after twelve years of marriage and two kids—I didn't know a thing about saving or investing."

Once Lauren got her divorce settlement, instead of investing the money, she put it in a savings account at her bank. Then she proceeded to spend it. She got herself a couple of credit cards—her first, since she'd never had one in her name. That would have been a fine idea if she'd kept them in her wallet most of the time and simply pulled them out to make purchases that she could pay off at the end of each month. (That way she could begin to build her own credit history.) Instead, she bought herself a few of the things she'd wanted during her marriage but never felt she could ask for. After years of wearing ill-fitting hand-me-downs from her sisters, she splurged on some new clothes. Then she bought a new car. She also began to treat herself to dinners out with the family and a few weekend getaways with friends. In addition, she made sure her two children always had the best of everything—from pricey tennis shoes and clothes to vacations in Hawaii, New York, and London.

Within three or four years Lauren's credit card debt had soared to $30,000. Then a legal secretary, she managed to just squeak by every month with the help of some creative money juggling. Amazingly, she managed to pay off her credit card debts a couple of times, but by then she was so used to spending money that she just incurred new debts all over again.

About that time the law firm she worked for scheduled a speaker to discuss investing for retirement. "I don't have any money to put aside for a 401(k)," Lauren immediately concluded after the presentation. Then she thought about what she'd heard. "I don't have to put that much money in for it to really start working for me," she realized.

So she made the commitment. Though every book she'd ever read recommended paying off debts first, knowing that she'd done that several times and was no further ahead than before, Lauren decided that she had to put some money away for herself as well. "When that money started accruing, that was a real motivator," she says. "I could see it." That reinforced her commitment.

Lauren now says, "I believe that when you put your mind to something, it can really happen. So I started focusing on saving money rather than spending it. I started contributing the full amount allowable (15% of my salary) to my 401(k). The first year was tight. Even so I managed to pay my credit cards down. Now I even have enough to contribute to a Roth IRA every year and have also built up an emergency fund to protect myself in case something happens."

In 2001, eleven years after her divorce, with the help of $60,000 worth of stock she sold, Lauren was able to buy a house, something she'd only dreamed of for years. "I can't tell you how great that makes me feel," she says. The fact that it's continued to appreciate in value hasn't hurt a bit either.

As Lauren put it so eloquently, the miracle she was sure she'd need turned out to be her.

THE DREAM TEAM

Though my paternal grandfather made only $100 a month as an attorney during the 1930s and 1940s (which would equate to about $1,200 a month now), he saved enough money to buy a small ranch in the Sacramento Valley of California. Focusing on a specific vision of what he and his family had agreed they wanted made putting money aside every month more meaningful and a lot easier.

To make your family's dreams (and the benefits you'll reap from them down the line) as tangible as possible, you might want to start a dream scrapbook—or even several. If you and your loved ones dream of owning a vacation home, then have every member of your family rip out magazine photographs of great homes and paste them into your scrapbook. Add vacation photographs and decorating ideas. Jot down any and all notions about how the place would look or feel, or why it's important to you in the first place. In short, use your dream scrapbook as a repository for anything that will remind you of the goals toward which you're striving. Should you and/or your partner feel yourselves weakening, actually seeing an image of your goals can help to strengthen your resolve.

Creating, expanding, or simply revisiting your scrapbook should inspire and encourage you and your family to discuss your financial situation as it relates to your dreams, and to reaffirm both your intentions and your commitment. So start gluing and gabbing!

Where Does Your Money Go?

As Lauren found out, sometimes the hardest part of investing is "putting your mind to it" and just getting started. Most of us don't realize how much money regularly slips through our fingers, money that could be invested in our futures. Not long ago one of my colleagues realized that he and his wife had been paying $50 a month for a DSL connection that they never installed and therefore never used. What with work and family, the couple was so busy that they simply hadn't taken time to carefully examine their bills. They just paid them. "That's six hundred dollars a year!" he confided in an appalled voice. "If we invested that, it could grow into a tidy sum!"

Most of us are guilty of that same lack of attention—if not about bills in particular then about where our money goes in general. Many of the day-to-day "needs" in which we indulge may be day-to-day luxuries that are sapping our bank accounts of potential investment funds. The Schwab Center for Investment Research calls this the "Doughnuts to Dollars" savings theory. For example, let's say that instead of buying an eighty-cent doughnut twice a week (at a savings of $83.20 per year), you invest that money. If you did this for twenty years and got a hypothetical 10% return, you would earn about $5,240. Or as another example, let's say you save $13 a week by not ordering an appetizer and dessert when you go out to eat; that amounts to about $675 per year. If you did this for twenty years and again earned a 10% return, you could have close to $42,000.

Of course, all of us have spent unwisely from time to time. For one thing, it's easy to get distracted by our immediate desires. Caught up in the moment, we can lose sight of our long-range goals, so we buy on impulse. We figure that the purchase is insignificant, and that the amount spent won't change our lives or our fortunes to any great degree. That's where we're wrong. All too often the little things become missed opportunities to invest, and consequently our ultimate dreams remain unfulfilled.

The bottom line? By reviewing your outgoing cash with your family members, you too can save money without giving up too much in the way of enjoyment. The returns could be well worth the negligible sacrifice.

THROW AWAY YOUR PLASTIC?

In a study reported in Belsky and Gilovich's *Why Smart People Make Big Money Mistakes,* researchers at the Massachusetts Institute of Technology auctioned off a pair of hot basketball tickets to two groups of volunteers. In both cases the auction was sealed, and the tickets went to the highest bidder. But here's the difference: The first group was told that the winner would have to pay for the tickets in cash, within the next twenty-four hours. The second group was told that the winner could put the expense on a personal credit card. If you guessed that the second group bid higher, you're right. But did you guess that they bid twice as much? Does this kind of reasoning sound familiar? Join the crowd. Most of us tend to devalue the money we spend on credit—a familiar but dangerous trap.

"Okay, already. I get the picture," I hear you say. "But we still just don't have enough to invest." Even if you live paycheck to paycheck and always seem to just make ends meet, I'll bet you're wrong.

Take Lauren, for example. When she started investing, her paycheck was stretched so thin that she'd pay the bills due in the middle of the month on the thirteenth to avoid any late fees or added interest, then pray that her checks wouldn't be cashed until she got paid two days later, on the fifteenth. But when she saw the presentation about investing in a 401(k), the fact that her contribution would be matched by her employer stuck with her. After all, that sounded an awful lot like free money. So she decided to put $100 toward her 401(k) every paycheck, figuring that she'd just have to juggle that much faster. Ironically, the difference after taxes was pretty negligible. "There was only about $60—or $30 a week—missing from my paycheck," says Lauren. "If you don't ever see it, you won't miss it. I sure didn't."

DON'T TOUCH THAT!

Sharing the ABCs of investing can be a wonderful way to home in on your family's dreams and financial priorities. As you probably already know, however, simply bringing up the topic of finances can easily be misconstrued by family members as a lack of trust. So getting your loved ones to the table to talk about investing and money requires that you clearly articulate what the discussion is designed to accomplish (getting everyone to participate in planning for the future) and what it's not (taking anyone to task).

The toughest part will be getting over the initial hump. Not many people are comfortable doing something for the first time. Go to a new aerobics class, and you feel like a klutz. If you've never taken an aerobics class at all, figuring out the steps seems that much harder. But when you hang in there, you soon find that it gets easier. Then you realize that it's not so bad after all, especially in light of achieving your goals.

Putting a face on investing by defining those values and dreams you want your money to support will help overcome the inertia most unseasoned investors experience. So will avoiding technical jargon. The concepts are really simple when the invest-ment-speak labels are omitted. So keep it simple—but not too simple. Just because your friends or family aren't familiar with investing doesn't mean they're stupid, so don't talk down to them. Respect will get you a lot further than condescension.

Finally, whether you're talking to your spouse, your best friend, your parents, or your kids, avoid assuming an advisory role. In her book *You Just Don't Understand: Men and Women in Conversation* (Quill, 2001), Deborah Tannen warns that pro-viding counsel effectively puts you in a power position. And that will do absolutely nothing to propel the conversation for-ward. A better bet: Ask whomever you're talking with for their opinion on the subject at hand, or to state their desires or con-cerns. Listen to what they have to say. Answer any questions. Then create a plan together.

Saving for Those Sudden Downpours

Once you've gone through the process of understanding where your money goes every month, it's time to start thinking about saving for your future. Everyone needs a rainy-day cushion to soften the impact of unforeseen life events such as illness, accident, or loss of a job. This comes under the heading of "first things first." Therefore, before you become an investor, make sure that you build up an emergency reserve that will cover at least two to six months of living expenses. This is the portion of your assets that you don't want to lose—ever. As you'll see later in this chapter, my father and I believe that cash-equivalent investments such as money market funds are good places to stash this cash.

It's crucial to realize, though, that *saving* for the future and *investing* for the future are two different things. *Saving* implies putting money aside in a safe place, such as a federally insured bank account. *Investing,* on the other hand, generally refers to uninsured brokerage accounts and products. As strange as it may sound, you can *save* too much. If you focus too much on short-term safety and limit yourself to savings accounts, you could end up depriving yourself of the long-term growth potential the stock market can provide. Inflation can eat away at your purchasing power if you don't put that money to work. That's why we say that saving is smart, but in the long term investing is smarter.

Time Is Your Best Ally

Once you've established your emergency fund, it's time to become an investor. Even if you have only a modest amount to invest, it's still worth it. Why? Because it's not just about how *much* money you have, it's also very much about how much *time* you have.

Let's illustrate this by comparing the hypothetical investing experience of a set of twins. Courtney is a starving artist, but starting at age twenty-five, she puts aside $2,000 every year in an IRA. She does this for ten years, earning a 10% annual return, then stops making any additional investments.

Her sister Jennifer, on the other hand, has always dreamed of being a lawyer and enrolls in law school right after college. Tuition is costly, and she has nothing extra to invest. When she graduates, Jennifer is still playing catch-up, and even though she has a well-paying job, she puts off that first IRA contribution. Finally, at thirty-five, she makes her first IRA contribution and continues to invest $2,000 a year until she's sixty-five. Like her sister, let's say that Jennifer earns the same 10% annual return.

Having heard this story, most people would assume that Jennifer would wind up with more money than her sister. But they would be wrong. Look at Table 2.1. Although Courtney invested only $20,000 over ten years (compared with Jennifer's $60,000

Table 2.1
Compound Growth and the Cost of Waiting to Invest

	Annual Contributions		Investment Growth	
Year	Courtney	Jennifer	Courtney	Jennifer
1	$2,000	$0	$2,200	$0
2	$2,000	$0	$4,620	$0
3	$2,000	$0	$7,282	$0
4	$2,000	$0	$10,210	$0
5	$2,000	$0	$13,431	$0
6	$2,000	$0	$16,974	$0
7	$2,000	$0	$20,872	$0
8	$2,000	$0	$25,159	$0
9	$2,000	$0	$29,875	$0
10	$2,000	$0	$35,062	$0
11	$0	$2,000	$38,569	$2,220
12	$0	$2,000	$42,425	$4,620
13	$0	$2,000	$46,668	$7,282
14	$0	$2,000	$51,335	$10,210
15	$0	$2,000	$56,468	$13,431
16	$0	$2,000	$62,115	$16,974
17	$0	$2,000	$68,327	$20,872
18	$0	$2,000	$75,159	$25,159
19	$0	$2,000	$82,675	$29,875
20	$0	$2,000	$90,943	$35,062
21	$0	$2,000	$100,037	$40,769
22	$0	$2,000	$110,041	$47,045
23	$0	$2,000	$121,045	$53,950
24	$0	$2,000	$133,149	$61,545
25	$0	$2,000	$146,464	$69,899
26	$0	$2,000	$161,110	$79,089
27	$0	$2,000	$177,222	$89,198
28	$0	$2,000	$194,944	$100,318
29	$0	$2,000	$214,438	$112,550
30	$0	$2,000	$235,882	$126,005

(Table 2.1 continues)

Table 2.1 (cont.)

Year	Annual Contributions		Investment Growth	
	Courtney	Jennifer	Courtney	Jennifer
31	$0	$2,000	$259,470	$140,805
32	$0	$2,000	$285,417	$157,086
33	$0	$2,000	$313,959	$174,995
34	$0	$2,000	$345,355	$194,694
35	$0	$2,000	$379,890	$216,364
36	$0	$2,000	$417,879	$240,200
37	$0	$2,000	$459,667	$266,420
38	$0	$2,000	$505,634	$295,262
39	$0	$2,000	$556,197	$326,988
40	$0	$2,000	$611,817	$361,887

Total Contributions		
Courtney	=	$20,000
Jennifer	=	$60,000

Final Results: 40-Year Period		
Courtney	=	$611,817
Jennifer	=	$361,887

Assumes a consistent annual 10% rate of return with investments made at the beginning of each year. The amounts shown for investment growth and final results do not consider any transaction costs or taxes. This represents a hypothetical investment and is for illustrative purposes only; the actual annual rate of return will fluctuate with market conditions.
Source: Schwab Center for Investment Research

worth of contributions), at the end of that forty-year period, Courtney would have $611,817 compared to Jennifer's $361,887.

It hardly seems logical. How could Jennifer's ten missed years cost her so much? It's due to the phenomenon of *compound growth*—one of the most important concepts you need to understand as an investor. In Table 2.1 you can see that not only does the amount you invest have the opportunity to grow, but so do all your gains, which gives the total amount the potential to grow at an accelerated pace. In fact, after seven years, Courtney's annual gain ($2,287, or $25,159 *minus* $20,872 *minus* $2,000) is larger than her $2,000 annual contribution.

Compounding is hardly a new concept. Benjamin Franklin has been attributed with calling it "the eighth wonder of the world." Certainly we all recall his famous saying that a penny saved is a penny earned. But did you know that if you took a penny and could actually double it every day, you'd have approximately $10.8 million after a month? Check my math: After the first day you'd have two pennies, and after the second day you'd have four. Easy so far. If you kept doubling that penny for twenty days, you'd have slightly more than $10,000—which still doesn't sound like much. But if you continued to double it for another ten days (thirty days in all), you'd have almost $10.8 million. In just one month! Of course, this famous hypothetical example assumes that the penny grew at a rate of 100% a day (or 36,500% a year), which obviously won't ever happen in the real world. But it does provide a clear, if inflated, sense of the concept of compounding.

Pay Yourself First

It's not hard to accept that we all *should* have the discipline to save that extra $1,000 a month and invest it in a way that we hope will grow over the long term. But we all know that's easier said than done. We procrastinate, we get distracted, we get swept away by other, more immediate concerns. So what can you do to overcome this? Before you pay any other bill—your mortgage, the utility company, the department store, *anything*—make sure you send that monthly check to your investment account. For many of us, a company-sponsored 401(k) plan is the best way to do this. Or if you're self-employed or not earning a salary, you can set up an automatic investment plan.

Basically, you want to take the whole business out of your hands, so it just happens. I always encourage clients to deliberately set up their plan so it's really hard to undo. Your easy path—the one of least resistance—should have you investing consistently, month in and month out, year in and year out.

THE PRICE OF PROCRASTINATION

It's human nature to avoid those tasks we find burdensome. We know what we're supposed to do, like saving money or reviewing our investment portfolios, so we resolve to tackle those "I should" projects—but just not quite yet. Frequently, instant gratification wins out over long-term benefits.

What's behind this? When it comes to investing, the sheer number of choices available (more than seven thousand individual stocks and more than thirteen thousand mutual funds) may be partially responsible. As reported in Belsky and Gilovich's *Why Smart People Make Big Money Mistakes,* psychologists Sheena Sethi and Mark Lepper set up a jam-tasting booth at an upscale grocery store to test how the number of choices affects our ability to make decisions. Half of the time the researchers offered twenty-four jams for tasting. The rest of the time they offered only six. (The jams were pretested to make sure that the quality and tastiness were comparable.) The result? Customers who had only six jams from which to choose purchased a jar 30% of the time. The customers who were able to sample twenty-four flavors made a purchase only 3% of the time!

Like the customers who were overwhelmed by having to choose among twenty-four jams, investors can easily succumb to "analysis paralysis" when trying to choose a mutual fund or a stock. For some this translates into keeping too much of their money in a passbook savings account or a money market account. For others, it may mean not being able to invest their 401(k) appropriately. The irony, of course, is that by not choosing a mutual fund or a stock—and instead keeping your money in a money market account—you're still making a decision.

The bottom line, though, is that procrastination does cost. As an investor, you have three primary tools to help you work toward your financial goals: the amount of money you invest, your rate of return, and the amount of time you have. By procrastinating, you are eliminating one of these—the benefit of time—and potentially dramatically compromising your overall return.

Another thing to realize is that the shorter your time horizon, the more pronounced the effect of procrastination. If you're not going to need your money for twenty or more years, waiting six months or a year may not have a huge effect. But if you have a ten-year time frame and don't invest it for a year, you may be seriously compromising your ultimate return. Let's look at some numbers: If you invest $100 a month for fifteen years and earn a 10% annual return, you'll end up with over $41,000. If you wait five years and have only ten years in the market, you have to invest about $200 per month to accrue the same amount (at the same 10% annual rate of return). As a rule of thumb, if your time frame is less than ten or fifteen years, for every five years you wait to start investing, you must double the amount you save to achieve the same result.

Realize that when I say "pay yourself first," I don't mean that you should place that money in a savings account. As you'll find in Chapter 7, one of the best things you can do is invest it in a retirement plan like an IRA or your company's 401(k) plan, both of which provide significant tax benefits that can further fuel the growth of your accounts.

"It's just a question of taking the steps," says Lauren. "The hard part is realizing that you do have enough money, then getting started."

The Power of Stocks

History tells us that the very best way for your money to grow over the long term—and to capture the power of compounding—is to invest in the stock market.

Figure 2.1
The Growth of a Dollar from 1926 to 2002

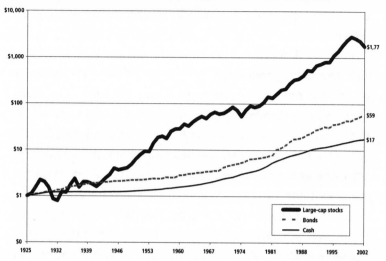

In Figure 2.1 you can see the growth in value of one dollar
invested in various financial instruments from January 1926
through December 2002.

If in January 1926 you had invested just one dollar in a mutual
fund that tracks the S&P 500 Index (which includes five hundred
of the country's largest companies), that dollar would have grown to
about $1,775 by the end of 2002. By contrast, if you had instead
put your money into intermediate-term U.S. bonds, it would have
grown to $59—or if you had invested in thirty-day Treasury bills
(T-bills), only to $17. Clearly, over these seventy-seven years, stocks
have outperformed both bonds and T-bills by a huge margin. In fact,
going back to 1926, the worst forty-year period for stock returns was
still better than the best forty-year period for U.S. Treasury bonds.
So yes, the stock market certainly has its ups and downs day to day,
month to month, and year to year. But the long-term historical trend
has demonstrated that stocks offer the greatest upside potential.

If you still aren't convinced that you should invest your money in
the stock market, think about inflation. Again, the rate of inflation

can vary widely from decade to decade—or even year to year—but in the last fifty-three years it has averaged 3.9% per year.

So let's say you started with $100 in 1950. Based on average inflation rates, it would have had to grow to $765 to have the same purchasing power in December 2002. Groceries (or anything else) worth $100 in 1950 cost $765 in December 2002. By next year they may cost $800. Fifty years from now they may cost $3,500.

Looking to the future, let's say you have $200,000 that you put in a can and bury in your backyard. When you dig it up in twenty years, that money will be worth far less, perhaps only $100,000 in purchasing power. That's why stuffing your cash under the mattress is such a poor idea, even if it doesn't get stolen!

THE RULE OF 72

The Rule of 72 is a handy way to estimate how long it'll take to double your money at different rates of return. Simply divide the number 72 by your rate of return, and you'll wind up with the number of years. If you invest $500 and could get 10%, for example, it will take just over seven years for it to grow to $1,000 (72 divided by 10 equals 7.2). If your return is 8%, you'll have to wait nine years for your money to double (72 divided by 8 equals 9). If you stick that $500 in a savings account that pays just 3%, you'll have to wait twenty-four years for it to double (72 divided by 3 equals 24). Of course, by then inflation, which generally is about 3% per year, will have eaten up most if not all of your return.

Grappling with Risk

When you're ready to embark on an investment program, the first things you need to think and talk about are your time frame and your willingness to assume risk. These two issues are both crucial on their own—and are also inexorably linked.

We all have our own individual tolerance for risk, one that changes over time and as family circumstances shift. I remember meeting a man who told me that when he was young, he'd ride his motorcycle cross-country, ski any hill he could find, and tackle any new adrenaline-pumping endeavor just for the thrill of it. But now that he has reached his forties and has three children, that has changed. "These days I think three, four times before I take on any kind of risk," he says. That attitude didn't confine itself to abandoning his former pastimes in favor of woodworking in his garage. It influenced how he dealt with his money as well.

Why is the concept of risk so crucial for an investor? Because as Figure 2.2 shows, the investments with the greatest potential for growth also carry the greatest potential for loss—at least in the short term.

This means that the more time you have, the more you can afford to place your money in investments—like stocks—that can be volatile in the short term but offer the best chance for your money to grow over the long term. Why? If you have ten or twenty years before you'll need the money, you can likely ride out most market downturns. Perhaps you can even use the market dips as opportunities to invest more. But if you know that you'll need your money in five years or less, all that changes. As many investors learned in the market decline of 2001–2002, if you assume too much risk, you may experience a significant and sudden loss. It's wise to remember that, as your time horizon shrinks, so should the amount of risk you take on.

In practical terms, this means using different strategies for different goals. An investment that is appropriate for a long-range goal is simply not appropriate for money you may need next year. If you're saving for your child's college in three years as opposed to your retirement in twenty years, you'll have to invest that money differently.

A friend recently learned this lesson the hard way: She left her son's college funds invested in the stock market after he'd entered college. When the stock market crashed, so did her son's tuition money. Unfortunately she didn't have time to ride out the lows, and she was forced to sell when the tuition bill was due. "I took on too much risk considering his time frame," she laments. She's absolutely right.

Figure 2.2
Three Basic Investments: Stocks, Bonds, and Cash

Lower ⟵ **Risk and Return** ⟶ Higher

Cash-Equivalent Investments	Bonds	Stocks (Equities)
Investments that are easily converted to cash, thus often known as "liquid assets."	Issued by a borrower, such as a public entity or corporation, seeking to raise funds.	Ownership of shares in a company. Categories include small-capitalization ("small-cap")[3] stocks, large-capitalization ("large-cap") stocks, and international stocks.[4]
Treasury bills (T-bills)	Corporate bonds • High-yield bonds • Investment-grade bonds	Common stock
Short-term certificates of deposit (CDs)	Municipal bonds	Preferred stock
Money market mutual funds[1]	Government bonds • U.S. government bonds • Zero-coupon treasuries (STRIPS)	Stock mutual funds[2]
	Bond mutual funds[2]	

[1]Money market mutual funds are managed to maintain a stable $1 share value. Investments in these funds are not insured or guaranteed by the U.S. government or FDIC, and there can be no assurance that the funds will be able to maintain a stable net asset value.	[2]Investment value will fluctuate, so shares, when redeemed, may be worth more or less than their original cost.	[3]Small-cap companies are subject to greater volatility than those in other asset categories. [4]International investing may result in higher risk due to political instability, currency exchange fluctuations, and differences in accounting methods.

Shorter ⟵ **Time Horizon** ⟶ Longer

A more prudent approach—and one that I always recommend—is to gradually move your money into more conservative investments as you get closer to the time when you will need to spend your money. My friend would have been wise to move at least a portion of her son's college account into a CD, a money market fund, or short-term bonds.

Retrenching, however, doesn't mean retreating completely from the stock market. My father and I strongly believe that you should always keep a portion of your funds invested for growth—even in retirement. What happens if you don't? Not only do you lose out on potential profits, but the rate of inflation can cause the value of your money (or at least your buying power) to shrink. And in these times when many of us are living so much longer than previous generations, none of us can afford *that*.

EXPERT ADVICE FROM THE SCHWAB CENTER FOR INVESTMENT RESEARCH

The Value of Time

One way to see how time can reduce the likelihood of a loss is to look at the returns of the S&P 500 Index from 1926 to 2002. According to research conducted by the Schwab Center for Investment Research, the S&P 500 was up 61% of the time over the course of one month. When the holding period was extended to one year, the S&P 500 was up 73% of the time. Over five years the trend was up 90% of the time.

In other words, the longer your time frame, the more likely you were to experience a positive outcome.

Diversify, Diversify, Diversify!

Still nervous about investing? Then you'll be glad to learn that a very simple concept can help reduce risk in your portfolio. *Diversification,* as it's known in the investment world, simply means not putting all your eggs in one basket. When you think about it, diversification makes complete sense. Since different investments respond differently to economic conditions, and because no one can consistently forecast which one will do best at any particular time, having a balanced mix of investments will help you stay your course.

In practical terms, this means that a smart investor doesn't look for that one hot stock, one hot sector, or even one currently hot type of investment. If you're still not convinced, just ask all the thousands of people who lost their nest eggs by investing vast portions of their stock portfolios in the skyrocketing high-tech sector that eventually lost its engines and came crashing back to earth. Had those investors been better diversified, their portfolios would have been much less volatile.

There are two equally important components to diversification. First, you need to invest in all three of the major *asset classes:* stocks, bonds, and cash-equivalents. Second, you need to be diversified *within* each class. This means that you need to own a mix of stocks of different size, in different sectors (such as health care and financials) and industries (such as biotechnology, drugs, and insurance) as well as both domestic and international companies. It also means that you need to own different *styles* of investments—that is to say, *growth* and *value.* The key is having the appropriate blend of investments—or *asset allocation*—that fits your particular goals, time frame, and tolerance for risk.

Just as a mutual fund that focuses on a single industry isn't going to help you with diversification, neither will owning fifty different stocks or mutual funds if they all cover the same thing. If you own shares in Coca-Cola, for example, as well as shares in a mutual fund that invests in Coca-Cola, you've duplicated your efforts and increased your vulnerability should Coca-Cola suddenly falter.

Therefore it's important to take your time and do your homework when figuring out what investments best fit your goals. This is not the time to be quick, impulsive, or reactionary. Only careful consideration will help you to get where you want to go, when you want to get there.

I know that deciding which investments to buy can be difficult, if only because you have so many choices. But once you define your objectives, all those possibilities start to narrow. As you continue to discuss and analyze those investment choices, your decisions will become clearer.

The good news is that it's never too late to start. You may have to get out of your comfort zone to grow financially, but you can do it. Lauren was forty-five when she first began to figure out how to invest in her future. If she could get a handle on all of that and make it happen, you can too.

Chuck's Two Cents: On Managing Risk

You mention the stock market, and most people have mixed emotions about risk and reward. Some seem to react almost viscerally to risk, particularly in a down market or a recession, when in the mind of the mass public risk turns into RISK!

Granted, as of this writing, we are experiencing one of the worst bear markets in history. In times like this it's extremely hard not to get emotional and want to run for the hills. But this is exactly when it's essential to maintain a long-term perspective. Every kind of investment has some inherent risk, whether the investment is stocks, bonds, real estate, or gold. In fact, risk is a part of everything we do—from investing to relationships to business. Risk is a part of life.

Given this reality, what is your best defense? Understanding how much risk is appropriate for your circumstances and creating a portfolio to match. In the late nineties, when the stock market was going straight up, investors didn't think too much about risk—it simply didn't seem real. But once people suffered severe losses, their tolerance for risk suddenly came into clearer focus.

Carrie tells me I'm a risk-taker: that I ski aggressively and that I'm a tough businessman. That may be true, but I would qualify that by saying that I take risk in a calculated way. I wouldn't take risks if I were skiing for the first time. I'd find an instructor and rely on help and advice from a pro. But because I have a fair amount of experience, I do ski fast—if the conditions are great. I go into the lodge as soon as things get ugly. My intention is to always stay in control.

I handle investing risk in the same way. I stay alert and informed, so that when I take a risk, I do so with awareness and understanding. And as an investor, you can do the same thing. As Carrie explains in the text, if you have the proper asset allocation and are adequately diversified, you will be able to take an appropriate risk. Of course I know there are no guarantees and that things can still go wrong. But I know also that I've done all I can to minimize unnecessary risk. And that, to me, is enough.

Dollar-Cost Averaging: A Prudent Strategy

Earlier I discussed the importance of "paying yourself first." Not only does it help you start—and keep—investing on an ongoing basis, it can launch you into a strategy that works well for a lot of investors. *Dollar-cost averaging,* as it's called, not only provides you with the structure and the discipline to invest consistently over time, it also works well for anyone who is feeling a bit hesitant about diving right in—and wants to spread out his or her investments over time.

This is how it works. Every month (or at any regular interval) you invest a set amount of money—regardless of how the stock market is performing. When the markets are down and prices are low, you wind up purchasing more shares for your money. Your friends will wonder why you're able to maintain your composure as the value of your stocks tumbles—but since you're in this for the long haul, a dip in the market means an opportunity to scoop up a greater number of shares at lower prices. When the market and prices are up, you'll buy fewer shares (just as you do when a sale ends and prices return to full retail). Over time your average share *cost* (how much you actually spend) can wind up being lower than the average share *price.* Table 2.2 shows the details.

Table 2.2
Dollar-Cost Averaging

Monthly Investment	Share Price	Shares Bought
$400	$10	40
$400	$8	50
$400	$5	80
$400	$8	50
$400	$10	40
Total: $2,000	$41	260

Average price per share:	$41 ÷ 5 = $8.20
Average cost per share:	$2,000 ÷ 260 = $7.69

In this example, the average share price ($41 divided by 5 months' shares) is $8.20. But because of dollar-cost averaging, your average share cost ($2,000 divided by 260 shares)—or the price you actually paid—is only $7.69. You paid 51 cents less per share than the average price during that five-month period!

This example shows you that dollar-cost averaging can work in your favor in a volatile market. Realize, though, that it doesn't assure a profit or protect you from a loss when stock prices tumble. So before you decide to adopt this strategy, make sure you're willing to invest during market declines. At the other extreme, if you could take out your crystal ball and know that the market is going straight up, you would be better served investing all your money as soon as possible. But for those of us who are less clairvoyant about the direction of the market, it can be reassuring to spread out our investments over time.

Tools of the Trade

Many of us neglect to talk to our spouses, our parents, and/or our children about investing because we feel uneasy about our own financial knowledge and skills. As we saw so clearly with Kate's dad and even her siblings, that uncertainty—or fear—not only leads to avoiding the topic of discussion, it can also lead to avoiding investing altogether. Like anything else, however, once you break investing down into its basic components, it's just not that complicated.

In this section I'll introduce you to the world of investment vehicles—from stocks to bonds to mutual funds. As you begin to learn (and talk) about them, you'll soon realize that each type of investment has its own advantages and disadvantages, as well as its own risks and rewards. Just remember that a properly diversified—or balanced—portfolio will include a mix of investments.

Once again this overview is directed primarily to beginning investors. If you're a bit rusty, you may find it a useful review. Or if you're encouraging a friend or family member to jump in, this could be a good place to start. Otherwise you can move on to Chapter 3, where we go into more detail about each type of investment and show you how they can work together in a well-balanced portfolio.

PAPERWORK MADE EASY

Whether you're a novice or a pro when it comes to finances, it's easy to miss things, even when you're trying to be conscientious and thorough. My suggestion? Organize your paperwork.

In Appendix A I'll provide some suggestions for how you can do this. Most of the clients I have worked with find that the process of getting organized not only helps them get acquainted (or reacquainted) with their finances, it also serves as a terrific vehicle for introducing a less-involved partner to the family finances. Many say that they obtain a better grasp of the big picture and, as a result, are in a better position to make sound decisions.

COMMON STOCK

A lot of people don't know that in 1983 Bank of America bought Charles Schwab & Co. lock, stock, and broker, with my dad staying on as chairman and CEO. Within four years he had bought back his company. But in those first few months of being under the Bank of America corporate umbrella, Schwab employees were offered the option of purchasing shares of BofA stock commission-free. Fresh out of college and just having received my broker's license—and never having actually placed a stock order for myself—I purchased two shares. Not two dozen shares or two hundred shares or two thousand shares. Just two shares, which I still own. I always joked that while my dad was one of the largest Bank of America shareholders, I was the smallest. Still, eighteen years later, with the two shares that I bought for $44 now grown to almost $400, a tiny sliver of that BofA pie remains mine.

Stocks (also referred to as *equities*) represent ownership. When you buy even a single share of stock, you're actually buying a piece of that company. That's what sets buying a stock apart from any other investment. Of course, this gives you not only the greatest opportunity for growth but also the greatest exposure to volatility if that company doesn't perform well.

Depending on the company's market value (the share price multiplied by the number of shares outstanding), stocks are classified as either *large-capitalization* (the top 5% of companies, generally with market value greater than $8.2 billion), *small-capitalization* (the bottom 80% of companies, with market value less than $1.3 billion), or *mid-capitalization* (the 15% in between). Both the Dow Jones Industrial Average and the S&P 500 Indexes are made up of mostly large-cap companies, with General Electric, and its more than $250 billion market cap, currently leading the herd. Though each category carries different levels of risk and reward, the object isn't to choose one among them but to come up with a mix.

Other terms you'll hear are *growth* and *value styles*. A growth stock is just what its name implies; its earnings (and usually its share price) are expected to grow rapidly. It pays negligible dividends because most of its profits are funneled right back into the company—to foster more growth. Growth investors are optimistic about the future of the firms in which they invest and are willing to pay a premium for this potential. This strategy has been most effective when new industries are developing and advancing, such as the rise of technology and biotechnology throughout the 1990s.

A value stock is a different creature. Investors who take a value approach are looking for fundamentally strong companies whose share prices might be depressed for any number of short-term reasons. Because a company's stock is believed to be underpriced, it is thought to represent good value. Value investors believe that, at some point in the future, the true value will emerge, the share price will increase, and they'll profit from buying at a lower price today. Some value stocks also tend to pay higher dividends, which may help increase your overall return.

EXPERT ADVICE FROM THE SCHWAB CENTER FOR INVESTMENT RESEARCH

It Pays to Be Style-Conscious

You have to look no further than recent performance data to see the importance of holding a mix of growth and value styles in your portfolio. In 1999 small-cap growth stocks rose 43% and small-cap value stocks fell 1.5%. In 2000 small-cap value stocks were up 23%, and small-cap growth declined 22%. In each year there was almost a 45-percentage-point discrepancy between styles. Given this, the real danger lies in trying to "chase" a previous year's performance. Investors who lost money in small-cap value stocks in 1999, only to switch horses to exclusively growth stocks in 2000, would have increased their loss. The key is to own both.

Many of us tend to think locally, but *international* stocks—or stocks of companies based outside the United States—are a part of any well-rounded portfolio. International investments do involve special risks, such as currency fluctuations, political instability, and foreign regulations—but they also balance out the domestic portion of your portfolio. In addition, because there is less correlation between the behavior of international markets and the U.S. markets than there is between the different stocks traded on the U.S. exchanges, adding international stocks to an otherwise domestic portfolio can reduce your portfolio's volatility—without decreasing your expected return.

Although only a handful of the largest global companies trade directly on the U.S. stock exchanges, American depository receipts (ADRs) allow U.S. investors to buy and sell shares of hundreds of other companies traded on foreign exchanges. As you'll see in Chapter 3, mutual funds are a particularly effective way of diversifying your portfolio overseas.

BONDS

During the last bull market, a newspaper editor I know became increasingly frustrated with his father, who stubbornly refused to add a single stock to his portfolio, which was 100% invested in bonds. At seventy-two, he simply wasn't interested in doing a thing that might jeopardize his retirement savings. To him, bonds, bonds, and more bonds were the answer.

So what's a bond?

Simply put, bonds are like IOUs. When you buy a bond, you're essentially loaning money to the government or to a corporation. In return, you get regular income in the form of interest payments (thus the term *fixed income*) as well as the promise that your entire investment will be returned when the bond matures. In theory, if you buy a $10,000 bond that pays a 5% yield and matures in March 2009, you will receive annual income of $500 until March 2009, at which time the original $10,000 investment will be returned.

Notice that I said "in theory." As a category, bonds fall somewhere between cash-equivalent investments (such as CDs or money market mutual funds) and stocks on the risk/reward continuum. In general, you get higher yields from bonds than from cash investments, but you don't have the same potential for growth that comes with stocks. Depending on the bond you purchase (with U.S. government bonds on the safe end of the spectrum and riskier, higher-yield corporate bonds on the other), you also assume more risk with bonds than you do with cash investments. This includes the risk of default as well as the risk that rising interest rates will erode the bond's value. Nonetheless, bonds are generally less volatile than stocks—provided they are high-quality issues that you hold until maturity. But if you deviate from this reliable strategy and start to trade bonds—or sell them prior to maturity—you are assuming a higher level of risk. I'll discuss this more in Chapter 3.

When you decide to purchase a bond, there are three basic types from which to choose, each with its distinct characteristics. In general, investors look to *government bonds* for greater safety, *munici-*

WHY DO INTEREST RATES AND BOND PRICES MOVE IN OPPOSITE DIRECTIONS?

Actually, this inverse relationship makes perfect sense. When current interest rates go down, bond buyers will pay more for an existing bond that yields 6% than they will for a new bond that yields only 5%. And on the flip side, if interest rates go up, a buyer will pay less for an old bond that is carrying a lower yield than the bonds that are now being released. Here's an example of how bond prices reflect the going yields. In June 2003 the yield on a five-year Treasury note with a face value of $1,000 was about 2.5%. But if you went out to buy a bond released several years ago yielding about 5%, you'd have to pay $1,100. Because current rates went down, the price of an older bond with a higher yield went up.

This effect is most pronounced for long-term bonds. When interest rates rise, the price of a 5% bond that won't mature for twenty years (in other words, a bond that will continue to yield 5% every year for twenty years) will fall more than a 5% bond that will mature in five years. And when interest rates fall, the price of a long-term bond will increase more than the price of a short-term bond.

pal bonds for tax-free returns, and *corporate bonds* for the higher yields. In very broad terms, the longer the maturity of the bond and the riskier the agency or corporation, the higher the yield.

Government bonds may be issued by the U.S. Treasury or by an agency of the federal government. Treasury bonds (10-to-30-year maturity), Treasury notes (1-to-10-year maturity), and Treasury bills (90-day-to-12-month maturity) together add up to more than $2.5 trillion in outstanding debt. Although changing interest or inflation rates may impact their value, in its more than two-hundred-year history, the U.S. government has never defaulted or delayed payment of interest or principal on one of its securities. As a result, U.S. Treasuries are considered the safest of debt instruments. Most other bonds issued by federal agencies are not guaranteed by the federal government but are still considered high-quality investments. In addition, the income from Treasury (but not Agency) bonds is exempt from state, but not federal, taxes.

A NOTE ABOUT THE END OF THE THIRTY-YEAR TREASURY BOND

In 2001 the Treasury Department stopped issuing new thirty-year Treasury bonds. Nevertheless, there are still about $525 billion in outstanding long-term Treasuries (with a maturity over ten years) available to investors in the secondary market.

Experts disagree as to the significance of this decision. Some believe that the government's objective was to lower long-term interest rates to the level of the ten-year Treasury note, thereby stimulating the economy. The government, on the other hand, maintains that the thirty-year bond was simply no longer needed to pay off the national debt.

Regardless, with the demise of the thirty-year bond, the new benchmark Treasury is now the ten-year note.

Municipal bonds (munis) are issued by state and local governments to raise money to build schools, roads, bridges, libraries, sewers, and other projects. Although muni bonds generally provide lower yields than federal and corporate bonds, they are free from federal tax—and generally from state and local taxes as well if they are issued by your state of residence. Obviously, the higher your tax bracket, the more advantageous a tax-free investment can be. As always, it pays to do the math.

COMPARING TAXABLE YIELD TO TAX-FREE YIELD

Let's say you're in a combined 20% federal/state tax bracket and you're trying to decide between buying a corporate bond that pays 10% and a municipal bond that pays 7%. To see which pays the higher after-tax yield, you can use the following formula:

equivalent taxable yield = tax-free yield ÷ (100% − tax bracket)

In this example,

$$7\% \div (100\% - 20\%) = 0.07 \div 0.8 = 8.75\%$$

Therefore, based only on their yield values, since the equivalent taxable yield is lower (8.75% for the muni bond), in this case it makes more sense to buy the 10% corporate bond.

Another way to compare yields is to use the formula:

equivalent tax-free yield = taxable yield × (100% − tax bracket)

Using the same example of a 10% taxable bond and a 20% tax bracket,

$$10\% \times (100\% - 20\%) = 0.1 \times 0.8 = 8\%$$

In other words, the municipal bond would have to yield 8% to equal the 10% yield from the corporate bond for an investor in the 20% tax bracket.

Corporate bonds are issued by corporations seeking to raise capital. In general, corporate bonds offer the highest yields and the highest risk of default. In March 2003 the corporate bond market was roughly $4.1 trillion in size.

In addition, some corporate bonds (as well as some Treasury and municipal bonds) have *call provisions*, which means that the issuer can call, or redeem, the bond prior to maturity. This happens most often when market interest rates drop substantially below the rate the bond is paying, and the issuer would like to reissue bonds at the lower prevailing rate. This makes perfect sense, as why would the issuer want to pay you more than the going rate? (It's a lot like a homeowner refinancing his or her mortgage when interest rates drop.) When your bond is called, the issuer gives you back your original investment or more, and future interest payments stop. In general, bonds with call provisions pay a higher return than those without—to compensate for this uncertainty.

BOND RATINGS

If all bonds were created equal, choosing among them would entail little more than comparing yields. But in truth they are far from equal, which is why they are rated on their credit quality by major rating services like Moody's and Standard & Poor's.

Bond ratings are based on the likelihood that the bond's issuer will default, failing to repay its obligation to investors. The highest-quality bonds receive a rating of AAA from Standard & Poor's (Aaa from Moody's). At the other end of the spectrum, bonds rated DDD or lower by S&P are already in default. As you might guess, lower-quality bonds generally offer higher returns as an incentive for investors to purchase them in spite of their higher level of risk.

Bonds rated BBB or higher by Standard & Poor's (Baa or higher by Moody's) are considered "investment grade"—that is, appropriate for consideration of purchase by prudent investors. Bonds with ratings below this threshold are considered noninvestment-grade or "junk." Junk bonds offer higher yields but are considered to be highly speculative investments due to the company's risk of default.

CASH-EQUIVALENT INVESTMENTS

For years, people like my friend Jim and his father sank their money into cash-equivalent investments, also known as liquid assets, because of how easily they could be traded in for cash. (If you need a visual aid, just think of how easily liquids pour from one container to another.) What would you guess they made on these ultrasafe investments that they could so easily jump back out of? You guessed it: not much.

The return you receive on your cash-equivalent investment depends entirely on the existing interest rate. If interest rates are low (a good thing if you're trying to borrow money), you're not going to make as much. In any case, you're not going to see a great return with these investments. They are essentially where you park either money you're planning to use in the near future, or your emergency reserve.

What kinds of investments are appropriate for this emergency-reserve category?

• **T-bills,** which are sold at discounted rates and then redeemed at their face value when they mature—in ninety days to twelve months. T-bills are backed by the federal government, so they're about as close to a sure thing as you'll ever find in the world of investing. But there's a price to pay for the low risk—and that's a lower return. An added benefit of T-bills is that they are free from state tax.

• **CDs,** or certificates of deposit issued by banks, as well as savings and loan institutions. CDs pay a fixed amount of interest until your investment matures. Depending on whether you've chosen a short-term CD or an intermediate CD, that time frame will fall somewhere between three months and five years; most people opt for CDs that mature in three to six months. The good news? Unless you're investing more than $100,000, your money is 100% insured (as long as the institution issuing the CD is insured by federal insurance programs, so check!). The bad news? If you need the money before your CD has matured, you'll have to pay an early-withdrawal penalty.

• **Money market funds,** or mutual funds that invest in short-term obligations from corporations and from state and federal governments. Although your money is not insured by the FDIC as it is in a bank account, the rate of return is usually higher. In addition, money market mutual funds generally don't charge a penalty for withdrawing your money no matter when you do it. Government regulations require money market funds to be invested in high-quality debt obligations; however, it is possible, if unlikely, that the value of your account will decline. So if you think you'll need access to your money but want a place to stash it where it'll earn more money than in your typical bank account, this is a good way to go.

MUTUAL FUNDS

A mutual fund is actually a company that gets its capital from investors and then invests that money in an array of other companies. Just like you, a mutual fund can opt to buy companies' stock or to invest in bonds or cash-equivalents issued by corporations or the government. By now it probably won't surprise you to find out that what they invest in determines both how much risk they entail and what kind of return they might bring.

When you buy a mutual fund, the price per share is based on the fund's *net asset value*—or NAV—plus any sales charges you have to pay. The per-share NAV is the fund's total assets minus its total liabilities, divided by the number of shares outstanding, and it is recalculated at the end of every business day. As we explain further in Chapter 3, if you buy what is known as a *no-load* fund, there is no sales charge, and the price you pay is the NAV. When you buy a *load* fund, you will also pay a onetime sales charge.

When you're choosing a mutual fund, you have lots of variables to consider. By law, all mutual funds must be sold with a written *prospectus* that outlines all of the fund's characteristics. We'll get into more details about what you should look for when you buy a mutual fund, and how to read a mutual fund prospectus, in Chapter 3. For now, I just want to mention three things: *past performance, fees,* and *after-tax return.*

First, be sure to look at a fund's *long-term* performance—at least three years or more—as compared to similar funds or relevant benchmarks. The second crucial factor is cost—both commissions and operating expenses. Even though fund fees may seem relatively insignificant, they can add up and significantly affect your return. And third, if you're buying a fund for a taxable account, you need to look at the return after taxes. See Chapter 3 for more details.

STOCK MUTUAL FUNDS

When you buy a single share of stock, you're buying a tiny part of an entire company, just as I did with my two Bank of America shares. But when you buy even a single share of a mutual fund, that share represents dozens if not hundreds of companies.

Investors have jumped into stock mutual funds in a big way. At latest count there were more than seven thousand (yes, you read that right) choices available—about as many as individual stocks! The two biggest advantages of mutual funds are automatic diversification and professional management. But be careful, because you have to pay for these benefits—and some funds have higher expenses than others.

Just like individual stocks, mutual funds come in lots of flavors— and it is important to understand the categories. There are funds that focus on growth, or value, or a combination of styles. There are funds that primarily buy large-cap stocks and funds that mostly hold small-cap stocks. There are international funds (that invest in non-U.S. companies), global funds (that invest in U.S. companies as well as international companies), and emerging market funds (that invest in developing regions of the world like Latin America). You can also buy funds that focus on a particular sector, such as health care, financial services, or utilities. The beauty of all this choice is that you find just that mix-and-match of size, style, and sector that suits your needs. Always keep in mind, though, that funds with a narrow focus, including those that invest internationally, may involve relatively more risk than those that have more diversified holdings.

INVESTING WITH YOUR CONSCIENCE

If you're among the increasing numbers of investors who want to make sure that your investments don't cause or contribute to social or environmental damage, a growing category of socially responsible mutual funds can help you keep your investments in line with your values. Although company practices are rarely black and white, you can choose funds that screen for a number of issues such as tobacco, alcohol, or weapons production; human rights violations; or practices that harm the environment. And you don't necessarily have to sacrifice your values for your bottom line, because some of these funds have achieved excellent results. Having a conversation about the investment practices of the various funds is a good way for you and your family to explore and articulate your shared values. For more information or help in finding socially responsible funds, check the websites www.socialinvest.org or www.socialfunds.com.

ACTIVELY MANAGED FUNDS VERSUS INDEX FUNDS

When you enter the world of mutual fund investing, one of your most important decisions is choosing between an *actively managed* fund and an *index* fund. As the name implies, an actively managed fund is run by a portfolio manager (or managers) who carefully selects and monitors the performance of each holding—buying and selling investments and attempting to optimize their overall fund return.

Index funds are a type of mutual fund designed to track a particular market index, such as the S&P 500 Index (an index of five hundred of the largest companies in America) or the Wilshire 5000 Index (pretty much the entire stock market). The way they do this is by simply buying each of the companies in the index (yes, that's five hundred stocks for the S&P 500) in amounts equal to the weightings within the index itself. So if GE represents 1% of the entire market capitalization of the S&P 500, $1 out of every $100 is invested in GE. Although no index fund will ever exactly duplicate the results of the index it tracks, if the index goes up 10% (or down 10%) in any given year, the index fund will generally go up or down by approximately the same amount.

Because index funds don't require the intensive day-to-day management that actively managed funds need, their expenses are generally lower and they are generally more tax-efficient (that is, they pass on fewer taxable gains to the investor). Ironically, though, large-cap index funds frequently outperform their costlier managed cousins. We'll discuss index funds in greater detail in Chapter 3 and explain how they can fill an important role in your portfolio.

BOND MUTUAL FUNDS

Like stock mutual funds, there are all types of bond funds—from those that specialize in Treasury securities (the safest, with the lowest return potential) to riskier funds that specialize in corporate bonds and offer potentially higher returns. Municipal bond funds usually offer lower returns but are generally tax-free. Regardless, bond funds allow you to take advantage of the same kind of diversification and professional management offered by stock funds. In addition, they can be a convenient way to get monthly income.

One word of caution, though: Unlike individual bonds, bond funds may not provide reliable income payments and do not have set maturity dates. Because a bond fund is a combination of many bonds, their income and principal values will vary based on market conditions and the fund's underlying holdings. Put more simply, when you decide to sell shares of your bond fund, you will get the current share price (NAV), which may be more or less than what you paid for it.

BALANCED MUTUAL FUNDS

If you want it all—growth and income, as well as stocks, bonds, and cash-equivalent investments—these mutual funds contain a mix of these three asset classes. Talk about well rounded! The beauty of balanced funds is that they spread out your risk among all the major types of investments, which can save you time.

One word of caution, though: Many balanced funds consist primarily of large-cap stocks and Treasury bonds—and may not include small-cap or international stocks. Therefore, if you buy a balanced fund, you need to look carefully under the hood; otherwise you may not be as diversified as you think.

PREFERRED STOCK

Preferred stock may *sound* a lot like common stock, but it generally behaves more like a bond. While a share of preferred stock does represent ownership (normally without the voting rights), it pays a fixed yield, like a bond. In general, companies issue preferred stock as a way of raising cash without diluting their common shares. The vast majority of preferred stock is owned by institutional investors, not individuals, and the price tends to be less volatile than common stock.

Preferred shareholders receive dividends before common shareholders, and if a company experiences a financial shortfall and suspends dividends, it is generally required to make back payments to preferred shareholders before it pays common shareholders. Also, in the case of bankruptcy, preferred stock owners are in line to get paid ahead of common stock owners. As a result, while preferred stock is less volatile than common stock, it doesn't offer the same opportunity for growth and its value is more affected by interest rates. As an added incentive, some preferred stock can also be converted into common stock.

Financial Help and Advice

Feeling like you and your family are in this alone and getting in over your heads? Don't! Though my father and I firmly believe that everyone should take an active role in his or her finances, most of us benefit from some professional advice—at least from time to time.

Let me digress for just a minute. A couple of years ago a friend gave me a gift certificate for several sessions with a personal trainer. I've been pretty active all my life, so my initial reaction was "I don't need that. I know how to work out on my own." But because I had the certificate, I made the first appointment. I'm sure you know where this story is going. That first session was great, and subsequent sessions even better.

In short, I was hooked. I started to see results and looked forward to coming back. I liked the companionship; it gave me that extra bit of incentive to work hard. I also liked learning new training techniques and ways to optimize my workouts. And when you meet a good financial advisor, the experience can be very similar. Not only can consulting a professional jump-start your financial fitness, but it can also help you hang on for the long term.

Chuck's Two Cents: When to Consider Professional Investing Help

Many investors come to a point when they consider getting professional help with their investments. Often time is the reason; they simply feel unable to give their investments adequate attention. Or maybe the reason is interest; some people just get tired of handling it all. A down market can also cause people to consider professional help; after some losses they decide that managing their investments themselves just isn't as easy as they thought it was. But whatever the reason, deciding to enlist the help of an investing professional can be one of the best investing decisions you ever make.

To decide if it's time to get professional help, think about where you are in your investing life. I see investors on a sort of continuum, from the completely independent investor who wants to manage his or her investments, to someone who wants a little validation or coaching along the way, to the person who wants to delegate all of the responsibilities that accompany managing a financial portfolio. For most investors, things are least complicated when they're at the beginning of their careers and just starting to invest. Over time people often move toward the middle of the continuum: Maybe they want some help with the fixed-income piece of their portfolio, but they feel confident in managing their equities. That's where I fit in at the moment. I use financial advisors in a couple of areas where I know I need some specialized expertise, but I'm very much involved in that big picture, sort of like the quarterback of the team.

If you too decide to get help, look for help that's expert, objective, and personalized. Know whom you're hiring and what they're pro-

viding for you at what cost, and make sure they know what you expect in return. And once you have help, don't coast. Stay involved and informed and knowledgeable, even if the person you've hired is handling all the day-to-day work for you. You owe it to yourself—and to your future.

Professional advice comes in all forms. Even if you're a veteran investor, a certified financial planner can help you look at your big financial picture, from insurance and estate planning to retirement, investing, and tax planning. Or if you have a specific goal or concern like balancing your stock portfolio or education funding, you may need to consult with an investment specialist on only an occasional basis.

No matter which route you choose to take, my father and I advise you not to hesitate. Some of us just don't have the time to fully research investments and stay on top of any changes. Others are looking for that extra psychological support. "I know in theory what I should be doing, but I can't distance myself enough to make the decisions I need to make," says one financially savvy investor.

Whether you decide to consult with an investment advisor on a onetime basis or choose to have him or her handle the ins and outs of your finances, you'll need to do your own homework beforehand and stay involved. Not convinced? Then let me share a story. Some of you may have read about the ex-Microsoft employee who entrusted his life savings to two separate brokers at a well-known— and respected—brokerage firm. Within sixteen months of handing over his $700,000 portfolio, which was largely the result of Microsoft stock options that he had gathered over his career, it was all gone. Completely. In fact, all he was left with was a $40,000 tax bill.

How could that happen? You could point a finger at myriad reasons, including the bursting of the technology bubble, speculative trading, greed, and perhaps even some dishonesty. But the bottom line is that this investor and his brokers didn't diversify his portfolio. They broke the cardinal rule of investing. Of course this case is an extreme. But within this cautionary tale are a couple of lessons that apply to everyone. First, the get-rich-quick mind-set of the

1990s just doesn't work. What we really need is to return to the tried-and-true methods of investing. Second, you have to stay involved. Don't ever just hand over your money to someone and walk away.

You can start your search for an independent, fee-based investment advisor with Schwab's complimentary AdvisorNetwork referral program. All the prescreened independent fee-based advisors listed already have met specified criteria. Another good method is to get word-of-mouth recommendations from professionals you know (like your attorney or accountant), relatives, or friends.

When choosing an investment advisor, it may be tempting to choose someone who charges nothing up front. Sounds like a good deal, right? Wrong—and I really can't stress this enough. Working with an independent, fee-based advisor (generally at the cost of 1% to 2% of your assets) who focuses on your goals—instead of someone whose income is based on a commission—provides you with less conflict of interest and more objectivity, two essential qualities in an investment advisor. In short, you want to know that the person giving you advice isn't going to profit from your trading activity or from selling you a particular product. Better that they profit from your overall performance.

Another alternative is to pay an hourly rate or a set fee for agreed-upon services. Those generally run $150 to $300 an hour or start at $1,500 for a comprehensive financial plan, which covers investment guidelines, retirement goals, tax implications, estate planning, and protection/insurance issues.

When choosing an advisor, much of the information you'll need is included on Part II, Form ADV, a legal document that registered investment advisors are required to file with the Securities and Exchange Commission. (Ask the advisor for a copy.) You're also going to want information about the firm and/or individual track record, so ask for whatever brochures, résumés, and additional written (or online) material they might have about themselves and their fee structure.

Ultimately, you're going to want to find someone with whom you feel comfortable talking. This means you're going to have to talk to

him or her first and to feel out his or her conversational and working style as well as the basic chemistry between you. You can ask
for a preliminary (free) interview and scratch from your list anyone
who won't grant one.

Once these basics have been established, ask your candidates to
describe their education (they should preferably have a CFP, or certified financial planner, certification), experience, background,
expertise, management style and philosophy, and investment pref-
erences. (Will they oversee your asset allocation, making sure your
portfolio is properly balanced and diversified?) You can also ask
about their track record with clients like you, and their willingness
to educate you along the way. It is always a good idea to ask for references.

You'll want to listen carefully for what they ask about you. Are
they questioning you about your current financial situation and
what you and your family want for the future? (A good sign.) Or are
they automatically trying to plug you into a ready-made formula?
(Next candidate!) Listen to your gut when figuring out if you feel
at ease around them. You'll need to share some of the most intimate
details of your family's life, so you'll need to feel good about opening yourself up to this individual.

Finally, you want to find someone who will spend time with you,
and not pressure you into making decisions or investments with
which you're not comfortable. You also want someone who's willing
to speak your language and not deluge you with financial terms you
don't understand. Most important, you'll want to make sure that
your advisor understands you and your family as well as your complete financial situation and objectives.

Once you've made your selection, speak openly and candidly
about your financial situation, even if part of it embarrasses you a
bit. You want to come up with a plan of action that will get you and
your family where you all want to go, within the context of your personal values and aspirations. Remember Pete and Eleanor, who
used their financial-planning sessions to reaffirm the life they had
together and the future they were planning? That's what it's all
about.

Something to Talk About

• *Do you spend your money in accordance with your overarching long-term goals? Is any of it slipping through your fingers? Are there any places you could cut back?*

• *What amount of risk is appropriate for your time frame and personality?*

• *Have you saved enough for a rainy day?*

• *Do you know how to use the Rule of 72 to figure out how long it will take to double your investment?*

• *Does your investment portfolio include an appropriate mix of different investment vehicles?*

• *Does dollar-cost averaging make sense for you? If it does, do you know how to get started?*

• *Have you organized and reviewed all of your financial records? Are there any obvious holes?*

• *Can you manage your finances by yourselves? Are you willing to spend several hours a month reviewing your portfolio and making what can turn out to be tough decisions? Or should you hire a financial advisor?*

3

Building Your Family's Wealth

It seems like just yesterday that we were in one of the biggest bull markets in U.S. history. Whenever I went to a cocktail party or an even less formal get-together, I would overhear people touting the hot stocks they'd just bought and sold. Often they would ask for my opinion—or approval. Even then their stories made me cringe, because even though they may not have known it, they weren't investing—they were gambling.

Unfortunately, misconceptions still abound. Phrases like "playing the market" sound far too much like "playing baccarat"—way too risky and complicated. So before we go any further, I want to emphasize that this is not responsible investing. To think otherwise is a myth. As Jane Bryant Quinn said in her parting column for the *Washington Post:* "Luck isn't a strategy. It's only luck."

That said, times do change quickly. The past couple of years have seen some serious ups and even more serious downs. As I write, all of the major stock market indexes are significantly below their highs of the year 2000, and we've seen countless investors lose significant portions of their wealth. So on the one hand, this is a sobering time to be writing about investing. On the other hand, it may be the best time of all. After all, downturns are a normal part of the stock market's cyclical behavior, and you have to be prepared to deal with the downs as well as the ups. The goal of this chapter is to give you *timeless* advice that will take you through the good times and the bad, so that in the *long term* you and your family will end up on top.

While everyone needs a sound investing strategy, your family's plan will look different from anyone else's. Having covered the nuts and bolts of investing in Chapter 2, it's time to get you thinking—and talking—about the strategy that best fits your individual situation and goals. To that end, we start this chapter with a questionnaire that will help you better understand yourself and your family members as investors and point you to an appropriate asset allocation. We then jump right in to help you evaluate different investments and create a well-diversified portfolio. If you feel you need a bit of a refresher on some basic rules of the road, turn back to Chapter 2.

One reminder before we start. With all this talk about money, you'd think that making that almighty dollar was the be-all and end-all. It's not. I've said it before, and I'll say it till the day I die: Money has no value in and of itself. It can, however, provide you with the personal power to make choices and pursue the life you want. In that capacity, it's downright critical. This means you need to know—and discuss—the fundamentals about investing it and managing it, so you and your loved ones can make the most of what you have.

Where Do You Stand?

As you and your family begin to plan your investment portfolio, first think about your time frame. Take a few minutes to jot down the various goals you have discussed and when you want to realize them. Your list might include retirement, college, supporting your parents, a new home, a vacation retreat, volunteer work, a year abroad—whatever. If you haven't yet discussed your short- and long-term goals, this is the time to do so.

Next, think about your tolerance for risk. My advice? Don't be hasty here. Assuming that you're an investor for the long term, you need to think carefully about how much volatility you can live with. That's the only way to stay the course through the stock market's ups and downs. Otherwise, if you've exposed yourself to too much risk and your portfolio drops precipitously, you are more likely to panic and sell at a time when the stock is low. One of the best ways to determine how much risk is appropriate for you is to *talk it out*— with your spouse or significant others.

Once you've had these discussions, fill out the questionnaire in Figure 3.1, which asks specific questions about your time frame, investing knowledge, and tolerance for risk. You might want to have your partner fill out the questionnaire as well—comparing notes may turn up some interesting insights!

Figure 3.1
Investor Questionnaire

Check the answers that apply to you. Then follow the instructions to select an asset allocation plan that suits you best.

1. **I plan to begin withdrawing money from my investments for retirement within:**

   Less than 3 years . . . . 1 point
   3–5 years . . . . 3 points
   6–10 years. . . . . 7 points
   11 years or more . . . . 10 points

   ____ **Points**

2. **Once I begin withdrawing funds from my investments, I plan to spend all of the funds within:**

   Less than 2 years. . . . . 0 points
   2–5 years. . . . . 1 point
   6–10 years. . . . . 4 points
   11 years or more. . . . . 8 points

   ____ **Points**

Subtotal A: Time-Horizon Score

   Enter the total points from questions 1 and 2.   ____ **Points**

If your Subtotal A score is less than 3, stop here.

A score of less than 3 indicates a very short investment time horizon. For such a short time horizon, a relatively low-risk portfolio of 40% short-term (average maturity of five years or less) bonds or bond funds and 60% cash is suggested, as stock investments may be significantly more volatile in the short term.

If your score is 3 or greater, please continue.

3. I would describe my knowledge of investments as:

None. . . . . 0 points
Limited . . . . 2 points
Good. . . . . 4 points
Extensive . . . . 6 points
____ **Points**

4. When I decide how to invest my money, I am:

Most concerned about the possibility of my investment
losing value. . . . . 0 points
Equally concerned about the possibility of my investment losing
or gaining value . . . . 4 points
Most concerned about the possibility of my investment
gaining value. . . . . 8 points
____ **Points**

5. Review the following list and select the investments you currently own or have owned in the past. Then choose the one with the highest number of points and enter that number.

Money market funds or cash-equivalents . . . . 0 points
Bonds and/or bond funds. . . . . 3 points
Stocks and/or stock funds. . . . . 6 points
International securities and/or international funds . . . . 8 points
____ **Points**
(Maximum possible score = 8)

6. Consider this scenario:

Imagine that in the past three months, the overall stock market lost 25% of its value. An individual stock investment you own also lost 25% of its value. What would you do?

I would:
Sell all of my shares . . . . 0 points
Sell some of my shares . . . . 2 points
Do nothing . . . . 5 points
Buy more shares . . . . 8 points
____ **Points**

7. Review the following chart.

We've outlined the most likely, best-, and worst-case annual returns of five hypothetical investment plans. Which range of possible outcomes is most acceptable to you or best suits your investment philosophy?

(The figures are hypothetical and do not represent the performance of any particular investment.)

Investment Plan	Average Annualized Return (1 year)	Best-Case Scenario (1 year)	Worst-Case Scenario (1 year)	Points
Plan A	7.2%	16.3%	−5.6%	0 points
Plan B	9.0%	25.0%	−12.1%	3 points
Plan C	10.4%	33.6%	−18.2%	6 points
Plan D	11.7%	42.8%	−24.0%	8 points
Plan E	12.5%	50.0%	−28.2%	10 points

____ **Points**

Subtotal B: Risk-Tolerance Score
Enter the total points for questions 3 through 7.   ____ **Points**

Now determine your Investor Profile.

Step 1

Enter Subtotal A here:
This number represents your time-horizon score.   ____ **Points**

Enter Subtotal B here:
This number represents your risk-tolerance score.   ____ **Points**

Step 2

Plot your time-horizon score and your risk-tolerance score on the Personal Investor Profile chart and locate their inter-section point. This shows the type of investor you may be.

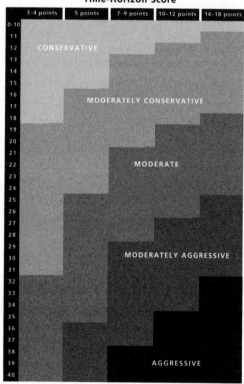

Now turn to Figure 3.2. Your point scores in the questionnaire will indicate which portfolio is most appropriate for you and your family—from Conservative to Moderate to Aggressive, or anywhere in between. Keep in mind, though, that the suggested percentages of stocks, bonds, and cash are only guidelines, not absolute rules. They are intended to give you a good idea—but not an exact figure—of how to split up your portfolio.

**Figure 3.2
Model Portfolios**

Choose your plan.
Match your investor profile with the corresponding asset allocation plan. The suggested percentages of stocks/stock fund, bonds/bond fund, and cash-equivalent investments are based on your answers to the Investor Questionnaire (see Figure 3.1) and the varying risk/return potential of each type of investment.

**Score 1–22
Conservative Plan**

This investment plan is for investors who seek current income and stability and are less concerned about growth.

**Score 23–30
Moderately Conservative Plan**

This investment plan is for investors who seek current income and stability, with some modest potential for increase in the value of their investments.

**Score 31–40
Moderate Plan**

This investment plan is for long-term investors who don't need current income and want some growth potential. Likely to entail some fluctuations in value but presents less volatility than the overall stock market.

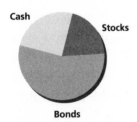

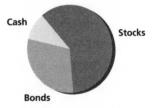

Stocks 20%
15% Large-cap stocks
5% International stocks
Bonds 55%
Cash 25%

Stocks 40%
20% Large-cap stocks
10% Small-cap stocks
10% International stocks
Bonds 45%
Cash 15%

Stocks 60%
30% Large-cap stocks
15% Small-cap stocks
15% International stocks
Bonds 30%
Cash 10%

(Figure 3.2 continues)

Figure 3.2
Model Portfolios (*cont.*)

Score 41–46
Moderately Aggressive Plan

This investment plan is for long-term investors who want good growth potential and don't need current income. Entails a fair amount of volatility, but not as much as a portfolio invested exclusively in stocks.

Score 47–58
Aggressive Plan

This investment plan is for long-term investors who want high growth potential and don't need current income. May entail substantial year-to-year volatility in value in exchange for potentially high long-term returns.

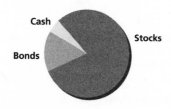

Stocks 80%
35% Large-cap stocks
20% Small-cap stocks
25% International stocks
Bonds 15%
Cash 5%

Stocks 95%
40% Large-cap stocks
25% Small-cap stocks
30% International stocks
Bonds 0%
Cash 5%

Source: Schwab Center for Investment Research with data provided by Ibbotson Associations, Inc.

So where do you fit in?

Let's say you're sixty-five years old and own your own home, your three children are grown and out of college, and you and your spouse plan to retire from your well-paying jobs within the year. You are looking for stability and a steady stream of income and are less concerned about growth. Your portfolio will be on the conservative side.

Or perhaps you're a thirty-five-year-old single parent of a five-year-old child, and you've just bought your first home. You want to set up a college fund as well as start to save for your retirement. As a result, you might be more concerned about growth than about current income. Your portfolio will likely be a blend between conservative and slightly riskier investments.

On the other hand, if you're twenty-five with a steady income, are now renting but know that you want to buy a house in about ten years, don't plan to have children, and won't be retiring for forty years, you can be more aggressive still. Your focus is on long-term growth, not on current income.

As you review these model portfolios, you can also see that they indicate suggestions for how you can further diversify the stock portion of your portfolio. For example, in the moderate plan, you might own 30% large-cap stocks, 15% small-cap stocks, and 15% international stocks in addition to 30% bonds and 10% cash. For a slightly more aggressive allocation this might shift to 35% large-cap stocks, 20% small-cap stocks, and 25% international stocks (in addition to 15% bonds and 5% cash).

Also notice that even the most aggressive of these portfolios has a portion appropriated to cash. According to the model portfolios, the percentage of your assets in cash may range from 5% to 25%, depending on your risk tolerance and time frame.

Also realize—as we mentioned in Chapter 2—that everyone, regardless of his or her time frame or risk tolerance, needs to have an emergency reserve of at least two to six months' living expenses in cash or cash-equivalents. No matter how much insurance you have (which we discuss in Chapter 9), this is essential. Therefore if you are just starting out as an investor and have a small portfolio, you will likely need significantly more cash than your model portfolio indicates. For example, if you have living expenses of $5,000 per month and a $30,000 portfolio, you need to keep a minimum of one-third of your assets in cash ($10,000) to cover two months of living expenses—even though this is more than is indicated by your model allocation. What this boils down to is that you need to build up your emergency fund before you become an investor.

Now let's get busy and figure out how you want to invest the equity portion of your portfolio—always keeping the vital concept of diversification at the forefront of the discussion. Depending on your individual circumstances, you can invest in stock mutual funds, individual stocks, or a combination of the two.

Chuck's Two Cents: Investing for Keeps

Investing, as experienced investors know, is a commitment, not unlike the commitments we make in other areas of our lives. It's an endeavor that involves persistence and the determination to hang in there, for better or for worse, during good times and bad.

Realize, though, that the greatest danger in the stock market isn't in what's happening to the Dow or the Nasdaq; it's in how you react. So when things get intense, how do you hang in there for better or for worse? It is said that we learn from experience and that there is no greater teacher than adversity. I've had more than forty years of investing experience and more than a few lessons in times of adversity. Here's what I've gleaned from those lessons and how to invest "for keeps":

1. Keep your emotions in check. When it comes to investing, your emotions can be your downfall. If you let them take over, you can get into real trouble. For example, panicking can cause you to sell an investment at its low. If, during a down market, you do some research and conclude that it's time to rebalance or to sell a less-than-sterling investment, that's different. But selling out of panic is usually a mistake. Remember that in these rocky times your gut is probably working against you.

The good news is that experience teaches you to handle those emotions. Experience deepens your understanding of the market's ups and downs and helps you to appreciate the value of basics such as diversification and asset allocation. Experience has taught me that it can even be wise to counter your emotions. Sometimes when I'm feeling a little anxious, I go against that fear—and I invest.

2. Keep your perspective. Perspective—by which I mean keeping a long-term view of the market's ups and downs—may be an investor's best friend. Once you've been an active investor for a significant period of time, a bear market probably isn't a new experience. You may even have expected it, which makes weathering the storm a little easier. When you're right in the middle of a down market, you can feel as though it's the worst one since 1929. At times like that, it can be very helpful to look at the big picture. A down market is a down market; that tough bear market we experienced from 2000 to 2002 was not that different from the one we saw in 1973–74 or 1987.

3. Keep the faith. *Keeping your emotions in check and keeping your perspective are two legs of a three-legged stool. The third and equally important leg is keeping the faith, by which I mean staying confident in the American economy. We live in a country of 285 million people and $10 trillion in gross domestic product, with a capitalization of $25 trillion. Those huge numbers are signs of a thriving economy. When we say we're having a bad time, that means our growth rate is going sideways, or maybe it's down a small amount in a recession. Even though our growth is cyclical, it is most definitely growth. In a down market, confidence in these facts can help get you through and allow you to overcome the temptation to act on your fear.*

Core & Explore™: Building a Diversified Stock Portfolio

There's no doubt that putting together a diversified equity portfolio can be complicated and time-consuming. But after looking at literally thousands of portfolio combinations, the Schwab Center for Investment Research has come up with a strategy that can make this job a lot easier. This strategy, which Schwab calls Core & Explore, is designed both to reduce your risk of underperforming the market and to provide you with the potential to beat the market—all within the context of your own time frame and tolerance for risk.

Central to Core & Explore is diversification. If this remains confusing, just think in terms of a balanced diet. To maintain good health, you should have a wide range of nutrition, including protein, vegetables, fruits, and grains.

Let's stay with that metaphor for just a minute. Your well-rounded selection of foods (read: stocks) represents the *Core* of your stock portfolio—or a wide range of U.S. companies. When one sector or stock category drops, which it will inevitably do at some point, it represents only a fraction of your holdings, so you don't take an overwhelming hit. Indeed, if more people had stayed diversified this way a couple of years ago, they wouldn't have been burned nearly as badly when the tech stock bubble burst.

But who wants to eat just meat and potatoes, along with the odd vegetable? Once you've got your Core set up, you can add in the *Explore* aspect of your portfolio. (Think desserts and appetizers.) This is where you get the chance to try to outperform the market—perhaps by buying small-cap and international stocks, or by buying more of a particular company, sector, size, or style, or perhaps by investing in nontraditional asset classes such as REITs or hedge funds.

Ultimately, your goal is to have the Core and Explore portions of your portfolio work together to give you the greatest probability of achieving your goals. Let's get started doing just that.

Investing Your Core

When it comes to buying investments, too many of us operate by the seat of our pants, following this tip or that instead of taking the time to talk out and then set up a cohesive investment plan. "You have to look at the bigger picture," insists one Schwab employee involved with investor education. "Otherwise you're just throwing the dice." That's a good analogy, because unless you establish a solid Core of investments, you're gambling in a game of luck.

Depending on your tolerance for risk and your time frame, your Core might represent anywhere from 40% to 60% of your stock portfolio (with Explore comprising the balance). For example, a conservative investor might want to allocate 60% to Core, a moderate investor might allocate 50%, and an aggressive investor closer to 40%. In other words, the more conservative you are, the more of your stock portfolio you will allocate to Core and the less you will allocate to riskier Explore holdings. See Figure 3.3.

Your Core should be a well-diversified portfolio of U.S. stocks that represent the many *sectors* (like health care, utilities, technology) and *styles* (like growth and value) of equity investing as well as both large and small companies. It can be in the form of individual stocks or mutual funds. If you're a longtime investor, you may well have created a diversified portfolio of individual stocks or mutual

Figure 3.3
Core & Explore™

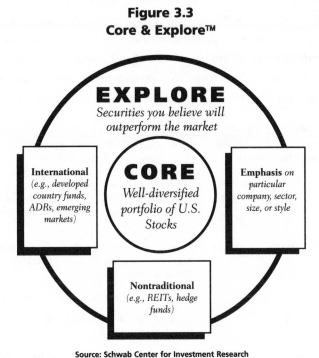

funds over the years. But if you're just starting out, or if you have less than $100,000 to $150,000 to invest in a *minimum* of 40 to 50 stocks, I highly recommend that you look into buying one or more broad-based *index funds* for at least a portion of your Core portfolio. They are by far the easiest and least expensive way to create a solid Core of equities.

EXPERT ADVICE FROM THE SCHWAB CENTER FOR INVESTMENT RESEARCH

Sectors

One of the best ways to help reduce market risk is to diversify your holdings across sectors. Typically a *sector* is the broadest categorization of a stock, which can be further divided into industries and subindustries according to the company's main business line. Health care, for example, is a sector; industries under that sector are health care equipment and supplies, health care providers and services, biotechnology, and pharmaceuticals.

Interestingly, different sources of information use different classifications of sectors. The sectors listed below are the Standard & Poor's Global Industry Classification Standard (GICS).

S&P GICS Sector	Industry
Consumer Discretionary	Auto Components, Automobiles, Household Durables, Leisure Equipment & Products, Textiles & Apparel, Hotels, Restaurants & Leisure, Media, Distributors, Internet & Catalog Retail, Multiline Retail, Specialty Retail
Consumer Staples	Food & Drug Retailing, Beverages, Food Products, Tobacco, Household Products, Personal Products
Energy	Energy Equipment & Services, Oil & Gas
Financials	Banks, Diversified Financials, Insurance, Real Estate
Health Care	Health Care Equipment & Supplies, Health Care Providers & Services, Biotechnology, Pharmaceuticals
Industrials	Aerospace & Defense, Building Products, Construction & Engineering, Electrical Equipment, Industrial Conglomerates, Machinery, Trading Companies & Distributors, Air Freight & Couriers, Airlines, Marine, Road & Rail, Transportation Infrastructure
Information Technology	Internet Software & Services, IT Consulting & Services, Software, Communications Equipment, Computers & Peripherals, Electronic Equipment & Instruments, Office Electronics, Semiconductor Equipment & Products
Materials	Chemicals, Construction Materials, Containers & Packaging, Metals & Mining, Paper & Forest Products
Telecommunication Services	Diversified Telecommunication Services, Wireless Telecommunication Services
Utilities	Electric Utilities, Gas Utilities, Multiutilities, Water Utilities

THE LOW-STRESS APPROACH: INDEX FUNDS

What if I told you there was a really easy way to invest your Core that involved a minimum of effort, just about guaranteed diversification, and frequently outperformed its competitors? Well, that investment is none other than the dependable, if unglamorous, broad-market *index mutual fund* (versus *actively managed funds,* which are designed to outperform the market but often don't accomplish that goal—especially when it comes to large-cap funds).

As we explained in Chapter 2, index funds are a type of mutual fund designed to track—rather than beat—a specified market index, such as the S&P 500 Index or the Wilshire 5000 Index.

Why invest in index funds? First, they provide diversification. For example, the Schwab 1000 Index closely tracks one thousand of the largest companies in the United States based on market capitalization (and represents about 90% of the U.S. equity market). As a result, one share of the Schwab 1000 Fund® represents a tiny portion of each one of those thousand companies, which include almost every industry imaginable. (Of course, if you opt for one of the smaller or more sector-specific index funds, you lessen that diversification. A narrowly focused index fund is *not* an appropriate Core holding.)

Second, if you subscribe to the *efficient market theory,* which holds that security prices fully reflect all publicly available information, you understand just how difficult it is to outperform the stock market. According to this line of reasoning, unless you're an "insider" (in which case you are legally prohibited from trading on this information), there is no way for you to have special information that will give you an edge over other investors. Of course this concept is not absolute, but when it comes to the best-known and most widely followed companies, it is likely close to the truth. As a result, when it comes to investing the large-cap portion of your portfolio, index funds, which are designed to keep pace with the market, make a lot of sense.

A third important factor that makes index funds attractive is their low fees. There's no expensive research team to pay and no high-salaried fund manager to compensate. The stocks in the index fund

REGULATION FD

Key to the concept of *efficient markets* is the fact that all pertinent information must be publicly available. To help make this happen, in 2000 the Securities and Exchange Commission passed Regulation FD (for *full disclosure*), which requires companies to release material information publicly rather than privately to Wall Street analysts. Included in this information is earnings information, mergers, acquisitions, new products or discoveries, and management changes.

are often simply determined by a computer program that analyzes the index that the fund is tracking, then makes sure that the percentages of the various companies in each match precisely. That doesn't cost much, so the *expense ratio* (or the fund's expenses expressed as an annual percentage of the fund's net assets) can run 0.75% or less, as compared to 1% to 2% for most actively managed

EXPERT ADVICE FROM THE SCHWAB CENTER FOR INVESTMENT RESEARCH

Check Out These Numbers

On average, an actively managed large-cap fund has an expense ratio of approximately 1.4%. The average large-cap index fund, however, has an average expense ratio of only 0.83%. This difference may not look like much, but through the power of compounding, a $10,000 investment over twenty-five years with a before-expenses return of 10% would result in an additional $10,817 (13.7%) for the index investor.

funds. That adds up! (See the box "The Ins and Outs of Fund Fees" on page 94 for a more detailed discussion.)

And finally, large-cap index funds by their very nature are generally tax-efficient. Because they trade less frequently than most actively managed funds, their realized capital gains are often lower, and distributions to shareholders can be minimal.

ANOTHER WAY TO INDEX: EXCHANGE TRADED FUNDS

Now that we've covered index funds, let's turn to exchange traded funds (ETFs), which are important newer indexing vehicles that are gaining in popularity. The first ETF launched in 1993, and by the end of 2001 a total of 202 such funds were available. Nonetheless, with a value of about $92 billion at the end of 2001, they still account for less than 3% of the value of equity mutual funds (about $3.3 trillion).

Like index funds, ETFs mirror certain indexes, like the S&P 500 (one of the best known is "Spiders"—the symbol on the exchange's ticker tape is SPY), the Dow Jones Industrial Average (or "Diamonds"— with the ticker symbol DIA), and the Nasdaq ("Cubes" because of its QQQ ticker symbol).

The key difference? Unlike a mutual fund, which can be bought only at the end-of-day price based on the fund's net asset value (NAV), exchange traded funds trade like a stock throughout the day on stock exchanges. Also like stocks and unlike mutual funds, you'll have to pay a brokerage commission every time you buy or sell an ETF. This can be a significant drawback if you trade or invest new money frequently. Let's say, for example, that you've set up your plan so that $100 is automatically invested every month. Good for you! But if you invest that in an ETF, you are probably spending several hundred dollars a year in brokerage commissions, money that you could have invested instead. In this case, it's better to use an index fund.

Both index funds and exchange traded funds offer broad diversification at a low cost, and they each carry pros and cons. Here's a snapshot of how ETFs stack up as compared to index funds:

Pros:

• ETFs sometimes carry lower operating expenses than index funds.

• If you hold an ETF for a long time, its lower operating expenses may offset the commission, and it might have lower overall costs.

• ETFs are designed to be more tax-efficient than index funds, so they may be better for taxable accounts. But this difference is usually very small.

• Some index funds require a large initial deposit, but you can buy as little as one share of an ETF. (Realize, though, that the commission may make a small purchase impractical.)

Cons:

• Because of the commissions, ETFs are *not* appropriate for investors who make relatively small or frequent purchases.

• Even though the larger and more actively traded ETFs are quite stable, some of the more narrowly focused funds may be a lot less predictable in terms of tax-efficiency and in tracking the underlying index.

• Unlike most index mutual funds, ETFs have no reinvestment option.

Investing the Explore Portion of Your Portfolio

Now comes your chance to shine—or in this case, to *out*perform the market and your Core holdings. Depending on your particular time frame and tolerance for risk, you can invest anywhere from 40% to 60% of your portfolio in Explore holdings (refer back to Figure 3.3 on page 85), which may include buying international equities, nontraditional asset classes such as REITs or hedge funds, or simply emphasizing a particular company, sector, size, or style. Two ways to do this are by buying actively managed funds and individual stocks, or a mix of the two.

ACTIVELY MANAGED FUNDS

By definition, actively managed funds (those shaped and guided by professional managers) strive to outperform the market, so they can be a great fit for the Explore portion of your stock portfolio. One of the biggest challenges is that there are literally *thousands* of funds from which to choose.

Research shows that active management can have the biggest impact with small-cap and international equities. (Remember the efficient market theory?) Statistics tell us that over the ten-year period from 1993 through 2002, 77% of actively managed large-cap funds underperformed the S&P 500 Index. Conversely, in this same ten-year period, 63% of actively managed small-cap funds *outperformed* their index, and 63% of actively managed international funds *outperformed* their index. It just makes sense that there would be a

EXPERT ADVICE FROM THE SCHWAB CENTER FOR INVESTMENT RESEARCH

Buying International

As we've mentioned earlier, international stocks can play an important role in your portfolio, providing you with extra diversification that can reduce volatility without reducing your expected return (and it may even increase your return). Somewhat understandably, however, many American investors tend to shy away from international stocks—perhaps partly because we're less familiar with foreign companies, and partly because it can be much more difficult to analyze and purchase foreign stocks.

Our advice is to persevere. Like so many other aspects of investing, however, it's a matter of balance. Just because we recommend that you have international exposure, it doesn't mean that you should go overboard. In general, most investors will derive the greatest benefit from having approximately 20% to 30% of their stock portfolio invested in international companies.

So how to best go about adding international stocks to your portfolio? For the largest foreign companies, you can buy ADRs, or American depository receipts, which are traded on the U.S. stock exchanges. But when it comes to smaller companies, trading is much more difficult. In addition, it is difficult enough to research a stock that is traded on a U.S. exchange and followed by financial institutions. But for smaller companies you not only need to speak the language, you also need to know the accounting rules and politics of the country, and understand the competitive landscape.

Therefore, unless you have special expertise, the best way for most Americans to invest overseas is through international mutual funds. And although you can certainly do this by buying an international index fund, statistics tell us that you are likely to get superior results by buying a well-managed actively managed fund.

Of course, whenever you invest, you are assuming a certain amount of risk – and when you invest overseas, you are subject to additional risks such as currency fluctuations, political and economic instability, and the country's legal and regulatory structure. This is why the fund manager's experience is so crucial, and why in the last ten years, actively managed international funds have outperformed the indexes 80% of the time. You'll pay a management fee, but when it comes to international investing, it is usually well worth the extra expense.

much better opportunity to find a diamond in the rough among smaller, less well-known, emerging companies.

Given this advice, should you restrict yourself to small-cap or international funds for your Explore holdings? Not necessarily. If you know what you're looking for and do your homework, a variety of actively managed large-cap funds—such as growth, value, or sector (industry-specific) funds—can also provide opportunities to outperform the market. Perhaps the best way to do your own research is to take advantage of the mutual fund screeners available online. At schwab.com, for example, you can screen more than ten thousand funds to find those that fit your criteria. Here are some overarching guidelines to help you make the best choices:

1. *Look at the big picture.* Think about how each prospective fund fits within the context of your overall portfolio. Are you looking for a small-cap growth fund, or a fund that specializes in a particular sector, such as telecommunications? One good way to narrow your search is to refer to Schwab's *Mutual Fund Select List®*, in which thousands of funds are screened against specific performance, risk, and cost criteria. Prepared by the Schwab Center for Investment Research, this list is arranged by category and is updated every quarter. Mutual Fund OneSource® no-transaction-fee funds are clearly separated from transaction-fee funds, and index funds are clearly separated from actively managed funds. I may be biased, but I always start my mutual fund search here.

2. *Look at the fund's long-term performance—at least three years or more.* This way you'll get a good sense of how a fund performs under varying economic and market conditions. Recent hot streaks often aren't sustained, so as enticing as those are, don't let them fool you into making a rash decision. Similarly, although you may not

EXPERT ADVICE FROM THE SCHWAB CENTER FOR INVESTMENT RESEARCH

Which Benchmark?

When interpreting the performance of your fund, be sure to use an appropriate benchmark, as follows:

Fund	Suggested Benchmark
Large-cap	S&P 500
• Large-cap value	S&P/Barra 500 Value
• Large-cap growth	S&P/Barra 500 Growth
Small-cap	Russell 2000
• Small-cap value	Russell 2000 Value
• Small-cap growth	Russell 2000 Growth
International	MSCI-EAFE (Morgan Stanley Capital International—Europe, Australasia, Far East)
Bond	Lehman Brothers Aggregate Bond

rule out a fund that has an occasional low, you probably want to avoid funds that consistently gravitate toward the bottom. A good approach is to look at the quartile returns for three years.

Also realize that in order to understand performance data, you need to compare the results to an appropriate benchmark. Don't make the mistake of comparing a fund that invests only in stocks to a fund that invests in both stocks and bonds, or a fund that invests in large-cap stocks to a fund that invests in small-cap stocks. You

THE INS AND OUTS OF FUND FEES

• A *load* is a onetime sales charge imposed by a fund. It can be charged when you either buy a fund (*front-end load*) or sell a fund (*back-end load*). It is important to understand that if you pay a load, only part of your investment actually gets invested. (Share classes indicate how a load is charged. In general, A shares indicate a front-end load, B shares indicate a back-end load, and C shares indicate a small back-end load and the maximum 12b-1 fees—see below.) *No-load funds,* on the other hand, do not incur sales charges, so all your money goes to work for you. By and large, if you have a choice between a load fund and a no-load fund, be sure to explore the less expensive no-load fund.

• Both load and no-load funds incur annual operating expenses. But these expenses, which cover things like management fees, administrative fees, and 12b-1 fees, vary considerably from fund to fund. (Small-cap and international funds tend to carry higher costs than large-cap funds, and load funds tend to have higher costs than no-load funds.) Together all of these fees make up the fund's *expense ratio,* or expenses expressed as an annual percentage of the fund's net assets, which is a good way to compare costs between funds. In general, you should be able to find a good large-cap fund with an

---

expense ratio no higher than 1%, unless it's a highly specialized fund that requires greater (and more costly) research and
management. In general, small-cap and international fund
expense ratios should run below 2%.

• 12b-1 fees are included in the expense ratio (see above)
but are worth thinking about separately. Even some no-load
funds include these annual fees, which are used to pay for
advertising and distribution costs. The regulatory cap on 12b-
1 fees is 1%, but as soon as they exceed 0.25%, the fund is no
longer considered no-load.

• Brokerage fees are incurred when a fund buys and sells
securities. In general, this fee is less significant (and more difficult to find—you have to look in the annual report) than
other fees.

---

would be comparing apples to oranges, and the comparison
wouldn't be that meaningful.

For example, let's say that your large-cap fund is up 8% for the year.
You feel pretty good about this until you look at the fund's relevant
benchmark, the S&P 500, which returned 12% for the year. On
the other hand, if your small-cap fund is up 12% and its relevant
benchmark, the Russell 2000, is up 9%, you should be justifiably
pleased.

3. *Look at costs—both sales charges (or loads) and operating
expenses.* Even though fund fees may seem relatively insignificant,
they can add up and significantly affect your return. See the box for
details.

4. *Don't forget taxes.* When you're buying a mutual fund for a taxable account, there are two statistics you need to check: the fund's
tax-efficiency rating and its after-tax return, both of which are available online, such as at schwab.com as well as on the Morningstar
Fund Ratings page at www.morningstar.com.

Why are tax considerations important? Whenever a fund sells a
holding, it is what is known as a *taxable event.* If a stock in the fund
is sold at a profit, that's a gain. If it is sold at a loss, that loss can

offset the fund's gains. But any overall gains at the end of the year are passed on to the investors as taxable distributions. (That's right, you pay the tax.) If the fund held any of those stocks for one year or less, those gains are taxed as regular income instead of as long-term capital gains (which, under current law, are taxed at 15%). In addition, "qualified" dividends (e.g., most stock dividends) are taxed at the long-term rate of 15%. "Ordinary" dividends (e.g., dividends from bonds and money market funds) are taxed at regular income rates.

One way to look deeper is to look at the fund's turnover rate, or the percentage of holdings that are sold each year. If the fund has a turnover rate of 50%, that means that half of the portfolio is being sold that year. If the fund has a turnover rate of 200%, the entire portfolio is being sold every six months. Clearly this leads to a greater possibility of capital gains distributions, which translates into higher taxes for shareholders. But if the fund manager is matching up the gains with losses, the level of turnover is less significant.

Also realize that you have to be especially careful when you buy a fund at the end of the year. Why? Most funds distribute capital gains in December. Therefore, if you buy a mutual fund in November or December, you may have to pay capital gains taxes on

TALK ABOUT A DAUNTING PROSPECT!

The only thing more intimidating than investing for the first time may be trying to make heads or tails of a mutual fund prospectus. So why bother? Because that's where you'll find a lot of the information that tells you if this is where you want to invest your hard-earned cash. Here are a few key sections to consult:

• *The fund's investment objectives and strategy.* This is where you'll find what the fund invests in (e.g., stocks, bonds, cash-equivalents, or a combination) and how it plans to make money. You might see a statement like "seeks long-term capital appreciation by investing in stocks of U.S. small-cap companies." Be on the lookout for ill-defined or risky strategies such as options trading.

• *Risk factors.* This is where you're apprised of any special risks inherent in the fund's holdings or strategy. If the fund's approach is especially volatile, it will be indicated here.

• *The fund's financial history.* Here you'll see the fund's performance for the last ten years, as well as how it compares to a given benchmark. (You need to make sure that this benchmark is the most appropriate one.) In the "Financial Highlights" table, you'll find other essential information such as the fund's total return for the last five years (the bottom line) and the portfolio turnover rate for the last five years.

• *Expenses,* which can include:

—Sales charge (front- or back-end load), a onetime commission.

—Operating expenses, which include management fees, distribution (12b-1) fees, and other operating expenses. All of these expenses will then be tallied so that you can see a total *operating expense ratio* (often called *OER*).

• *Management.* If management has changed recently, you'll want to evaluate the new team or manager.

• Other useful information such as how to purchase and redeem shares and initial and subsequent investment minimums.

---

an investment you've held only for a short time, even though you haven't received the benefit of the increase in price.

The bottom line? At the end of the day it's not how much you make that counts but how much you get to keep. Even if a fund is incredibly tax-efficient, it's the after-tax return that counts.

5. Finally, *check the manager's record.* Is the person in charge now the same individual who made the fund worth considering? Fund managers do move around, and if someone new is at the helm, the fund's performance could change in a hurry. It's always a good idea to keep an eye on who's captaining your ship, even after you invest.

WHEN TO SELL A MUTUAL FUND

If you're a long-term investor, buy-and-hold can be the easiest and most effective strategy. But about once a year you should reevaluate your funds and make sure that they are still the best choices for your portfolio. Where to start? Once again, by comparing your fund's performance to its peers and to its relevant benchmarks. If your fund is down 10% for the year but similar funds are down 15%, that's a good result. If your fund is up 10% and similar funds are up 15%, that's not so good. Performance alone—without comparing it to a benchmark—is *not* a reason to sell.

In fact, if you do fall into this trap and sell on the basis of out-of-context performance alone, you could be missing the next upward trend. Frequently a particular style of fund will be down one year and up the next. Small-cap value stocks fell 1.5% in 1999; in 2000 they rose 23%. If you had sold your well-managed small-cap value fund at the end of 1999, you would have missed the boat. The bottom line? Consider selling a fund if it has performed worse than most of its relevant peers or benchmarks for the last year; if it has been a relative underperformer for two or three years, that's a clear sell sign. If your fund has been in the bottom quartile (it has performed worse than 75% of its peers) for even a year, that's also probably an indication to sell.

Second, consider selling when a fund's objective changes. If you bought a small-cap fund that has now gravitated toward large-cap equities, and you already own as many large-cap funds as you need, it's probably time to look for a true small-cap fund. Similarly, if your small-cap funds have increased in value and are now a disproportionately large part of your overall equity portfolio, you may want to sell some in favor of other funds.

And finally, you should reevaluate your fund if it has a change in management. This is not a clear indication to sell, but remember: Your fund is only as strong as the person who is calling the shots.

INDIVIDUAL STOCKS—FOR THE LONG TERM

When people think of investing, they invariably think of stocks. But before you jump right into stock picking, realize that even though individual stocks might represent a terrific growth opportunity, they also carry a high level of risk, especially in the short term.

"I always thought that when investing online, there should be a box that asks you to identify your financial goal," says a colleague. "It's too easy to get on there and make an impulsive decision to buy a stock instead of thinking, 'Is this stock going to get me where I want to go in five, ten, twenty years from now?'"

That's exactly the question you'll want to ask yourself when you're selecting stocks. Before you write that check or click that box on a website, make sure you understand how this purchase will fit into your overall plan. Once you've figured that out, it's time to do your homework. First, make sure you understand the company's basic business plan and are familiar with its financial condition. Some investors have been quite successful by buying the stocks of companies whose products they know and like. But that doesn't give you a complete picture. You also have to research the company's financial picture, its competition, the health of the industry in general—and how all of this affects the company's future prospects.

TWO SCHOOLS OF RESEARCH

In very broad terms, stock research falls into two general categories: *fundamental analysis,* an examination of the company issuing the stock, and *technical analysis,* an evaluation of the performance of the stock price itself. Fundamental analysis focuses on things like the company's products, its competition, and its management. It also takes into account the company's financial health—whether it has consistent earnings growth, a low debt ratio, and a strong cash flow. Technical analysis, on the other hand, looks at the behavior of the stock's price over time—but doesn't attempt to explain the forces behind that movement.

Another way of looking at the difference between these two approaches is to think about a stock's *intrinsic* value, which fundamentalists believe can vary from the stock's market price. (If you believe that the intrinsic value is higher than the market price, you're a buyer; if you think that the intrinsic value is lower, you'll sell.) Technicians, on the other hand, disregard this type of evaluation and are much more likely to buy or sell on the basis of a trend or chart pattern.

In general, technical analysis is most useful for active traders or other investors with a short-term horizon. If you're a long-term investor, there is no substitute for evaluating the fundamentals. Although most investors are not likely to get involved with in-depth fundamental analysis, they can obtain a wealth of pertinent data from publicly available resources such as on schwab.com.

Admittedly, this is a lot of information to compile and review—but online tools like the Charles Schwab Stock Analyzer and the Charles Schwab Equity Snapshot, both available at schwab.com, make that job a lot easier.

Here are some basic fundamentals to check out before you buy:

1. *Earnings.* Over the short term stock prices will fluctuate for any number of reasons—from investor sentiment to the time of year. But over the long term it's a company's earnings that count. If earnings go up, so should the share price. Earnings per share (EPS) is the company's net income (after taxes), minus preferred dividends, divided by the shares outstanding. A rising EPS indicates increasing profitability.

2. *Revenues.* This is the amount of money a company takes in from the sale of its products and services. Make sure you understand a company's sources of revenue and prospects for growth.

3. *Price/Earnings (P/E) Ratio.* This highly quoted figure is the stock's price divided by its earnings per share. If a stock is priced at $50 and the company is earning $2 per share, its P/E is 25. A high P/E indicates that investors are paying a higher price for earnings and have a lot of faith in the company's prospects for future earnings. A low P/E, on the other hand, indicates lowered expectations. In general, growth stocks carry high P/Es (for example, a high-tech

company might have a P/E of 50 or higher), while value stocks generally have lower P/Es (for example, an out-of-favor stock might have a P/E in the low single digits). Whether you lean toward one or the other, be sure to compare a company's P/E to that of other companies in the same industry.

4. *Profit Margin.* This is the percentage of sales the company gets to keep. To increase its profit margin, a company has to either increase its sales or decrease its expenses. In general, technology stocks tend to have higher profit margins as well as high volatility. Many consumer staples (such as food distributors), on the other end, have low profit margins but generally more stable performance. Again, when looking at this number, you have to compare a company to its peers.

5. *Debt/Equity Ratio.* This ratio shows how much a firm has borrowed long term as a percentage of its stock equity. In general, you should be wary of companies with a higher debt ratio than their industry. Realize, though, that debt is not necessarily a bad thing. For example, if a company borrows money at 10% and makes a 20% return, that's a positive. Similarly, debt may not be a problem if a company has ample income to cover its interest payments.

Of course, no matter how careful you are, you may suffer some setbacks. I know all about that. Sometimes when I buy a stock, it immediately drops in value. Each time my heart sinks right along with that stock, but I tell myself that the company and the industry are sound and that this is just part of the normal ride.

The fact is that unless you're some kind of genie (and if you are, we'd like to meet—and hire—you), you're probably never going to see everything going up at once. The probability that you will pick every stock at its all-time low is just about nil. But as long as the big picture is up, a temporary dip may actually represent a buying, rather than a selling, opportunity. This is where that famous phrase "buy low, sell high" comes in. This is also where diversification comes in. If you're well diversified (that is, you own a variety of investments in each asset class), most likely some of your holdings will be going up while others are going down. As long as the losing stocks don't represent more than a small portion of your investments, you can afford to take—or take advantage of—the hit.

The bottom line? No matter how much research you do or how much you want to invest a large sum of money in a particular stock, you *must* remain diversified.

INTRODUCTION TO MARGIN LOANS

After you've been investing for a while, you're sure to hear someone talking about margin loans. So what are they, and are they for you?

In a nutshell, a margin loan allows you to borrow money from your brokerage company, using the securities in your account as collateral. You can use these funds for a variety of purposes, but the most common use is to buy stock "on margin." This is how it works. Let's say you want to buy one hundred shares of stock priced at $100 per share. If you pay for the entire amount up front, that will cost you $10,000 (plus commission). If the price of the stock goes up to $150, your investment is now worth $15,000. Not bad. But instead of paying for the stock in full, a margin loan will usually allow you to borrow up to half of the purchase price. Although you will eventually have to pay back the $5,000 loan (plus interest), in the short term you're only out of pocket $5,000 plus the commission.

While this concept is straightforward, and can certainly work in your favor, margin loans can entail a significant amount of risk. Continuing with our example, let's say that instead of rising to $150, the stock falls to $50. With a straight purchase, the value of your initial $10,000 investment falls to $5,000. But if you had initially bought this stock on margin, paying $5,000 and borrowing the other $5,000, you would have lost your entire up-front investment. Now let's take this scenario even further and say the stock falls to $40. In this case, the value of your shares is now $4,000, or $6,000 less than the purchase price. Now your loss exceeds your up-front investment and an additional risk is introduced—margin "calls" and margin "sellouts." Using the example of the stock falling to $40, if this decrease in price causes your account to fall below your brokerage firm's minimum maintenance requirement, your broker will either make a "margin call," asking you to deposit sufficient funds and/or securities to your account, or sell (a "margin sellout") some or all of the securities in your account to bring it back to the required minimum maintenance level. Be aware that your broker has the right to sell your securities without consulting you first if your minimums are not maintained in the required timeframe. And once that sale goes through, you have no opportunity to recoup your loss. In essence, that's the up- and downside of leverage. It's great when it works in your favor, but it can get very painful, very quickly, when it doesn't.

So what's an investor to do? Following are a few questions to ask yourself before you take out your first margin loan:

• Do you completely understand all of the rules and regulations associated with margin loans? For example, if the value of your margined stock falls below a certain level, you will be required to deposit more money or risk losing the position.

• How long have you been investing? As a general guideline, you should have at least five years of experience in the stock market before you buy on margin.

• What is your risk tolerance? If losing a large percentage of your investment would be devastating, buying on margin is not for you.

• How large is your portfolio? If you have less than $50,000 invested, a margin loan is probably not appropriate.

• How diversified is your portfolio? If you don't own a broadly diversified mix of investments, margin debt is probably too risky.

In sum, when it comes to margin loans, a little caution goes a long way. Like any other debt, margin loans can be a great tool—but only when used appropriately by a knowledgeable investor.

WHEN TO SELL A STOCK

Figuring out which stocks to buy is challenging enough, but somehow knowing when to *sell* a stock is even harder. Certainly if you hold a diversified portfolio and did your homework when you selected the stock in the first place, a drop in price alone is no reason to sell. Remember: Stock investments are generally long-term commitments; the day-to-day blips on the chart are generally not a trigger to act.

So when should you sell? In general, I use three criteria:

1. *The stock's fundamentals have changed.* When deciding whether to hold or sell, analyze the stock in the same way that you did when you decided to buy it. If it no longer passes muster, this may be an indication to sell.

2. *Your diversification is out of line.* Suppose your target is to hold 50% large-cap stocks, 25% small-cap stocks, and 25% international stocks. But large-caps now constitute 75% of your portfolio. You should consider selling the underperforming large-caps (and buying more of the others).

3. *Your personal situation has shifted.* If your circumstances have changed, perhaps due to a marriage, a divorce, or a death in the family, and as a result either your time frame or your risk tolerance has shifted, you may want to reallocate your portfolio.

EXPERT ADVICE FROM THE SCHWAB CENTER FOR INVESTMENT RESEARCH

Concentrated Positions: The Antithesis of Diversification

A concentrated equity position occurs when an individual stock makes up more than roughly 20% of your total portfolio. The danger is that the performance of your entire portfolio may be significantly affected by that stock, and as a result you may be exposed to more risk than you are comfortable with.

This concept holds for sectors and industries as well as individual stocks. You don't have to look back any further than the fall of Enron or the tech wreck of 2000 to see how concentration in any one company, industry, or sector can wreak havoc with your returns.

How do you acquire a concentrated position? Often it results from receiving shares of your company's stock in your 401(k) plan or from receiving shares in an inheritance. When you review your portfolio, you should be aware that in addition to individual equities, the concentration may be less visible but still lurking in your 401(k), IRA, or mutual funds. Do yourself a service and check them all. It may be time to rebalance.

Adding Balance with Bonds

Intelligent investing is all about balance. If you look back at the various model portfolios on pages 79–80, you'll notice right away that the more conservative the plan, the larger the percentage of bonds. This is because when *done carefully,* investing in bonds can provide a dependable stream of income and greater price stability.

But you need to be careful. The world of bond investing is huge and complex, and it's easy to get misled. You also have to keep in mind that bonds *intrinsically* don't have the ability to grow like stocks do. That's why my father and I suggest only a few ways to invest in bonds—that will provide you with the diversity you need to balance out the other investments in your portfolio, without taking on undue risk.

In Chapter 2 we talked about *trading* bonds versus holding them until maturity. If you buy an investment-grade bond and hold it until it comes due, you're almost guaranteed that you will get your original principal back (plus interest along the way). But trading (or buying and selling prior to maturity) carries other risks. Because the price you pay for a bond depends on the prevailing interest rates (bond prices go *up* when interest rates go down, and vice versa), you can certainly lose money by buying and selling at the wrong times.

You also have to consider time frames. Some government bonds don't mature for up to thirty years. (Even though the government stopped issuing new thirty-year Treasury bonds in 2001, many will remain in circulation for years to come.) But even if you have the safety of the U.S. government backing up your investment, just think what the ravages of inflation could do to your investment in thirty years!

In my mind (and my father's), five years may be the ideal time frame. Five-year Treasury notes are safe, provide a steady stream of income, and don't tie up your money for an unreasonable length of time.

LADDERING

We don't want to get too tricky (because we really do believe in keeping bonds as simple as possible), but there is one strategy, called *laddering,* that can help stabilize the bond portion of your portfolio—much as dollar-cost averaging helps even out the price fluctuations in your stock portfolio. Here's how it works:

Instead of buying bonds that are all scheduled to come due in the same year, when you ladder you buy bonds scheduled to mature at evenly spaced future dates. The idea is that if the rates go up, you can renew your maturing bonds at the better, higher rate. But if the rates go down, then you'll still have your other bonds locked into higher rates.

For example, say you invest $60,000 equally among three bonds that mature in one to three years. Bond A yields 5%, bond B yields 5.25%, and bond C yields 5.5%. In the first year your portfolio will generate an average return of $3,150 (5.25%) from the three bonds.

In a year bond A matures, and you invest the proceeds in bond D, which matures in three years. If interest rates have gone up, let's say to 6%, your new portfolio will generate a return of $3,350 (5.58%).

But if interest rates have fallen, you still buy the new bond at the lower rate. Although your yield will be lower for this bond, you will have the peace of mind of knowing that you locked in a higher rate for your other bonds. In other words, you're in good shape regardless. If interest rates go down, you've locked in a higher rate. If interest rates go up, you can continue to buy bonds that pay higher yields.

MUNICIPAL BONDS

A second type of bond investment that might make sense for you—especially if you're in a high tax bracket—is tax-free municipal bonds. When you buy a muni, your interest is generally free of federal income tax, and if the bond was issued by your state of residence, you generally won't have to pay state or local taxes either. But there are a couple of potential bugaboos. First, some types of muni bonds could be subject to the alternative minimum tax (AMT), an additional tax system created to ensure that people who claim many deductions still pay their fair tax bill. In addition, tax-exempt interest can impact the taxable status of your Social Security benefits. Be sure to double-check your situation with your tax advisor.

TIPS ON TIPS AND OTHER INFLATION-INDEXED OFFERINGS

While many of you have been offered tips on investing, this may be the first time you've gotten tips on what's commonly known as TIPS—Treasury inflation-protected securities. Introduced by the U.S. Treasury in 1997, TIPS are fixed-income securities, sold in multiples of $1,000, whose principal value is indexed to the Consumer Price Index (CPI). This helps you—the bondholder—

offset the risk that inflation will decrease the value of your principal.

Why is this worthwhile? While Treasuries carry almost no risk of default, they are subject to the ups and downs of interest rates. Therefore, if you want to sell a Treasury bond before it matures, the value of your principal may be less than what you paid. The other concern is that although you are sure you'll get the full value of your principal back when the bond matures in, say, ten years, your purchasing power will likely be reduced due to inflation.

If you buy a TIPS, however, the semiannual interest you receive is calculated as one-half of the interest rate (determined at auction) multiplied by the inflation-adjusted principal. This means that you will always receive a real rate of return above the inflation rate (but in the unlikely event of deflation, your interest payments will decrease). At maturity, the bond is redeemed at its inflation-adjusted principal amount or its par value, whichever is greater. Therefore, you will likely receive more at redemption than you paid at purchase. You can't receive less.

Which is better for you to hold: regular Treasury bonds or TIPS? The answer isn't absolute, but, as a rule, if you think inflation is rising, you'd do better with TIPS. But realize that you have to pay income tax each year on the inflation adjustments you receive from TIPS—even though you won't get the actual cash until the bond matures. This makes TIPS most appropriate for tax-deferred accounts. In addition, you should probably only buy a TIPS if you plan to hold it until maturity. Unlike many traditional bonds, it can be difficult to sell a TIPS.

Note: Other variations of principal-protected notes are available in the marketplace. Inflation-indexed savings bonds (I-Bonds), a variation of the tried-and-true U.S. government savings bonds, are also indexed to provide a hedge against inflation and are sold at face value in increments as small as $50. These bonds offer a guaranteed annual rate that remains in effect for the life of the bond as well as an additional rate that is tied to the CPI and adjusted every six months. I-Bonds can be cashed out without a penalty if you own them for five years—but if you withdraw the money before that, you will lose three months' worth of interest, much as you do with a CD. In addition, other inflation-indexed notes are assembled by third-party suppliers, but be sure you check the issuers and the fees before investing in them.

ZERO-COUPON BONDS

Another variation in the world of fixed-income investments is the zero-coupon bond. Unlike most bonds, which make interest payments semiannually, zeroes pay nothing until the bond comes due, at which time you collect all of the compounded interest in addition to the principal you invested. The advantage is that you can buy a zero at a very deep discount. The disadvantage is that you have to pay taxes on the interest you have accrued—even though you haven't collected it. This can be a real problem in a taxable account. But zeroes can be a great way to save for retirement or for your child's education—especially in a high-interest-rate environment. More on this in Chapter 6.

CHOOSING BETWEEN INDIVIDUAL BONDS
AND BOND MUTUAL FUNDS

As you know by now, individual bonds offer income payments and maturity values that do not fluctuate, as long as you hold the bonds to maturity. But when you buy a bond mutual fund, income payments and principal values will fluctuate based on market conditions. When redeemed, bond fund shares may be worth more or less than you originally paid.

Diversification also enters into this picture. When you buy individual bonds, the management—and diversification strategy—is up to you. Like other mutual funds, bond funds can provide you with diversification and professional management.

The costs of investing in individual bonds and bond mutual funds also differ. With an individual bond you pay a commission or a markup on each transaction. With a bond mutual fund you pay a percentage of invested assets each year for the operating expenses and management of the fund.

So what should you do? To help you decide, the Schwab Center for Investment Research has come up with some guidelines.

Consider investing in individual bonds if you:

• Have $50,000 or more to invest in bonds (provided that you buy high-quality bonds such as Treasuries; you need considerably more money to assemble a well-diversified corporate bond portfolio)
  • Want a fixed level of income or are saving for a specific goal
  • Want to be actively involved in managing your own money

On the other hand, you might consider investing in bond mutual funds if you:

  • Have less than $50,000 to invest in bonds
  • Are investing in corporate bonds
  • Can tolerate fluctuations in your level of income and in the value of your principal (the longer the maturity, the more volatile the bond will be)
  • Are looking for monthly income. While most bonds pay interest semiannually, bond funds usually pay dividends monthly. In order to receive monthly income from individual bonds, you would have to create a portfolio of six bonds according to their payment schedule.
  • Seek professional management and additional diversification

Are REITs Right for You?

Have you ever dreamed of investing in commercial real estate but didn't have the assets or experience to get started? REITs, or *real estate investment trusts,* may be worth considering.

REITs are companies that own, and in most cases operate, income-producing real estate such as apartments, shopping centers, office buildings, hotels, and warehouses. They have existed since Congress decided that small investors should be given a vehicle to invest in a larger "pool" of commercial real estate and enacted the Real Estate Investment Trust Act in 1960. It wasn't until years later, however, when tax shelter laws were changed (limiting the deductibility of interest and restricting the use of "passive losses") and REITs were given broader range to *operate* as well as *own* real estate, that they really started to gain in popularity.

Today individual REITs are traded on the major stock exchanges, and you can also buy REIT mutual funds that invest in a pool of REITs. Both individual REITs and REIT funds give you a practical and effective way to include professionally managed real estate in your investment portfolio, also providing the diversification of investing in a portfolio of properties rather than a single building.

When you're trying to decide whether a REIT or a REIT fund will be a good addition to your portfolio, there are several things to think about. First, most REITs are in the small- to mid-capitalization range (in July 2003, Equity Office Properties Trust, the largest REIT, had a capitalization of $11.8 billion; most REITs fall into the $1 or $2 billion range), so it should be no surprise that their performance is closely correlated to small cap stocks. If you already own your full allocation of small cap stocks (and in particular small cap *value* stocks), REITs may only provide limited additional diversification.

Second, many investors who are seeking income are attracted to REITs because they pay dividends (by law they are required to pay out 90% of their taxable income to shareholders). Realize, though, that this income comes at the cost of high volatility. REITs are subject to fluctuations in interest rates, rental and leasing demands, property values, vacancy rates, and other factors that affect real estate. In 2000, REITs as a group provided a total return of 26% (17% price increase and a 9% dividend), but in 1998, REITs *lost* 17% (they had a 22% price *drop* partially counteracted by 5% dividends).

The bottom line? If you're looking for a way to include real estate in your portfolio, REITs can be a great way to do that. But when it comes to income, they are not a replacement for lower-risk bonds.

Hedge Funds—Becoming a Household Word?

If you have only recently become aware of hedge funds, you aren't alone. Formerly the provenance of the affluent only, hedge funds are now being reformatted for a broader audience. However, before we discuss how hedge funds are changing, it's important to state what they have been.

Traditional hedge funds are loosely regulated structures that use a much wider range of investment strategies than do mutual funds. In essence, they employ whatever strategy, or combination of strategies, they believe will provide positive returns—whether the market is up, down, or flat—including:

• Arbitrage, or attempting to exploit pricing inefficiencies between related securities or currencies

• Selling short, or "borrowing" a security from a brokerage house and then selling it in the hope that when it's time to buy the stock back, the price will have fallen (and thus capturing a profit)

• Trading options, which gives the manager the right—but not the obligation—to purchase or sell optioned shares of a corporation at a specific price, thereby leveraging stock price movements

• Leverage, or using borrowed money to enhance returns

• Attempting to take advantage of price movements in mergers or hostile takeovers

Depending on the strategies used, traditional hedge funds carry varying degrees of risk and volatility, as well as large differences in performance. As a group, however, their lack of regulation, lack of liquidity (with strictly limited redemptions), and wide range of strategies have made them riskier investments than diversified mutual funds. Their primary filter has been their high price of entry—typically a minimum investment of $500,000 to $1 million as well as net worth requirements. In this way, hedge funds have excluded the less wealthy, and presumably less sophisticated, investor.

But now, in the spirit of economic "glasnost," newly regulated hedge funds are available with minimum initial investments of $50,000, opening them up to a larger pool of investors.

Another shift is that the new breed of hedge funds can be marketed publicly, which means that you can expect to see even more media dollars promoting them. Along with this advertising and new structure comes increased regulation, closer to what is in place for mutual funds. While the regulations are designed to advise prospective investors of the risks involved in these types of funds, we want to emphasize that hedge funds are not for everyone, no matter what the minimum investment or number of investors allowed in the pool. Proceed with extreme caution.

DON'T TOUCH THAT!

As we've repeatedly pointed out, building wealth is definitely not something you want to do in a vacuum, as the whys and wherefores involving how your money is invested—or spent, for that matter—affect your entire family. The good news is that by opening all this up for discussion, you may foster a whole new connection with your spouse, your kids, or even your parents. After many years a friend finally took the plunge and learned some finance and investing basics. "Listen to you!" exclaimed her delighted father when she ventured to contribute an opinion during a money-related conversation. "We can actually talk about all this now."

Of course, once you've initiated these discussions about your family's investment plan, you'll almost certainly find yourselves at loggerheads at some point. Don't give in to the temptation to cut the conversation short or avoid it thereafter. But don't just keep going around and around either—arguing won't get you anywhere but in trouble. If you can't agree on how to get where you want to go, it may be time to bring in the pros and turn to a financial advisor for some objective third-party advice. On the other hand, being sensitive to the generational differences that color these topics may help break the impasse.

For starters, remember that while you and your spouse may have similar money philosophies, your parents and children probably don't. "Each generation is driven by unique ideas about the lifestyle to which it aspires," write J. Walker Smith and Ann Clurman in *Rocking the Ages: The Yankelovich Report on Generational Marketing* (HarperBusiness, 1997). And those disparate ideas are shaped by the era in which they grew up. People who were raised during the Depression, for example, may not feel comfortable with their adult children's easy acceptance—and even expectation—of affluence and all that goes with it. Additionally, the fear of losing their money may influence how open they are to the notion of hiring professionals such as financial planners or attorneys, or even investing at all. On the flip side, the Gen-Xers to whom you're close may not behave the same way you did at their age. In short, pragmatism may outweigh their urge to be on their own—which could mean that they'll wind up at home longer than you did.

Understanding how each individual participating in the conversation perceives money will help you address those underlying issues. Keep in mind that money represents independence and dignity to an awful lot of people. Threaten one, however unintentionally (by suggesting to your parent that you might take over paying their bills, for example, or that he or she might need your financial help), and you threaten the other. As much as possible, you'll want to offer your help without even hinting at incompetence.

Finally, never forget that using money discussions to connect with people—rather than control them—will prove a whole lot more fruitful in the end.

Maximize Your Return—Year In, Year Out

The bottom line is that you want to make the most of your family's investments now and in the future. The best way to do that? Invest now, and then stay invested for the long term.

The market's in a slump? Don't panic! The worst thing you can do is to overreact and sell at a low.

People who talk about the "hot market" and "hot stocks" make it sound as if your investment must be timed just right to be successful. I caution you not to fall into that trap. It's nearly impossible to perfectly time the stock market on a regular basis, so don't even try. At Schwab we have a saying that it's *time in* the market, not *timing* the market, that matters. In fact, for all the sweating we do about putting together our portfolios, the length of time your money is invested matters even more than which stocks you choose—assuming, of course, that you have a diversified portfolio.

If you look at Figure 3.4, which reflects a study done by the

Figure 3.4
The Power of Starting Now

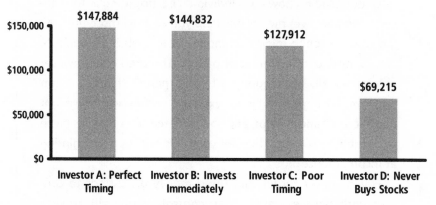

Consistent Investing versus Procrastination:
Ending Wealth for Four Hypothetical Investors (1983–2002)

Source: Schwab Center for Investment Research

Schwab Center for Investment Research, you'll see what happens to four very different hypothetical individuals who invested $2,000 a year for twenty years (starting in 1983) in four different ways:

Investor A is either very smart or very lucky, because he invested at just the right time. He placed his $2,000 in the market (represented by the S&P 500) every year at its low.

Investor B took the simple approach. Each year, once she received her $2,000, she immediately invested it in the same investment at the earliest possible moment. No decisions—just a simple, consistent approach.

Investor C suffered from terrible timing, or maybe just bad luck. He invested his $2,000 each year at its costliest peak.

What about Investor D? She left her money in Treasury bills every year and never got around to investing in the market at all. She was always convinced that lower prices—and therefore better opportunities—were just around the corner.

So let's look at their results.

Of course, Investor A did great, accumulating $147,884.

The most unexpected result is that of Investor B, who came in second with $144,832—only $3,052 less than A over a twenty-year period. This relatively small difference is really surprising because Investor B simply put her money to work as soon as she received it each year, without any guesswork or timing at all.

Investor C's results are also encouraging. While his poor timing left him with around $17,000 less than Investor B, he still earned a total of $127,912, almost $60,000 more than he would have had he not invested in stocks at all.

And what about Investor D, who kept waiting for just the right moment? She fared worst of all, garnering only $69,215. She was so worried about investing at the market high that she paralyzed both herself and her chances of earning a substantial return on her money. Ironically, even if she *had* bought in at every single yearly market high (which, no offense to Investor C, is darn near impossible), she could have earned over three times as much over the twenty-year period.

As you can see, whether the market is high or low over any given year is less important than just making sure you invest in a diversified mix of holdings. And although we have shown the data for only the twenty-year period from 1983 to 2002, virtually all twenty-year periods show the same result. The reality is that investing is not about market timing—it's about consistent investing over time. That means investing today and for the long term.

Let's look at it another way. Figure 3.5 shows that the annualized return for the S&P 500 Index for the ten-year period from 1993 to 2002 was 9.3%. But if you were out of the market for just the best ten days, your return would have only been 4.3%—more than 50% lower. And watch what happens if you missed the best twenty, thirty, or forty days. Your return begins to fall and drops all the way down to −5.4%! To me, the message is clear: Trying to time the market is nothing short of a gamble—and a time-consuming one at that!

Sometimes investors get so caught up in the day-to-day changes that they lose sight of the big picture. In that big picture of investing, what you want to achieve is a healthy portfolio that is appropriate for your time horizon and risk tolerance—and that will serve you and your family not just today but throughout all your tomorrows as well.

Figure 3.5
The Effect of Missing the Top Ten Days, 1993–2002

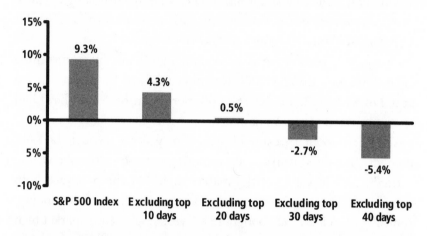

Source: Schwab Center for Investment Research® with data provided by Standard & Poor's. Data is annualized based on an average of 252 trading days within a calendar year. The year begins on the first trading day of January and ends on the last trading day of December and daily total return index closing levels were used for the period 1993 through 2002. Total return includes reinvestment of dividends. Indices are unmanaged, do not incur fees or expenses, and cannot be invested in directly. Past performance is no indication of future results.

Whatever approach you take to dealing with risk, the bottom line is that you have to be able to live with your decisions. It's your life, it's your money, and investing wisely is the task of a lifetime.

So don't count on someone else to do it for you. Get in there and make it happen for yourself and those close to you. And when you do, just remember four things:

• Stocks have historically outperformed other investment vehicles over the long run.

• The earlier you start, the less you usually need to invest to achieve your goal.

• Market volatility is par for the course. If you look at the history of the market, downturns are simply part of the natural order, just as a two-year-old's tantrums and teen rebellions are inherent to growing up. Despite the occasional steep declines, which admittedly are frightening, history has shown that the long-term trend of the stock market is up.

- To achieve the most predictable results, you must be diversified within and across asset classes.

Keeping Up with Yourselves

Staying in the market for the long term doesn't mean that once you determine your asset allocation you walk away and never look back. As your life changes, you and your loved ones will need to periodically revisit your dreams and your portfolio to make sure that everything is still pertinent and in sync. Also realize that when I talk about your portfolio, I am referring to all of your investment holdings—including your 401(k), IRA, and taxable accounts.

So sit down with your family members and a cup of coffee next Saturday or Sunday morning and go over your investments together. As my father explains in the accompanying text, staying on track involves assessing the performance of your individual holdings and, perhaps more importantly, making sure that your asset allocation is still on target. If a stock or fund has consistently underperformed, you'll have to decide whether to hang in or jettison it. On the other hand, if a stock has done brilliantly, in addition to celebrating, you may need to talk about rebalancing your portfolio by selling some of that stock and investing in something completely different. Why? Because that success probably means that your carefully planned portfolio is now out of kilter.

I realize that this may sound counterintuitive. You may well be inclined to stick with a stock or an asset class that has done well, and sell the stock, fund, or asset class that has underperformed. But your overarching goal is to maintain the appropriate allocation and to be diversified within each asset class.

As a rule of thumb, I recommend that you review your asset allocation about once a year—or more frequently if your circumstances have changed. If any one asset class is more than 5% off your target, it's probably time to take action. Otherwise, you may be assuming a lot more investment risk than you realize—which is probably the opposite of what you want to do as the years go by.

Chuck's Two Cents: Knowing When and How to Rebalance

One of the keys to achieving financial long-term success is creating and maintaining a balanced portfolio. A balanced portfolio is one that is based on an appropriate asset allocation model (given the investor's time frame and tolerance for risk) and that is adequately diversified within and among asset classes. But once you have that beautifully balanced portfolio, you don't just ignore it, any more than you ignore any other part of your life. You maintain it, which means that, now and then, you make sure it has kept its balance, and if necessary, you do some rebalancing, which simply means bringing your portfolio back to its original percentages.

Over time, due to market fluctuations, the proportion of stocks, bonds, and cash-equivalent investments that you chose originally can change. For example, suppose you start out with 60% of your portfolio invested in stocks and 35% invested in bonds (with 5% in cash). Two years later, you find that, as a result of an increase in stock prices, you now have 75% of your portfolio invested in stocks, with only 20% in bonds. Or after a down market you may find that you have 55% in bonds and only 35% in stocks (with 10% in cash). What do you do?

First, ask yourself if you're unhappy with those new percentages. True, they aren't what you originally chose, but it may be worth your while to reexamine where you started in terms of asset allocation. If you decide that the new percentages are acceptable, all is well. You don't need to do anything else for now. If not, it's time to do some rebalancing.

If you choose to rebalance, you can do so in a couple of ways:

• Buy more of what's low. This is the easiest approach and, to my mind, the most advantageous, if you have the money to add to your investing pot. You simply buy more of the investment that's low. In the first example above, you would buy enough bonds (or bond funds) to bring the percentages to the mix you wanted. In the second example you would buy more equities.

• Sell some of what's high. Selling off some of the holding that's too high and reinvesting that money in the holding that's low also works. In the first example above, you would sell some stocks and reinvest that money in bonds. Or if you had just been through a mar-

ket decline, as in the second example, you would sell some of your long-term bonds and buy more equities.

Realize, though, that if you're rebalancing a taxable account, you have to consider the tax implications—that is, if you sell an investment that has appreciated, you may incur capital gains. As a side note, I'll add that as a long-term investor, I generally don't even consider selling more than once a year, thanks to the tax advantages of a buy-and-hold strategy.

My wish for you is that you and your family will take these suggestions to heart. After all, reevaluating your portfolio together can give you the opportunity to stay in touch emotionally as well as fiscally. As you keep on talking and planning, you're well on your way to financial independence.

Something to Talk About

• *Where do you stand in fulfilling your financial goals such as saving for your retirement, saving for college for your children, helping your parents as they age, or buying a home or a vacation retreat?*

• *Have you figured out the best way to get started working toward your goals? If you've already initiated the process, what's next?*

• *Have you figured out the most appropriate asset allocation for your time frame and risk tolerance? When it comes to the equity portion of your portfolio, how big a percentage do you want in Core versus Explore investments?*

• *Do you know how to choose a mutual fund? An individual stock? Should you hold on to the investments you already have, or can you find better value?*

• *Do index funds or exchange traded funds make more sense for you?*

• *Should you consider adding either individual bonds or bond mutual funds to your portfolio?*

• *When is the last time you revisited your portfolio? Are you meeting your goals? Do personal or market changes now mandate a shift in your asset allocation?*

4

Joining Forces

Like so many young couples, when my husband Gary and I got married in 1985, we basically lived on a shoestring. Gary was a sportswriter for the *Washington Post,* and I was a new broker at Schwab. Our incomes weren't large, but we managed to pay our way with Gary's salary and to bank mine. We even bought our first home—a town house located outside of Washington, D.C.

Looking back, I realize we never really talked that much about money. But we were lucky because we shared the same (and at the time unspoken) values as well as the sense that we should save for the future. We didn't know exactly where we were going at first, but we did know we'd need resources along the way. As a result, when those turning points came, as they do in everyone's life, we had choices.

As time passed, our financial dealings evolved along with the rest of our life together. We learned to discuss money issues and make decisions as a team. In short, we learned how to stay in step with each other—a true feat, when you consider our track record on the dance floor. We may have argued ourselves right out of the ballroom dancing class we took early on in our marriage, but when it comes to money, we've gotten pretty good about knowing the moves and not tromping on each other's toes.

It takes awhile to build up enough trust to lead and follow each other and to develop the same kind of fluidity that long-married couples have when they fox-trot together—which is exactly why financial arrangements tend to evolve right along with relationships. Of course, the more we know about each other, as well as about our financial alternatives, the more readily we can get in sync. Some of the best lessons I've learned about dealing with this money dance have come from my professional as well as my personal life. Seeing how my friends and clients who are married, who have remarried, or who live together handle their various financial situations has taught me more than any textbook strategy ever could.

Take my friends Anna and Josh. When they decided to get married, each was determined not to repeat the mistakes of their first marriages. Anna needed to ensure that she would not lose her sense of identity—or autonomy—as she did with her first husband. Josh was concerned about protecting his separate property this time around. So they made sure to do what they had previously neglected: They talked together about their fears, about their desires, and about how they could make their plans and dreams come true.

Their discussions started when they decided to draw up a prenuptial agreement. Although it's widely assumed that "prenups" are necessary only when the rich marry "beneath" them, a prenup is actually a great way to get all kinds of money issues—from sharing expenses to sharing responsibilities—out in the open. Even if you never formalize the document, a prenup can provide the outline for these vital conversations, walking you through all you need to cover.

Anna and Josh decided that they each wanted to have their own money—separate funds they could draw upon without consulting each other. At the same time they wanted to feel like a family unit. Their solution was for each to put a set amount each month into a communal pot to pay for all joint expenses, including the mortgage, food, utilities, taxes, and insurance premiums, as well as joint savings that funnel into a joint brokerage account. Since Josh earns more than Anna, he puts more in the pot; otherwise he'd be left with a lot more personal discretionary money than Anna. This bothered him at first. But after talking about it, he realized that he didn't want to be able to drive a sports car while his wife drove a clunker (unless, of course, that was how she chose to spend her separate money). The way they see it, this arrangement allows them to be equal partners no matter how much money they make independently.

It took many discussions—and a fair amount of discomfort and stress—to reach this financial accord. This process of articulating their needs was new to both Anna and Josh, and not wanting to hurt each other's feelings made it even harder. But once they'd finalized the agreement, their sense of relief was rivaled only by the new sense of closeness that the process had engendered.

While Anna and Josh's particular arrangement may not work for you, their process will. And even if you've been married for decades, the issues we address in this chapter—from dividing financial responsibilities, to making joint decisions, to openly discussing all things financial—are just as relevant for you as they are for newlyweds. Some of you will want to create a legal document such as a prenuptial agreement or a cohabitation agreement (or even a postnuptial agreement if you're already married). That's a personal decision. (And if you do decide to go that route, you will need to consult an attorney, preferably one who specializes in family law.) But whether you make your agreement legal or not, your time spent talking will be worthwhile; by resolving differences early on, you'll sidestep a multitude of conflicts down the line.

Although many couples perceive family financial decisions as all-or-nothing propositions, they don't need to be. How you handle your money and how your partner reacts, what he or she agrees to, may be a marker of where you stand in the relationship—and what you may need to work on. The good news is that you'll be able to apply what you learn in terms of negotiating about money to all other aspects of your relationship. As Anna and Josh found, talking things through brought them closer together, provided a foundation for their relationship, and made it easier to talk not just about money but about everything else as well.

Chuck's Two Cents: Of Money and Marriage

I want to underscore Carrie's point about the importance of married couples talking over financial matters. Certainly we've all heard about the havoc that money issues can wreak on a marriage. And it is my belief that money is always an issue, even when it doesn't seem to be. Therefore my advice is to take the time not only to know the numbers but to understand your feelings about money and any differences between you and your spouse. For example, if one of you comes from an affluent family and the other doesn't, that can affect all of your dealings with money—from how you save, to how you spend, to how you invest.

If you're already married, it's never too late to start the conversation. If you're the primary wage earner and the one paying the bills, ask your spouse if he or she has a clear picture of where you stand. And if your spouse is the one who takes the money lead, be specific about where you're in the dark. If you're just starting out—either newly married or about to be—meeting with your family lawyer or financial advisor to go over the details of your financial lives is one of the best things you can do for your future. You may or may not want a prenuptial agreement; the conversation and the understanding it engenders are what's important. It's been my experience that the potential rewards—a stronger financial future and a stronger marriage—are well worth the effort.

THE EXPERTS WEIGH IN

There's nothing simple about talking to the ones we love about money. Money has so many psychological overlays—from our childhood, from past relationships, from our careers, from you-name-it—that the resulting feelings can interfere with communication.

For starters, most of us are hypersensitive to criticism from the ones we love. If you don't believe me, just think about how you felt the last time your significant other didn't compliment you on how you looked or for a job well done. And that wasn't a dig! When those negative comments hit, and they're bound to in even the best relationship, even the mildest censure or judgment can feel devastating.

Psycholinguist Deborah Tannen calls this the paradox of family. "You want the one you love to be an intimate ally who reassures you that you're doing things right, but sometimes you find an intimate critic who implies, time and time again, that you're doing things wrong," she writes in *I Only Say This Because I Love You: How the Way We Talk Can Make or Break Family Relationships* (Random House, 2001). "It's the cumulative effect of minor, innocent suggestions that creates major problems."

According to Marcia Millman, in *Warm Hearts and Cold Cash: The Intimate Dynamics of Families and Money* (Free Press, 1991), "In far too many families, money (often in the form of gifts) is used as a gauge of love—or a substitute for it. In families, there is a constant activity of accounting, both emotional and financial, with deep expectations and definite, if unspoken, rules of exchange. Though we commonly romanticize the family as the one place where all is shared and where nobody measures, in fact there is probably more counting in families than in any other close circle. What may start as a grievance over attention or love that was desired and not received is often converted into a financial debit."

This only complicates an issue that surely doesn't need further misinterpretation. Again, the only way around this quagmire is to talk. Unfortunately, many of us continue to resist. Most of those who acknowledge that they're hesitant to discuss money in their second marriage, for example, admit that financial issues contributed to the demise of their first marriage. How ironic! By refusing to break through their reluctance and discuss the money issues that surface in every relationship, they're dooming themselves to repeat the same mistakes and conflicts and, more than likely, the same outcome. Statistics bear this out: Second marriages fare just as poorly as first marriages.

Making It Legal and Making It Clear

When it comes to marriage, it's best to examine and define your financial relationship well before you tie the knot. If money squabbles and misunderstandings contribute to most divorces, your best defense is a good offense, which means getting those financial conversations going from the start.

For many couples, like Josh and Anna, a prenuptial agreement—or a legal document that not only spells out how a couple's assets will be distributed in case of divorce, but that can also include agreed-upon financial terms for the marriage—may be the best answer. Others may not want or need to go the formal written route. I'm not an attorney, so I can't provide legal advice, but I can tell you that I believe firmly that *every* couple entering into a committed living-together relationship—whether a marriage or not—needs to thoroughly discuss ahead of time how they plan to merge their financial lives.

Granted, a prenup isn't the most romantic notion. But if you think that's unromantic, consider a messy divorce. Though prenups have traditionally looked ahead to the demise of the marriage, my feeling is that handled correctly, they can actually improve the present and long-term health of your relationship. Why? First, because preparing a written document compels you to talk about what every couple must discuss. Second, it eliminates the possibility of either of you forgetting a discussion or remembering it differently. And third, it gets everything out in the open.

Certainly you don't need to be rich or famous to consider a prenuptial agreement. Josh and Anna weren't. In fact, prenups make a lot of sense for a lot of people. Just look at the following list of possible scenarios:

• One of you is coming into the marriage with significantly more money or property than the other.

• One or both of you has significant assets, such as a home, stock, or retirement funds, that you want to protect.

• One or both of you own all or part of a business that you've built up over years.

• One or both of you are expecting to receive a sizable inheritance.

• One or both of you have children from a previous marriage.

• One or both of you have alimony responsibilities from a previous marriage.

• One of you will be supporting the other through college or graduate school.

• One or both of you have significant debt.

In every one of these situations (and more), a prenup will be able to help you clarify your issues *before* they have a chance to turn into a problem or a source of dissension. At the very least, you should talk through how you will deal with your situation in a way that is fair for both of you.

WHAT BELONGS IN A PRENUP?

Property. First and foremost, a prenup should indicate how your assets will be divided if you and your mate split up. In this case, *property* refers not only to your savings, investments, income, home, car, and jewelry but also to your retirement plans, stock option plans, and interest in your business. In other words, it's everything. (Tip: Draw up your list of assets before you arrive at the attorney's office since time, as they say, is money.)

In general, there are two ways to go here. First, you can consider all property that you acquired prior to your marriage as separate, and all property that you acquire after your marriage as joint. Alternatively, you can continue to keep your assets separate, even after you are married (but to pull this off, you will have to be very careful not to commingle your accounts or their appreciation). Or you can come up with whatever combination of these plans works for you—provided, of course, that you're both clear and it is in writing.

Splitting up financial responsibilities. Although this is optional, many couples choose to stipulate how they will split up household expenses after they are married. In this section, you can indicate which expenses you agree that you should share (for example, your mortgage, utilities, groceries, etc.), and those you want to keep separate (perhaps your clothes, personal entertainment, etc.).

Spousal support. If you divorce, will one of you continue to support the other? If you have particular conditions that you feel strongly about, this is your time to write them down. Or if you want to waive spousal support, that's another option in most, but not all, states.

Illness and disability. If one of you becomes disabled or has significant medical expenses, you can indicate how you will pay for this as a couple.

Estate planning. Although a prenup is not a substitute for a will or trust, you may want to stipulate that certain separate property will pass to your children, for example. Be careful, though: You must make sure that your provisions completely dovetail with your other estate planning documents. See Chapter 8 for details about estate planning.

Debts. A prenup is a great place to indicate how you will handle any debts incurred prior to and during marriage.

Filing tax returns. Will you file a joint return? In almost all cases, this is the wisest choice, but there are exceptions.

A sunset clause. If you want, you can specify a period of time— perhaps ten years—when you will reevaluate the terms of your prenup.

A severability clause. If one part of your prenuptial agreement isn't enforceable, such as an agreement on religious practices, child-rearing, or personal responsibilities, the rest of the prenuptial is still enforceable.

Dispute resolution. Decide how you will deal with conflict and how you will proceed if a dispute arises. For example, you can agree in advance to use mediation.

WHAT DOESN'T BELONG?

Child custody or support arrangements never belong in a prenup (and are not enforceable). But if you or your partner already has children, you can use this opportunity to get any care-related issues out on the table early. You may even want to discuss parental care, no matter what age your parents are.

Any arrangement that will be considered "unfair" to one of you. In addition to creating distrust, courts will not enforce prenuptials that are unfair or, in legal terminology, "unconscionable."

PRENUP ETIQUETTE: HANDLE WITH CARE!

Also realize that the process you use to arrive at your goal is crucial. For example, treating your beloved as a business rival and driving a hard bargain may make it hard—if not impossible—to have a mutually supportive relationship once you're finished. This doesn't mean that you won't have disagreements as you try to come to terms with an arrangement you both can live with. Of course you will. Those differences of opinion, however, needn't be daggers in your hearts. This is where you can take a lesson from the children around you. Kids barter and make deals all the time. If one wants to play marbles and the other hide-and-seek, they find a way to work it out, albeit loudly sometimes. It's called give-and-take. And while you don't usually wind up with everything you want, you come away with an arrangement that's fair. When you get right down to it, the do's and don'ts of marital financial agreements—or prenup etiquette, if you will—are pretty simple:

• Don't spring the idea of a prenup, let alone a completed document, on your mate. The more time you have to discuss the notion, as well as the arrangements, the better.
• Stress how this process can strengthen your relationship by resolving areas of potential conflict, as well as crystallizing how you each feel about—and deal with—money.
• Negotiate as loving partners, not as business rivals out to best each other.
• Never issue an ultimatum.
• As in all family money conversations, find a spot where you're both equally comfortable and equally empowered. That means your

private den or office is out, but the living room, kitchen, or dining room might work just fine.

• Keep this between the two of you. You can certainly consult your friends and family about whether you want a prenup or what to include. But when it comes to the actual negotiating, bringing them in to support your position is not playing fair. Make sure that you go over each paragraph after the document is complete to ensure that each person feels comfortable with the details. Use this review process to bring up any lingering doubts or feelings.

The decisions you make now may well need to be revisited periodically as circumstances change down the line. Like everything else that has to do with relationships—and money, for that matter—this too is an ongoing process. The real trick is to talk openly now and in the future, if you really want to give your relationship the foundation to grow. So whether you decide on a prenup or not,

COHABITATION AGREEMENTS

If you decide to move in together without getting married, I agree with the lawyers who recommend that you go through the same sort of process as a couple contemplating marriage. Like a prenup, a *cohabitation agreement* can record your intended financial responsibilities and obligations to each other and clarify your joint and separate property. It also will prompt you and your partner to discuss crucial issues, thereby helping you to have an open and rewarding relationship. Cohabitation contracts are an especially good vehicle for same-sex couples whose unions are not recognized the same way by state law, thereby depriving them of whatever protection their state marital laws might have provided. Also like a prenup, cohabitation agreements should be in writing and reviewed by your individual attorneys.

discussing money basics and histories—from goals and feelings to income sources and levels to what you own and what you owe— must be a priority. If you want to talk about spoiling romance, just let this stuff simmer and don't address it.

"These are things people should talk about in a first marriage," says Anna. "Unfortunately, most people don't get around to them until their second."

For Richer, for Poorer

Often the adage "opposites attract" seems to apply just as much to our money attitudes as anything else. Sometimes it's easier to detect these differences in others than it is in our own relationships. Have you ever noticed that your friend who spends money freely is married to a penny-pincher? Or perhaps what attracted you to your spouse in the first place—like their generosity or laissez-faire, easygoing attitude—is the same trait that bothers you later on and can even threaten to break you apart? To keep this from happening, your first step is to figure out not only how compatible you are when it comes to basic money and investing styles but also how to work around those areas of incompatibility.

Meet Max and Bridgette. When these clients married in 1994, they knew that their financial upbringings couldn't have been more different.

Max had been raised wanting for nothing. His father, a lawyer, was determined to provide the best for his family. He sent his two sons to private school and then put them through college and graduate school, during which time they lived in nice apartments rather than more typical student housing. While Max's parents didn't exactly live in the lap of luxury, they drove around in it—and were always impeccably dressed and groomed. Then came the reality check, when Max's father's law office experienced a downturn. Suddenly all those hefty bonuses were history. Eventually the firm went, too. Although the situation was never discussed, Max could see the impact that the reduced income had on his parents, who had been so busy spending their money that they had never saved enough. Understandably, Max became a money control freak or, to use his own term, a tightwad. Determined never to allow himself to fall into a similar situation, he'd watch every penny that came in and went out of his and his wife's joint checking account, which he checked every morning before going to work.

To say that Max's obsessiveness didn't work for Bridgette would be an understatement. Her father—a frugal produce manager who had spent the last thirty years working for the same supermarket chain—was about as different from Max's father as night from day. So too was her reaction to how she was raised. Denied the chance to spend money on herself growing up, she jumped at the opportunity as an adult.

Each morning when Max would see a new department store expense, he'd go ballistic. So each night they'd fight about it. "I was putting a lot more into our account than she was, but she was spending a lot more," he recalls. Figuring that there was no reason to deprive himself if she wasn't going to deny herself anything, Max made a few expensive purchases. Naturally, that did nothing to resolve the problem. So they fought even more. In short, their diametrically opposed money styles brought out the worst in each other. "It was so ugly and painful," recalls Max. "It was horrible."

Five years into their marriage a $2,000 credit card bill finally got them talking.

"I'm probably too protective of our money and don't trust you enough because you overspend," he admitted to his wife, managing to censure her even in his confession.

Then came the surprise.

"You know what," replied Bridgette, "I do it just to get back at you sometimes, because I know it makes you mad."

Resentful of the control Max was trying to impose, she would overspend just to prove that she was still independent—which would make him try to control her even more.

A single suggestion—sitting down and talking about what each of them wanted—helped shatter the vicious cycle that had threatened their finances as well as their relationship. Looking and feeling good were important to Bridgette. Saving money was important to Max. "So why don't you take a certain portion of our income and put it away?" his wife asked. He proceeded to do just that. In addition, "I just let go," he says. "That really helped out tremendously." For out of respect for her husband's willingness to trust her, and realizing that she had to uphold her part of their bargain, Bridgette made a concerted effort to cut down on her spending.

That was two years ago. "Once we overcame that hurdle, we suddenly had money to invest. We've started the whole process of putting together a financial plan, reorganizing our finances, and setting a shared monthly goal," says Max. "I cannot tell you how much that's helped our relationship."

Who Takes the Lead?

Even in relationships where money isn't a source of conflict, there's usually one person who manages the money while the other remains less involved. In our family I'm the one who takes the lead. Gary and I talk about any and all money-related decisions, but I'm the one who pays the bills, balances our checkbook, prepares our tax return, and researches investments. Of course, that means that every now and then I let myself in for a little ribbing, especially when the value of the stock I buy falls. But Gary, a sportswriter turned author, knows from experience that I've done my research and invested in sound companies. In short, he's learned to ride out the inevitable downs as well as to appreciate the ups.

Gary freely admits that he leans heavily on me when it comes to investing and money management. "We play to our strengths. She handles the finances, and I write the thank-you notes," he quips. The first time he met my dad, he laughed as he said that the only thing he knew about the stock market was that it was listed in the back of the sports page. Later, when my father tried to convince him to go back to school and get an M.B.A., Gary said, "Hey, I already cover the NBA."

Get the picture?

Still, despite Gary's self-deprecating jokes, he has a tremendous amount of knowledge about our investments. Like so many couples, our perspectives seem dramatically different. Whether we're investing in stocks or buying a house, I tend to be more willing to push beyond my comfort zone and take a chance, while Gary's more cautious and risk-averse. When we bought our second home in Atlanta right after our second son was born, Gary literally couldn't sleep nights for fear that we wouldn't be able to afford it. He was sure that we'd be forced to sell within six months.

In the end it worked out fine. And even if we don't have major discussions about every single investment, I evaluate any comment Gary makes, no matter how lighthearted, and we make our decisions together. We both recognize that this contrast in our money philosophies provides a good balance in our family.

Decision-Making at Its Finest

Although one of you may function as the primary money-person in your family, making decisions as a couple shouldn't be like a round of Follow the Leader. Too often one partner handles the finances while the other, whether because of control issues, or his or her own reluctance to become involved, is kept in the dark. In a healthy relationship, however, each partner has financial autonomy and knows exactly what's going on with the family's financial affairs (especially since your spouse's bad credit is also yours). In addition, since every decision will affect both parties, each partner needs to participate in determining how the family money is invested or spent.

This is where issues of self-sufficiency, respect for differences, cooperation, trust, and mutual support come into play. And the only way to figure out the rules of the road—in this case, how you want to handle your money as a family—is to discuss them in a way that mirrors the financial relationship you want to set up. "Family talk is a matter of finding just the right blend of responsibility, caring, and independence—the right footing, in other words, on a continuum between hierarchy and equality," writes Deborah Tannen. Similarly,

BRIDGING THE SALARY GAP

Does one of you make a lot more money than the other? Traditionally, of course, men have earned more. That didn't seem to pose a problem for anyone, since it supported our socialized notion of men being both the protectors and the providers. But more and more women these days are earning higher salaries. And what should seem like a cause for celebration is proving downright thorny for many couples.

But just as net worth doesn't equal self-worth, how much money a person contributes to the pot is not a gauge of how much he or she contributes to the relationship or the family. This is especially true when one parent decides to put his or her career on hold to care for and raise the children. Sacrificing one's professional ambitions for the good of the family shouldn't mean sacrificing one's autonomy as well.

"My wife decided to stay home when our son was born. That was a really tough adjustment for her, because all of a sudden she wasn't kicking in her hunk of money," says Zach Piper, a Schwab colleague. "But by going in jointly and looking at our household as a business—this is how much money flows into Piper and Piper, Incorporated, and this is what we need to allocate out—it works just fine."

Nor is how much a person contributes a gauge of who's stronger or better or "wearing the pants." So let's move past those stereotypes and look at each other as people rather than as wage earners whose merit is defined by how much money or income they contribute.

Of course, that's not going to happen overnight, even if you both philosophically agree that how much each of you earns shouldn't matter. So how do you deal with those issues that will inevitably rear their ugly little heads? You talk about them.

family money is a matter of finding just the right blend of responsibility, caring, and independence on a continuum between autonomy and operating as a unit to support the family team.

Those concepts aren't mutually exclusive. You and your partner should value the fact that you're both independent people who lead individual lives. But you can also treasure your life together. This balance is really important for couples, but it doesn't necessarily come right away.

Trust and intimacy grow gradually, no matter how stellar your relationship. As reported in Patricia Schiff Estess's *Money Advice for Your Successful Remarriage* (Betterway Books, 1996), Anita Metzen, former executive director of the American Council on Consumer Interests, and her husband, Dr. Edward Metzen, a consumer and family economist at Purdue University, delineate five stages of trust. Although originally conceived for remarried couples, I believe that this progression carries over to first-marrieds as well.

1. *The Rose-Colored-Glasses Stage,* in which romance rules and money talk seems completely unnecessary if not irrelevant.

2. *The Don't-Rock-the-Boat Stage,* during which feelings of resentment or anger are suppressed for fear of ruining the budding relationship.

3. *The Lay-It-on-the-Table Stage,* where feelings, frustrations, and fears are honestly, albeit roughly, shared with each other.

4. *The Getting-It-Together Stage,* during which a mutually agreed-upon lifestyle, as well as a workable financial arrangement and decision-making process, have been put into place.

5. *The Achieving Stability Stage,* where integrated perspectives and common goals mean smooth sailing together no matter how rough the waters might become or what other changes the future holds.

Of course, in the process of striving for equality, you'll both have to engage in the dreaded event known as compromise. The good news is that as bitter as those concessions can taste going down, they often mean that things work out better in the end.

Even though Gary and I share common goals, along with the intense belief that family comes first, life- and money-related decisions aren't always easy. When my career prompted us to move to the San Francisco Bay Area in the summer of 2001, Gary was reluctant to go. The kids were happy in their school, and our quality of life was terrific and cost a whole lot less than a comparable setup in the Bay Area. So, as Gary says, "we fought our own Civil War over moving," and "Atlanta burned again."

It was a long haul for us, but we worked it out. We talked, although the discussions weren't easy. We discussed what the move would mean for us as a family—leaving our friends, having our children leave their school, leaving a community we all loved—and what the move would mean for Gary and me individually. We had to deal with some anger, as well as some conflicts between our personal and career goals.

Along the way we had to learn to sort out what Deborah Tannen calls the *metamessage* from the *message*. Simply put, the message is what a person literally says, like "I'm hungry." The metamessage is what the speaker implies ("You need to feed me") or what the listener assumes is implied ("By not feeding me, you're not taking care of me properly").

"Everything we say to each other echoes with meanings left over from our past experiences—both our history talking to the person before us at this moment, and our history talking to others," writes Tannen. "This is especially true in the family—and our history of family talk is like a prism through which all other conversations and relationships are refracted."

Being able to distinguish what's actually being *said* (whether verbalized or implied) from the *inferences* we superimpose on the words helps clean up messy conversations. But it does nothing to dispel disagreements, which are inevitable in any relationship. Which brings me right back to my family's controversial move to the Bay Area.

Once Gary agreed to leave Atlanta, we had to start our relocation process. Step one? Finding a place to live that we both liked. After seeing a dozen houses, we found the one we wanted. We were about to bid when Gary pulled back. "The price is way out of line," he announced. "I don't think we should go there." So we didn't, even though the house had everything we were looking for.

I was extremely disappointed, of course. I loved that house, and I wanted to have a sense of being settled. But Gary suggested that we wait a couple of months to see if the price would come down. Two months later his strategy paid off when we bought the house for substantially less than we would have had to pay the first time around. And I learned the value of compromise, and talk, yet again.

DON'T TOUCH THAT!

What are the four words many men hate to hear? "We need to talk."

Considering how much financially related psychological baggage we all carry around, it stands to reason that "we need to talk about money" sounds just that much worse. That's exactly why approaching this topic in a nonthreatening way is so critical.

For starters, no one likes to be preached to, so make sure you engage in a dialogue as opposed to an extended monologue.

Separate what's actually being said or implied from any additional—and inappropriate—messages you might be adding. When in doubt, ask. For example, although you could easily assume that a request for separate accounts indicates mistrust, it may simply have to do with a desire for autonomy. At different stages in their lives, many people need to have a sense of self-determination in order to have a sense of self or self-worth. And that's usually good for a marriage, as long as you talk about it together.

Remember that making financial decisions together doesn't mean that you're asking for permission. Communal money simply requires communal agreement.

Keep others out of your discussion. Using your friends' or family's opinions to buttress an argument will simply make your mate defensive.

Pick your moment. Hitting your partner with a situation you've been stewing about all day the second he or she walks in the door probably isn't an ideal time.

Instead of confronting a family member with a problem, you might try presenting it in terms of a possible solution (such as specific ways you might cut back and save money). Those of you who tend to phrase ideas and wishes as questions or opinions (i.e., "Do you think we might turn down the heaters at night to economize?") may need to take a firmer stance (i.e., "Turning down the heaters will save us money—I'd like to do that") in order to be heard. You may want to avoid suggestions that include the words "Let's do that" with partners who are particularly sensitive to control issues, suggests Tannen, since that expression can be misinterpreted as a command rather than a suggestion or preference.

Try to understand where your partner is coming from rather than indulging in one-upmanship. In this same vein, showing your own fallibility will foster a connection rather than a competition between you. Remember, this is not about winning, it's about working things out.

Once you finish talking, take an emotional temperature reading to see if you're both okay with the discussion as well as its outcome.

Show Me the Money

No matter who manages the money in your family, both parties need to have equal access to the family assets, as well as full knowledge of what's what—from where your banking, savings, and brokerage accounts reside to how that money is invested. Even though what you don't know won't necessarily kill you, it sure can cost you financially and emotionally. A woman in her forties, who introduced herself after a speech I gave, told me that her husband had invested heavily in commodities futures without her knowledge. They wound up losing everything, including their home.

Nothing can change what happened to that unfortunate woman, but at least we can learn from her devastating lapse. Don't just assume that your mate is doing things correctly, even if he or she is the one most comfortable with handling your family's finances. Take some ownership, and know what's going on in your accounts. We'll talk about how to make sure that you're both in agreement about those investments later in this chapter. For now, simply familiarize yourself with them. Which brokerage house do you use? What stocks and mutual fund companies have you invested in? What other holdings do you have? How are they performing?

Just as you need to participate in your family's investments, so too must you learn about each other's business-related dealings. As a young woman, my client Tory married a friendly, outgoing, and very wealthy man with whom she quickly had three girls. Consumed by her new marriage, motherhood, and day-to-day life, she was more than happy to let him handle all their finances. They never talked money at all. He didn't even share his work life with her. So she had no way of knowing that his business was failing. By the end, he'd sunk in all the capital he had. When the marriage failed, she came away with worse than nothing: As his ex-wife, she inherited his debt as well.

Ironically, Tory's new marriage seems to be structured much like her last. She and her new husband live in a house that's registered in his name only (a big mistake—for more on this, see "Taking Title," page 149). She's sold her car to buy a more family-friendly minivan that is registered in his name alone. Is she taking the same financial backseat she did last time around? It sure looks that way.

The good news is that just because you have a certain arrangement in place now doesn't mean that it can't be changed. Whether you're just joining forces or have been together for many years, you can always review—and even rewrite—the terms of your marital financial contract simply by talking about them. In their book *Money Shy to Money Sure: A Woman's Road Map to Financial Well-Being* (Walker & Co., 2001), Olivia Mellan and Sherry Christie recommend starting out slowly to minimize the chance for conflict. After telling your mate how much you appreciate his or her handling of all your affairs, explain why you want to become more involved. Your reasons could include that you feel this will help foster a sense of self-esteem, security, competency, responsibility, or even togetherness. If you're female, you could also add that women live longer than men, and you don't want to wind up helpless if he predeceases you. Then suggest that you take on a money-related chore, like updating your family budget or researching a mutual fund in which you're considering investing. Once your mate has gotten used to this switch, you can suggest other chores. The trick is not to jump in all at once but simply to jump in, period.

The same advice applies to those of you who have been trying to get resistant partners more involved in the family finances. Start slowly. Ask for help with one of the tasks you routinely handle, and provide enough assistance and encouragement to guarantee success.

As Aretha Franklin might put it, including even a hesitant partner in your family's financial knowledge, planning, and decision-making spells R-E-S-P-E-C-T. No matter how late you get in the game, having a financial partnership will only enhance your romantic partnership. I was reminded of this fact by a story that Libby, a financial advisor I know, recently told me.

Lawrence and Marian, among her longest-standing clients, are in their seventies. He's a big man, with a big voice and a big, hearty personality. Marian, on the other hand, is petite, elegant, and so soft-spoken that Libby often has to lean forward in her chair to hear what she's saying.

During their financial review Lawrence had always been the dominant partner, asking all the questions and interpreting the answers. Meanwhile, Marian had always sat silently in her chair watching the process and smiling. Libby always made it a point to address at least half of her questions to Marian in an effort to involve her in the process. But Marian would simply agree with what Libby said, or defer to Lawrence, and then try to blend into the office woodwork.

That changed a year ago, when Libby took both of them out to lunch. She had brought along a male colleague, and he and Lawrence were actively involved in discussion. It was then that Libby felt Marian's hand alight delicately upon her shoulder. As Marian leaned forward to speak, Libby leaned forward to listen. "When my father died, my mother was completely at a loss," she said in a soft voice. "She didn't know what they had or how to take care of it." She dropped her voice even further. "The other day I realized that I've been setting myself up to be in that same position. I don't want to be that vulnerable if Lawrence dies. Can you help me?"

What Libby didn't realize at that point was that behind Marian's soft-spoken facade lay a fiercely intelligent woman. She attacked learning systematically and with great dedication. They chatted on the phone, she attended investment seminars, and they followed up with a one-on-one meeting where Libby walked her through the details of the couple's portfolio. On her own Marian read a couple of investing primers and started to read the business section of the newspaper. Over the course of one year she gained a real grip on the basics of investing and the particulars of her portfolio.

Their next meeting was completely different. Lawrence was still as colorful as ever, but this time Marian—newly empowered by her financial knowledge—played an active part in all the discussions. And every time she spoke, you could see the astonishment, pride, and new respect in Lawrence's eyes, as if he were watching a rare creature he'd never laid eyes upon.

After the meeting Libby was walking the two of them down the hall when she felt that same gentle touch on her arm. When she turned to her, Marian leaned forward, her brilliant blue eyes smiling. "I just wanted you to know," she said in a conspiratorial tone, "this has been the best thing that has ever happened to our marriage." And this at seventy-plus years of age.

SWEET CHARITY

Part of being a couple involves wanting to bring out the best in each other. What better way to do that than by teaming up to give to others?

For starters, simply discussing your feelings about philanthropy, and then drawing up and reviewing candidates for your joint charitable contributions, provides you with an opportunity to revisit your values in a way that's not at all threatening because it's not pointed at the two of you. Once you've come to terms with where you both want your money to go, knowing you've joined together for a cause you both believe in can bring you closer as a couple.

Of course, giving as a couple doesn't have to be limited to money. You can also volunteer your time. Whether you decide to serve Thanksgiving dinner at a homeless shelter, spend a week as counselors at a cancer camp, help clean up the beaches or your community, or pick up a hammer or a paintbrush and build for Habitat for Humanity, doing it together will make it that much sweeter. Besides, just as with all your other goals, making a volunteering commitment to—and with—your mate will increase your chances of following through. Once you do, you'll see why that old cliché "It's better to give than to receive" is so true. I promise you unreservedly that you'll come away feeling like you're the one who just made off with all the goods.

Marrying Your Financial Lives

Like so much of life, merging your money doesn't have to be an either/or proposition. As long as you figure out a system that allows for each other's individuality and self-determination, while ensuring the welfare of the team, you're in business.

Gary and I started our married life with separate accounts. But since we were essentially paying our bills with his salary and investing what I made, that didn't make much sense. We had essentially pooled our money anyway, so combining our checking accounts was the next logical step.

Today Gary and I also share our primary brokerage account. In addition, I have a much smaller separate brokerage account that consists of modest inheritances from my two grandmothers. Gary jokingly refers to it as my Swiss account even though it's not a lot—but he knows that it's important for my sense of independence, and he respects that. Regardless, we're perfectly content having most of our funds commingled. We're a family, I figure, so everything each of us makes should get thrown into the same pot, and whatever anyone needs gets taken out. Our basic philosophy: What's yours is mine, and vice versa.

This logic may work well for young couples who are just starting out—but not always. Just ask Lynn. At the age of twenty-four, having just completed graduate school and entered the workforce, she married her husband, George. George still had a year to go, and even though he worked, money was scarce. "We had absolutely nothing," Lynn says. "These days people who are getting married keep separate accounts. We didn't have any money to put into one account, let alone two."

All that changed within the next few years as Lynn and George's careers (and family) grew. Still, there seemed to be no reason to stop pooling their money. Sure, Lynn resented George's growing tendency to make compulsive purchases without consulting her, but she figured it was mostly because he had grown up feeling that he didn't get what he wanted and this was his way of compensating. Of course, by not expressing her misgivings, Lynn's sore spots about George's spending were like bruises begging to be bumped.

Then came the final straw. Although the couple had agreed to redo their kitchen sometime in the not-too-distant future, George went out one day and bought a $20,000 piano. Not only did he not consult Lynn, he didn't even tell her about the purchase. She figured out what he'd done when she happened to find the financing agreement.

A year later the sight of the piano in her living room (or worse, tripping over the piano bench) still makes Lynn see red. Though George knows that the purchase angered her, they still haven't discussed the matter. "It's water under the bridge," says Lynn. Her face, which turned five shades of red during the telling of this story, belies this.

Let's face it: When all your accounts are merged, you really must talk about every single major expense. Not only do you need to determine how much money is available to be spent, you also have to decide whether that's how you both want to spend it. If you know in advance that you're going to want to make those kinds of decisions without consulting a soul (let alone your soul mate), then you need to have your own account.

Indeed, whether you're an income-earner or not, having your own individual account is often the only way to sidestep these kinds of relationship-threatening clashes. Remember Max and Bridgette? Once they talked out their money differences, they decided to shift from sharing a single joint checking account to individual accounts, and a third shared account just for household expenses. Separating their money this way made it much easier for Max to stop micromanaging his wife's spending and allowed them to begin the process of planning for their future together.

Josh and Anna took this one step further. To make sure that each would have the same amount of discretionary money to spend each month, they first reserved the same specified sum for their own private expenditures, then they put the balance of their earnings in their joint account. The latter would pay for all shared expenses and joint savings. Individually, they'd be responsible for their own car payments, their own wardrobes, and any personal needs or indulgences. In essence, they found that this system allowed them to be separate in some respects but still equal.

At the other extreme, some couples choose to keep everything completely separate from the start. Gloria Steinem and her husband, David Bale, for example, have chosen to commingle their lives but not their money. As reported in *BusinessWeek*, Steinem states, "We keep our finances separate. We often find ourselves arguing over whose turn it is to pay for things when we go out, and each one insists it's their turn. So far, there hasn't been any difficulty." For glamour couple Vanessa Williams and Rick Fox, separate finances even entail separate homes (he owns one on the West Coast; hers is in the East). Why? Fox, a professional basketball player, witnessed financial battles that helped tear apart his parents' marriage as a child, then experienced his own money conflicts as an adult with a girlfriend. Former Miss America–turned-performer Williams, whose first husband—also her manager—handled all the finances, never wanted to be in the dark about her money again or to hand over its control.

So when all is said and done, I figure that how you choose to marry your financial lives is a question of whatever works for you and your mate. Of course, this arrangement is subject to change as your needs—or your sense of each other—change. Susan and her husband, who have been married for ten years and who dated for seven years before that, still keep their savings and checking accounts separate. Each has specific household expenses (which have been apportioned equally) that they're responsible for paying. All other money decisions, from investing to spending, are handled separately. For a few years after the couple had their children, they joined their accounts, since Susan sacrificed time at work (and therefore income) to be home with the babies. Once the kids were old enough for her to return to work, however, the couple reverted to the original plan. If it ain't broke, they concluded, why fix it?

Of course the discussion shouldn't stop with your current situation. When Anna and Josh married, they continued to explore the many possibilities down the road: for example, what would happen if one of them lost their job or became disabled? When Josh suggested that the other would finance both of their monthly draws (which would obviously have to shrink to accommodate the loss of one income), Anna expressed reservations about still taking that money if she wasn't able to contribute her fair share. Josh didn't miss a beat. "That's what we talked about," he insisted. "In rough times the other of us is right there."

To me, that's what a solid relationship is all about. So whether you or your partner decide to marry all or part of your finances, communicating that you'll be there for each other through thick and thin can make a world of difference.

Investing Together (or Not)

If you can come to terms with an investment approach that works for both of you, combining all—or part—of your investments can be a great way to plan for your future together. Obviously if you completely disagree about how and where to invest your money, you'll want separate investment portfolios. But you don't need to completely agree either. Even if one of you is more prone to risk it all while the other's more conservative, the disparity can operate in your favor by balancing you—and your joint portfolio—and naturally prompting the very diversification that will maximize your chances for investment success.

Should you decide to merge your assets, you'll want to rebalance the joint portfolio. Just as you need to make sure that your asset allocation doesn't become skewed by performance, you'll want to look at the new big picture and make sure that your combined forces aren't now overweighted in some areas and underweighted in others. Remember that if different mutual funds invest in the same companies or sectors, your diversification—and protection from the impact of a drop in a particular stock or sector—has been compromised. Similarly, if you both work for the same company and both hold a lot of that company's stock, you may want to consider selling a portion of that and diversifying into something else.

Of course, investing together doesn't need to be an all-or-nothing proposition. If you each come into the relationship with your own assets, you can maintain them separately and then establish a joint account. That's what Anna and Josh did. He has his, she has hers, and at about their one-year anniversary, they established their joint brokerage account. "It took about a year for the dust to settle, for us to know what our expenses were going to be month in and month out and what we'd have left over to invest," says Anna. "We also used that time to look into the future and think about what we wanted. Now it's fun. We can talk about our investment choices, make those decisions jointly, and remind each other about the goals we're shooting for."

Home Sweet Home

If you haven't already bought a house together, the question is *should* you?

Past practice and wisdom used to make that a moot point. Whether you were embarking on your first marriage or your third, it was assumed that you would start life together in a new house if possible.

Today's real estate prices, however, make owning your own home tougher than it used to be. And in some cases it makes less sense as well. Unlike investing your money in the stock market, when your goal is to increase the value of your portfolio, buying a home is not about having your money grow. It's about the quality of your life.

When Win, our second child, was born, we realized that we needed a bigger house. After all, he couldn't exactly spend his entire childhood sleeping in the living room, which is where we were initially forced to set up his crib. By then we were living in Atlanta, where we'd moved when Gary accepted a job offer from the *Atlanta Journal-Constitution*. So we went house-hunting and found a home we absolutely loved. Gary was convinced that it was way out of our league; I got out my calculator and number-crunched like crazy. After running through all the calculations, I was able to reassure Gary that even though we would no longer be able to live on one salary and bank the other, we could afford it.

Thankfully, my calculations had factored in the cost of repairs. I didn't, however, plan on most of them being needed all at once, let alone right after we closed escrow. Within a few months of buying the house, everything started to fall apart. Every week we'd have to spend another $200, and to make things worse, the plumbers were forced to knock gaping holes in two parts of the house to get at the pipes. Naturally, this debacle happened right when six members of my family were coming to see our new home and stay with us. It got to the point that we had to laugh about it. It was either that or cry!

The decision to buy a house—surely the largest single investment most of us will ever make—should be based on wanting a home and that lifestyle first, and on making an investment second. In addition to debating whether you're inclined, ready, and able to take on this kind of financial responsibility, you must determine how much each of you can contribute financially and who's going to pay for what, including upkeep and monthly dues if you're investing in a condo or town house.

If you decide to take the plunge, make sure you figure out what you can afford for a down payment, just how far you can stretch for your monthly mortgage payments, and where you're willing to bend to make the numbers work. A rule of thumb is that your house payments (including mortgage, taxes, insurance, and maintenance) shouldn't exceed 28% of your gross monthly pay. Once you've found the house, double-check your figures (as opposed to your realtor's or real estate agent's). No matter how much you love the house at the outset, you won't love it for long if it compromises the quality of the rest of your life. Then have it checked out thoroughly to avoid the repair nightmare that Gary and I faced. Your best bet? Line up your own independent home inspector to avoid potential conflicts of interest. This is not the time to take shortcuts, as there's a lot of money at stake and probably a lot of years in the dwelling as well. So don't act impulsively. Do your homework, which might include reading Ilyce Glink's excellent book, *100 Questions Every First-Time Home Buyer Should Ask* (Times Books, 2000).

If you're moving into a partner's preexisting home, you might consider contributing your own equity so that the house will feel equally yours (and then changing the title to the property accordingly). When Anna moved into Josh's house, for example, she matched the money he'd already invested in it. They put 20%

toward paying down the mortgage. The rest they used to remodel the house, thereby making the house feel like theirs instead of his.

TAKING TITLE

When you're finally ready to buy a house, make sure to think carefully about how you take title. This decision may seem simple on the surface, but it is actually complicated, and it's easy to make a costly mistake. My advice? Review and debate the alternatives below, but double-check with an attorney or other professional before you sign on the dotted line.

First, make sure you register the title in both your names. This is the best way for married couples to protect their separate interests, and it is also essential for unmarried and same-sex couples whose family members might otherwise claim ownership. For estate-planning purposes (see Chapter 8 for more details), many couples benefit from registering their house title in the name of their revocable living trust. (This is definitely an area in which you need to consult an attorney.) Depending on your state, there are different ways to hold title:

1. *Joint tenancy with right of survivorship* is usually the best way to hold property if you live in a non-community-property state. Joint tenancy means that each of you owns 100% of the property (not fifty-fifty)—a bit of an odd concept—but in practical terms this means that if one of you dies, your share immediately passes to the other without probate. (The survivor now owns 100%.) Therefore this type of ownership will not allow either one of you to will your portion to someone else—which could be a problem if, for example, you want your children from a previous marriage or other heirs to inherit your portion.

A benefit is that when one partner dies, that person's portion is passed on to the surviving partner on a stepped-up tax basis, minimizing the amount of tax the survivor will owe. For example, let's say that you and your spouse bought your house for $100,000, and it is now worth $500,000. If you die, the cost basis for your half is "stepped up" to $250,000. The cost basis for your spouse's half is $50,000 (or half of the original price of the house). Added together, the new tax basis is $300,000. Therefore, if your spouse decides to sell the house after your death, he or she will owe taxes on a $200,000 gain. Joint tenancy with right of survivorship is not limited to married couples and can be appropriate for life partners as well.

2. If you live in a community-property state (Arizona, California, Idaho, Nevada, New Mexico, Texas, Washington, and Wisconsin), it's usually best to register your house as *community property.* (But the laws differ somewhat among community property states, so you should consult an attorney.) Community-property ownership means that you each own 50% of the whole and do not necessarily have a right of survivorship. (Each of you may pass your 50% share to whomever you name in your will.) But community property does have the additional benefit that the step up in tax basis applies to the entire property, not just to the half that is being transferred—thereby providing even greater tax benefits (see Chapter 8 for more details). This form of ownership is available only to married couples.

3. A relatively new way to hold title in most community-property states is *community property with right of survivorship,* which combines features of joint tenancy with right of survivorship and community property. This means that when one spouse dies, the other will own the home outright—so this type of ownership is not appropriate if you want to will your portion to someone other than your spouse. On the other hand, if you do want your spouse to obtain 100% ownership at your death, with this ownership he or she will receive the benefit of a stepped-up basis for the entire house. Again, this is for married couples in community-property states only; you need to check on the specific law in your state.

4. Another possibility is to establish *tenancy-in-common,* which stipulates that you each own a predetermined share of the house. That share can be bought and sold without the other's consent and does not automatically pass to the other owner(s). With tenancy-in-common, you can will your share to whomever you want.

Something to Talk About

• *Do you and your partner spend enough time talking about the values you want to live by, the dreams you're striving to realize, and your financial goals?*

• *How do you make financial decisions as a couple?*

• *What money-related issues cause you and your partner to argue? Spending? Bill-paying? Debt? Investing? Not being consulted?*

• *What mistakes did you make in a prior marriage? What have you done to avoid making these mistakes in the future?*

• *Do you need a prenup or cohabitation agreement? How can you make sure it feels fair to each of you?*

• *How do you want to merge your financial life with that of your partner?*

• *Do you and your partner know everything you should about each other's finances, including assets, income, investments, money history and obligations, business dealings, estate planning (see Chapter 8 for more on this last point), and financial institutions and handlers (i.e., bankers, brokers, etc.)?*

• *How can you best share financial responsibilities and family roles?*

• *Are both you and your partner up to speed on your family finances? If not, how can you change that?*

• *Have you considered donating time or money to charitable causes recently? Do you know your partner's favorite charities?*

• *If one of you makes a lot more money than the other, are you comfortable with how you address that?*

• *Have you identified ways to deal with money incompatibilities in areas such as spending or investing?*

• *Should you buy a house together? How should you title it?*

• *Do you share common investing goals? Do you want to invest together?*

5

Raising $mart Kids

There is no question that talking about money helps promote healthy adult relationships. But the discussions don't stop there. Once you become a parent—or a parent-figure—it's time to extend the conversation to include the kids as well.

There's a lot to address. Like most parents, Gary and I want so much for our children. We want them to grow up to be competent, caring adults who face life with a strong sense of independence and confidence. We want them to have fulfilling personal and professional lives and to eventually be in a position to give back to those who are less fortunate. We want our children to have choices and to live life to its fullest.

A tall order to be sure, but one that parents across the country face every day. Not only does it mean providing our children with the best possible education, it also means that as a family we live by a value system we jointly respect and embrace. From how we spend our time to how we spend our money, Gary and I realize that the example we set and our unspoken messages can be much more powerful than our words.

Finding the proper balance between protecting and providing for our children—and letting them learn to provide for themselves—

presents another challenge. Personally I know that although I want to give my children wonderful experiences and a memorably happy childhood, I don't want to furnish them with so much that I take away their incentive to do great things on their own. Nor do I want to deprive them of that early experience of saving for something they really want. Certainly many parents have learned the hard way that overindulging their children simply doesn't work. So how *do* you raise money-wise kids who will turn into productive, motivated adults?

This chapter is devoted to helping you achieve just that by examining some of the best ways we know to raise responsible, money-wise children and teens. Having spent our careers counseling families about their finances, my father and I feel very strongly that children should learn the ABCs of money and investing just as they learn to read and write. Regardless of whether you're raising an entrepreneur, a concert pianist, a teacher, or a second baseman, we believe that your kids will benefit from receiving a solid foundation in money basics and money values. Realize, though, that it doesn't happen by magic, and it doesn't happen overnight. It's a process that you can begin when your children are quite young and continue as they mature. This chapter will get you started on that most important journey.

Money-Savvy Children, Teens, and Young Adults

"It pays to talk" may never be truer than when it comes to your children. What better opportunity to break through the traditional taboos and misperceptions surrounding money?

A Harris poll that Schwab sponsored in 2000 shows that most parents believe that they, rather than schools, should teach their kids about money. That would be terrific, as they could share their own values about life in general—and put money into a meaningful context. There's only one problem—it isn't happening.

We don't hesitate to tell our children not to touch a hot stove or not to talk to strangers, to look both ways when they cross the street, and what time to come home at night. We may even feel justified in telling them whom they should or shouldn't date. But our

Harris poll revealed that less than one-third of parents regularly talk to their children about money and investing. Financial topics—along with sex and drugs—share the dubious distinction of being the American family's least-discussed topics.

Compounding the problem, personal finance and money management are rarely taught in school. Since kids, like the rest of us, don't learn by magic, they're not learning at all.

As you embark on the important journey of raising money-wise children, there are a few rules of the road to keep in mind. First, no matter how old your children are, you should treat them the same way you want your parents to treat you—with candor and respect. Second, the specific topics you choose should depend not only on your children's age but on their developmental stage as well. It's never productive to burden children with problems that they're not equipped to deal with or to weigh them down with concepts they can't relate to. Third, realize that with children it's not just what you say but also how you say it and the example you set that colors their perceptions from early on. And finally, not only do parents need to talk to their children more, they also need to talk to each other more. As you struggle with how to deal with your child's relentless yen for acquisition, don't just talk to your spouse, talk to parents in other families. Share your values with your friends and close colleagues. Share what's worked for you, and ask about their solutions. This isn't top-secret information. To the contrary—pass it along, the more frequently the better.

Damage Control

In the past decade of extravagant consumerism and one-upmanship, *peer pressure* and *media influence* took on gigantic proportions. "Members of history's most indulged generation are setting new records when it comes to indulging their kids," Nancy Gibbs reported in a *Time* magazine article entitled "Who's in Charge Here?" (August 6, 2001). Teenagers didn't just get cars, they got Mercedes. And these kinds of indulgences don't start when the child hits sixteen.

Only recently I was talking to a friend who was planning to rent two ponies (and two human assistants) for her daughter's fifth birthday party. Rather surprised at the excess and the message it would send her kids, I asked, "Why two?" She must have received a similar response earlier because she immediately responded, "Well, at least I didn't rent an elephant!" As it happens, I knew what she was referring to—that same *Time* magazine article in which Carrie Fisher (Princess Leia in *Star Wars* and daughter of famous Hollywood stars) acknowledged with some embarrassment that she had rented an elephant for her daughter's twelfth birthday party.

While this is an extreme example, parents of all income levels struggle with how much they should give their children in the way of material possessions. We don't want to spoil our children, but we don't want them to "do without," either. Although some of the effusive gift-giving and extravagant parties have hopefully tapered off due to the changing economic climate, vestiges remain. Brand names are big, even for kids as young as five. Many kids still prefer shopping in a mall to family outings or hikes, and they define their self-worth by their belongings. Keeping up with the Joneses—or at least their kids—is a big deal, a message the media consistently reinforces. So even if you've managed to keep "affluenza" down to a low roar in your household, those nasty influences seem to lurk around every corner.

This raises the next issue—how do you teach financial responsibility in the absence of need and in an era in which satisfying a child's every whim seems to have reached epidemic proportions? Certainly most parents try to instill the right values in their children, to guide them along the way, and to help them learn from the decisions—both good and bad—that they make. Realize, though, that your attitudes and values communicate themselves. If having the newest, priciest car on the block or the most current top-of-the-line flat-screen TV is important to you, your children may become more materialistic than they would otherwise.

So start by asking yourself what values and sense of responsibility you want to impart. More often than not this big-picture perspective can make all the difference. I remember, for example, being troubled when a friend bought a car for her daughter on her sixteenth birthday. What I didn't understand was that along with this gift of independence came the added responsibility of helping drive her younger siblings to and from their many extracurricular activities. This, of course, proved a tremendous help to her parents—and also helped bring the family together in a new way.

Also realize that you're never going to be able to completely mold your children. Despite your best efforts, they may turn out differently than you wanted or expected. You can only do your best, which may involve taking a good hard look at your own life.

Chuck's Two Cents: A Grandfather's Perspective

Talking to your kids about money can be a tricky business, and I want to ease your mind by saying from the start that there is no perfect way to raise a money-savvy child, any more than there is a foolproof way to raise a perfect child in any other area. As in any part of parenting, you do what you can—and then hope for the best. It's another part of parenting; it's tough—and it's completely worthwhile.

That said, I do have some suggestions, based on my experience with the things I think I've done well with my own kids or grandkids, as well as with the things I wish I'd done better.

First, think about what you want your kids to understand about money. It's my view that we want our children to value money and to understand the important truth in the old adage that money doesn't grow on trees. We want them to understand what money can do for them and, more important perhaps, what it can't do: that it can't buy self-esteem, or confidence, or self-worth; that it cannot produce the personal rewards that come from hard work.

Second, start your teaching early. Teaching kids to value money is like teaching them any other value, such as honesty or integrity or respect for others. You don't just have a talk with them when they're eighteen; ideally you teach them their whole lives, by modeling the behavior you want them to learn. Let them see examples of the ways in which you value money, so that by the time they leave home, they get it. Much of that teaching is implicit, not through words but through examples.

There are also some more explicit things you can do. You can try to sneak in a lesson when your kids don't realize they're being taught. When I was a kid, I learned a lot about money through games. When we'd play for a few nickels or dimes, I was always more interested, and I learned that if I played well, I was rewarded. I do the same thing with my grandkids. The minute that money is involved, the attention level goes way up. All of a sudden there's some incentive, and the game is more meaningful.

You can encourage your kids to get a job, anything from mowing a neighbor's lawn to working part-time at the supermarket. Working teaches kids what money does for them—that it gives them choices. A twelve-year-old with some money of her own learns that she can buy a CD without asking Mom. No money, no choices. And when the time is right, there are some specific skills you can teach. You can teach your children about budgeting their allowances, and you can teach a high school kid to balance a checkbook.

Third, be aware of how your financial situation influences your teaching. Sometimes affluence—the very presence of money—can lead to not talking about it as much as we should. In a family where money isn't a problem, sometimes less care and attention are given to teaching kids how to handle it. If, on the other hand, things are a little tight, you're less likely to hand over a $20 bill so easily or to forget to ask for the change. In a family where money is an issue, kids are often very aware of what $20 means and how long it's supposed to last. And they're often more motivated to get part-time jobs when the parents aren't handing out pocket money so readily. These are generalizations, I know, but the point is that it's important to look at how your current financial picture influences your attitudes about money—and the attitudes you're passing on to your kids.

Finally, customize your approach as much as you can. No two children are alike, and one of the best things you can do is to give your children tailored educations. That's tough to do, as is much of parenting. But there really isn't any cookie-cutter approach to teaching anything, whether the subject is skiing or tennis or cooking or algebra or money. Some kids take to it and some don't, simple as that. While we do owe it to them to try and instruct them, be forewarned that trying to teach even the most basic financial skills to a child who isn't interested is a real challenge, and part of the eternal parenting challenge of trying to give good advice to our kids.

Your children's financial life isn't everything. It's only a chunk of their lives, but it is an important chunk, because it gives them choices. Teach them to be interested, and to take responsibility for this part of their lives. When it comes down to it, teaching kids about money is really a way of nurturing independence. And that's one of the best gifts you can give.

Teaching Kids by Words and Deeds

What's the most effective way to talk to your young children about money? By letting money-awareness-raising activities do most of the talking for you. A six-year-old who wants a PlayStation 2 isn't interested in whether you can afford it. And she certainly won't understand the concept of saving for it. But she can learn.

Just as you teach your children to read by sharing bedtime stories and pointing out signs as you drive down the street, the best way to teach them about money is to make it a part of their everyday life. So the next time you go shopping for soccer shoes or groceries, do some comparison-shopping out loud. Take advantage of every opportunity to reinforce the messages about money and saving.

OPENING GAMBIT

Even very young kids need the chance to handle money early on. In *Kids, Money and Values* (Betterway Books, 1994), authors Patricia Schiff Estess and Irving Barocas suggest giving your preschooler a dollar to buy herself a nutritious snack. "Let her pay for the snack herself, get a receipt, hold the purchase in her own paper bag and keep the few coins in change from the transaction."

Of course, children differ wildly in their interest in and affinity for finances. Remember Pete (the executive) and Eleanor from Chapter 1, who renewed their marriage vows after reassessing their relationship? Their teenage son doesn't care at all about money or investing. In contrast, their eleven-year-old daughter watches the financial shows on TV, just as her father does. "Tough day at the market?" she'll ask her dad by way of greeting when the Dow has gone south.

Even if your children don't exhibit that kind of spontaneous enthusiasm, you *can* encourage their interest by demystifying finances and making money-talk relevant to their lives. Whether you're talking about how current events affect the economy, or how purchasing decisions affect your child's life, the conversations can be both instructive and fun. In the process, you'll find that money, rather than being a dry, irrelevant topic, is actually a perfect way to ground your children in solid values and grown-up decision-making.

Joline Godfrey, CEO of Independent Means, a company that provides solutions for raising financially fit kids, maintains that "both personality and developmental stages will have an impact in how your kids acquire financial skills and language. Start where they are, not where you want them to be—make money, language and concepts relevant to their lives and stage of development."

In the years to come, your kids' growing understanding—or wonderfully naïve misunderstanding—of financial terms and concepts is bound to surprise you. My colleague Tom has an eight-year-old who collects dollars. Literally. The way he sees it, only the brand-new bills—"crispies," as he calls them—have value.

When my colleague Lynn noticed that the house next door was up for sale, her family's conversation touched on whether the neighbors' attempts to sell it for "565" (shorthand, of course, for $565,000) would be successful. A few weeks later Lynn's sister came to visit from Denver. "Wouldn't it be great if you could buy this house next door and live next to us?" Lynn's eight-year-old son Oscar announced to his aunt. "It's only $5.65. I could give you that money!"

MAKING FINANCE FUN FOR THE WHOLE FAMILY

Entertaining, money-related activities that parents and kids can both participate in are a terrific way to educate and spark further conversations down the road. Here are a few ideas taken from programs offered by Independent Means:

• Turn a grocery-shopping trip into a budgeting game for your seven-year-old. At the beginning of each aisle, give her an item to buy and a budget. (Example: Can she find two rolls of paper towels for $3? How much under or over can she come?)

• Give your twelve-year-old a budget of $20 and ask him to plan and shop for dinner for six. (If your family is smaller than that, have him invite friends!) Reward him with movie tickets if he makes his goal; if not, work with him to make the goal the following week. Make sure you help him prepare dinner, and make it a family affair. If he figures out that he can buy three pizzas for $18 and one large bottle of water for $2, go with it. He's met the goal. (Quality of the buy is a lesson for later!)

• Role-play with your thirteen-year-old to negotiate for pay. Those early jobs (mowing lawns, shoveling snow, taking care of kids) have value because they help kids deal with such issues. Next time your daughter and her friends are having a sleepover, try this out: Tell them you're willing to pay them to clean out one of your closets, but that you need to know how much they will charge. Ask each one separately, and see what each says. Don't necessarily take the lowest bidder; push them a little to find out who makes the best case for the job! Some kids will say "Whatever you want to pay," others will under-charge, and others will overcharge. Talk about how you find out "going rates" and value of time. It may be the most instructive sleepover these girls ever have!

• If your kids are at least ten years old, start a family giv-ing circle. This is a means of developing family values about money and philanthropy. Set up a weekly meeting (at first) to establish what causes each family member feels strongly about. Set an amount that will be given every year by the whole family (it could be $50 or $500 or $5,000, depending on family circumstances; the amount is less important than the learning experience), and then decide on a process for determining how to make the donation. Will you all agree on one cause? Will there be more than one? Must it be a unanimous decision? Working out the process of how and what will help kids understand both the complexities of giving as well as the importance the family places on giving as a family value.

• For kids thirteen and over, start a family investment club. It may become more sophisticated over time, and in some families the kids may want to start their own club with adult supervision. But the first phase of a family investment club will help establish values, communicate language, and demystify the process. Most important: Take your kids seriously. Remember that every twelve-year-old knew before every grown-up that Harry Potter was BIG!

• Set up a kids' barter day in the neighborhood. Have your kids invite all their friends to bring toys or clothes that they want to trade for equal value. You will need an adult to act as arbiter, but it will help teach the value of equivalence and fair trade.

Once you stop smiling at these misconceptions, you can use them as opportunities to teach a few more lessons.

Three excellent books for explaining financial concepts include *Ultimate Kids' Money Book* by Neale S. Godfrey (Simon & Schuster Books for Young Readers, 1998) for tykes as young as seven, *The Kids' Guide to Money: Earning It, Saving It, Spending It, Growing It, Sharing It* by Steve Otfinoski (Scholastic, 1996) for kids nine and up, and the previously cited *Kids, Money and Values: Creative Ways* to *Teach Your Kids About Money* by Patricia Schiff Estess and Irving Barocas (Betterway Books, 1994) for parents of preschoolers to preteens.

He Heard, She Heard

Pete and Eleanor made a special point of exposing their savvy daughter to a wide variety of financial concepts. Research shows, however, that when it comes to conversations about money, many parents speak to their daughters differently from how they speak to their sons. Our Harris poll revealed that parents tend to talk to their daughters about saving (associated with security and independence) and to their sons about investing (associated with power and profit). Probably as a result, most girls grow up not knowing as much as boys about the stock market or about how to make money grow. Instead, they focus on saving it, which puts them at a significant disadvantage in the long run.

Does this sound familiar? Do you talk to your daughter the same way you talk to your son? It might be worth a listen. You could be surprised at how unconsciously we fall into stereotyped patterns.

Computer games like Roller-coaster Tycoon, where kids create and then operate a virtual roller-coaster amusement park, present a great way to counteract this kind of gender bias. Ten-year-old Sabrina could scarcely be torn away from the theme park she had created on her computer. Not only had she designed the rides and set up concession booths in order to attract more visitors, she kept to the prescribed budget, met payroll, and paid both start-up costs and subsequent expenses. "You want to see the best part?" she cried. "I have maintenance staff, and I have to pay them virtually as well!"

Will the notion of starting a business faze this little girl when she grows up? Possibly, but now that she has caught the entrepreneurial bug, I believe that she is more likely to want to meet the next challenge.

From Piggy Bank to Bank Account

Perhaps the most important concept to teach young children is that money can be saved instead of simply spent. Two of the best ways to do that are about as old-fashioned as ice-cream sundaes: piggy banks and kids' savings accounts.

Lynn's two young sons, Oscar, eight, and Daniel, four, share a Pooh Bear bank that stands about a foot high. The bear is fed with spare change lying around and the odd quarter given to the kids, and over time it actually fills up. Two years ago and again this year, when the kids couldn't shove in another dime, they emptied out their bank. Both times the total came to about $300, and Lynn tromped her kids into one of the few brick-and-mortar banks that still give out savings account passbooks. Shortly thereafter Oscar received a couple of birthday checks. "That would be a good thing to put in your bank account," Lynn suggested. Now he can't wait to get that money into his savings account. (No wonder he thinks he can afford to buy his aunt a house!)

Joline Godfrey suggests, "If you want kids to develop the savings habit, make sure that when they are five years old you set up three jars for any money they receive. Have one jar marked for spending, one for saving, and one for giving away. Whether it's a birthday gift or unexpected money from grandparents, divide it into those three pots. By the time the child is ten, up the ante; now their allowance can be allocated in the same way. When they get their first job—whether baby-sitting or computer tutoring—the rules remain the same: separate accounts for saving, spending, and giving money away. When kids get the same message at each step of the developmental process, the habit becomes ingrained as a life skill."

Eventually, like Lynn, you'll want to take your child to the bank so she can open a savings account. If you can find a bank that still provides passbooks, so much the better. Having a teller note each deposit is wonderfully reinforcing. (Tip: The bank will need your child's Social Security number to open the account, so be sure to bring your child's Social Security card as well as that initial deposit.

Also be sure to ask about minimum balance requirements and monthly service charges before you go; sometimes if you already have a checking account at that bank, they will waive the fee for the savings account.)

Explain to your child that a savings account will help her money grow, since the bank pays her for letting them use the money she deposits. You may even want to point out that by making it that much harder to access her money, the bank makes it easier for her to resist the temptation to spend it. Once she's started to save, conversations about how that money is growing and what it's ultimately destined for will further encourage her to think about the future. That's a critical aspect of a child's money-related development, since thinking long term, after all, is what financial planning is all about. And that's something you can instill in your child at any age.

The Ins and Outs of Allowances

When I was a child, I didn't get an allowance. I scoured the cushions for dimes and quarters when I needed some pocket change or, reluctantly, asked my mother. I didn't really *need* money, of course, but I *wanted* money—my own money. I think all kids do, not because of greed or materialism but because they want to experiment with being independent.

In my opinion, that's what getting an allowance is all about. With a regular allowance children have cash of their own to touch, experience, and learn to value. Let's face it. We've all seen kids whose parents shower them with money, teaching them absolutely nothing about sound money practices. More important than the amount you give is the context in which you give it, and the discussions you have surrounding that money and what it means.

Talking about it, however, doesn't mean dictating how it's spent. Allowances give children the chance to deal with money on their own from a very young age. Telling them what to do only defeats the purpose. Only by making their own decisions—and their own mistakes—can they develop the skills they'll need later on. As a parent or any other concerned and involved adult, your job is to guide them in that process. Two essential components of that guidance entail helping them:

- Distinguish between an impulsive want, a deep-seated desire, and a need.
- Understand how to manage—or budget—their money wisely. That means that "if the money disappears at the arcade in one day, you don't give in to any child-applied pressure for an advance on the following week's allowance," write Dr. C. Diane Ealy and Dr. Kay Lesh in *Our Money Ourselves: Redesigning Your Relationship to Money* (American Management Association, 1998). "One thing you're trying to teach is responsibility. That includes learning the difference between wise and unwise choices."

How much allowance you give your children will depend on how old they are, the going rate where you live, and your financial situation. I learned this lesson the hard way when I gave a little financial talk to my son Ross's class. Naturally, the conversation quickly turned to allowances. When we informally polled all the students about how much allowance they received, it turned out that Gary and I were the chintziest parents of the bunch. "You see!" my son exclaimed triumphantly in front of all his classmates. "I told you!" The result of our showdown? I upped his allowance from $2 to $5 a week. On the other hand, he's now expected to pay for his own school snacks. That's part of the equation as well. The more you want your child to buy out of pocket instead of relying on your wallet, the more money he or she is going to require. As your child ages, her allowance and what she's responsible for buying with it should increase as well.

All of these variables make it difficult to provide you with firm numbers for how much allowance to give. As a general guideline, consider giving six-to-eight-year-olds $2 to $3 a week, nine-to-eleven-year-olds $5 to $7, and twelve-to-fourteen-year-olds $7 to $15. Clearly, the more your child relies on her wallet rather than yours, the more she'll need. In addition, remember that these amounts depend on where you live and may prove high for some areas and low for others.

You'll also want to make sure that the allowance is big enough to allow him to save part of it. Your best bet? Talk to your friends and the parents of your child's schoolmates to see how much they're paying and what the child pays for out of that weekly sum. (That'll be important information to have when your son confronts you with the information that his friend is getting 50% more than he is.) Then figure out whether that's enough to cover your child's spending and saving needs as well as regular charitable contributions.

Finally, most child experts and financial psychologists believe that allowances and family chores should be kept separate. There are certain unpaid responsibilities that simply go along with being part of a family. That doesn't mean you can't pay kids for extra work they do around the house or the yard. Allowances, however large or small, should come with responsibilities but no extra strings attached.

FAIR'S FAIR

Even if you're as careful as can be, if you or your spouse have kids from a prior marriage and children together, you also have a great potential for resentment. Spend money on the first batch, and questions about how much you've spent on the others are bound to come up. If one divorced parent has more money to lavish on a child than the other, it can all get even tougher.

Only by talking about these thorny issues openly and bringing up any lurking resentments can you hope to reach an agreement or understanding that feels right to everyone.

First Jobs

We parents ride a thin line. On the one hand, we want to protect our kids; on the other, we want them to become independent adults. We know that there's a difference between protection and overprotection, between raising strong, independent children and raising those who will never be able to fend for themselves.

How does that translate to money matters? Kids need to develop their money muscles, according to Joline Godfrey, whether they like it or not. And they can't do that if you make life so easy that they never want for anything. Instead of coddling our children and providing them with everything on a silver platter, we also need to make them work for it. In addition to instilling the kind of ethic that can make or break them as adults, working also teaches them the value of money.

When I was twelve, I had a paper route. Every morning my alarm clock would go off at dawn. Even though it was often still dark, I'd climb out of bed, jump into my clothes, and make my way to the front of my house, where I'd load up my pushcart with the *Oakland Tribune*. Then I'd walk the neighborhood for over an hour, hurling papers onto people's front stoops.

Kids' paper routes seem to be a thing of the past. That's too bad, since the job not only teaches money-handling and bookkeeping, it also trains kids to get themselves out of bed and show up on time. Of course, plenty of other endeavors can teach kids those work-related basics—as long as you as a parent or grandparent reinforce the effort.

Let's say your daughter decides to set up a lemonade stand. Announcing how "cute" she or her idea is diminishes the endeavor as well as her role, says Godfrey. "Let's sit down and figure out how to best make this work" augments it. With older kids you might even want to sit down together to create an operating budget so that they'll know what it will take to turn a profit.

You want to make the most of these kinds of kid-initiated, kid-driven learning opportunities, which means *not* taking them over. "'Okay, so here's what we'll do,' my dad would have announced if I'd ever wanted to open my own stand," says a San Francisco lawyer who considers himself hopeless when it comes to managing his business affairs. "He then would have delegated all the tasks and run the show."

The point *isn't* for you to run the show, it's to let your kids do it. Similarly, you don't want to succumb to the need for speed, or at least efficiency, at the expense of the learning activity itself. The object here isn't to make money, it's to make the most of this moment. That's a lesson that all too often escapes success-driven parents.

A friend recently told me about seeing a man and his young daughter selling Girl Scout cookies along Manhattan Beach, California's oceanside strand. With all the foot traffic on that sunny weekend day, it proved a bonanza. As the father busily took all those preorders, virtually ensuring that his daughter would be the highest cookie salesperson of the troop, his daughter stared out at the waves and halfheartedly solicited more customers. All she learned that day was that her dad was quite the business guy. I'm afraid that could prove an expensive lesson down the line.

You simply have to allow room for your kids to do it on their own. If it doesn't work out as expected or even if they slip up completely, that's okay. Mistakes are allowed. Indeed, they're required for learning purposes. Your role? Providing support. "How can we change this plan to make it work better?" you might want to ask. Then constructively steer your child's analysis in the right direction. With all the fund-raisers schools now seem to have, you'll have no shortage of opportunities to try and try again, until you and your kids succeed. Speaking of fund-raising, it could be an educational experience to walk your children through the steps of figuring out whether enough money is being raised for the effort expended. First find out how much money was spent to stage the event. Once the total amount raised has been computed, calculate the profit. Then figure out together how much time was expended to achieve those results, and discuss whether the venture might have been organized differently to improve the rate of return.

Finally, try to see that your kids don't fall into stereotyped gender-based jobs. To this day many girls tend to gravitate toward caregiving by relying on baby-sitting opportunities. In a stretch they'll clean, hold a bake sale, or open that proverbial lemonade stand. Boys tend to be more entrepreneurial: They pick weeds, sweep walkways, shovel snow, and wash cars. Many, however, will avoid work that entails looking after children or cooking. Rather than cementing these limiting notions, it's important to broaden your children's sense of choice. At this stage they need to gain the kinds of experiences that will boost their confidence and open up new horizons.

LET'S WORK IT OUT

The easiest place for kids to find work is right at home. Sure, certain responsibilities like making their beds, cleaning their rooms, setting and clearing the table, and helping with the dishes or the laundry are part of being a family member. Still, there's plenty of other work that could be done for pay, according to Jayne A. Pearl, author of *Kids and Money: Giving Them the Savvy to Succeed Financially* (Bloomberg Press, 1999), including:

• Housecleaning, including dusting, vacuuming, floor mopping, bathrooms
• Houseplant care
• Garden maintenance (weeding, raking leaves, lawn mowing)
• Baby-sitting
• Pet care (walking, feeding, grooming)
• Window washing
• Car washing
• Snow shoveling
• Home office tasks (including filing, collating, stamping, and sealing outgoing mail)

Of course, many of these jobs are also available in the neighborhood. Looking around for needs that aren't being met (think neglected yards, for example) or overhearing neighbors complain about certain tasks (like grocery shopping) can pro-

vide opportunities. So will a little self-promotion and net-
working. One enterprising young girl printed business cards
for her dog-walking business, which she handed out liberally
to all her neighbors and family friends.

Budding entrepreneurs should think about what they could
sell. Steve Otfinoski's *The Kids' Guide to Money* suggests the
following salable products:

- Lemonade and brownies
- Old clothes and toys
- Homegrown vegetables
- Flowers and plants
- Handmade jewelry and other crafts
- Handmade birthday cards
- Gift baskets

To Spend—or Save?

Once your children have opened up savings accounts, do what you
can to encourage them to save even more. If they have their eye on
something big, don't automatically buy it for them. Instead, encourage them to save their allowance or any other money they earn.
Teaching children how to save for a big purchase teaches them
more than the fact that they can work for and eventually get what
they want. They learn that they can count on themselves.

As kids grow older, you can have them pay for some of their discretionary items, such as sports- (or music- or art- or whatever-)
related expenses, contribute to a college fund, or help pay for a special opportunity. Once you've reviewed why saving money is important, you can bolster their savings practices by offering to match
their total at the end of the year. After all, if it encourages you to
contribute to your 401(k) at work, the concept should work for your
children as well. Call it an irresistible one-two punch.

Of course, this whole savings effort will fizzle like a dying fire if
you're in the habit of throwing money at your children whenever

they ask for it. Just because that's the way it's been in your household doesn't mean that's the way it always has to be.

My colleague Deborah decided that instead of forking over a handful of $20 bills every time her fourteen-year-old daughter wanted new clothes, she would provide her with a lump sum every three months. The understanding? Her daughter would be responsible for—and totally in charge of—buying whatever clothing and footwear she needed during that time. Deborah gritted her teeth when the teenager announced that she planned to spend the entire clothing allowance on lingerie. Knowing that experience would prove the most effective teacher, however, she said little beyond suggesting that this might not be the wisest course of action. And four weeks later, when her daughter's gym shoes needed replacing and the money was gone, Deborah didn't jump to the rescue. The lingerie mistake hasn't been repeated.

You can introduce your children to the concept of value in the same way. Roy, a Schwab broker, only had to ask his eleven-year-old daughter once, "If you spend your money on that toy, how long do you think it'll last?" Viewed in this new light, it didn't take her long to decide to hang on to her money. Of course, you have to be prepared to go along with your child's decision, no matter how wrong you think it might be. If the toy breaks or your child loses interest almost instantly, you can use that as a reminder when the issue of value comes up again. Just beware of the "I told you so" mode; that doesn't sit well with kids any better than it sits with anyone else.

Introduction to Investing

As soon as the kids in your life begin to take an interest in finances, you can also start teaching them about the difference between saving money and investing it. Explain that although investments are generally riskier than a savings account, they also have the potential to grow more over time.

I explain the concept of stocks to my kids the way my dad did for me: that they're buying a little piece of a company, and that its value can rise or fall as the company succeeds or fails. Keeping the concept tied to a particular company gives them something to hold on to, especially if it's a company that produces a product they use or like. Actively involving them in the market is even better.

Marcus, a Schwab broker, remembers his father sitting down with him and his sister when they were still in middle school. "Okay, we have some additional money," his dad told them. "What would you like to invest in?" Naturally, both kids drew a blank. "What are you using at school?" he prompted. When Marcus and his sister answered "Calculators," their father made a few calls to find out who made calculators and researched the companies. The kids, with their dad's guidance, wound up investing in Hewlett-Packard, way back when. Watching the stock's fluctuations and eventual growth taught them more than words could ever have done. It also gave them the confidence they needed to invest and trade on their own when they grew a little older.

My son Ross has already been bitten by the investment bug, courtesy of a finance program in his school that encourages kids as young as eleven to create a "virtual portfolio." Even before he began this pretend-trading, however, he wanted his very own Schwab stock. So I bought him a single share and presented him with a framed certificate for his eleventh birthday. He was thrilled. In a similar spirit, my friend Anna gave her Gap-crazed daughter a Gap gift certificate accompanied by a company stock certificate for her sixteenth birthday. Anna was rewarded with the same excited reaction. And both kids got the same incentive to then follow "their" companies' ups and downs in the stock market.

Of course, getting your kids interested is just the first step. I found that although Ross was caught up in trying to be the most successful virtual investor in his class, he wasn't necessarily learning essential concepts such as how to manage risk. That came only later, when I made it personal and explained diversification in terms he could relate to: getting good grades across the board instead of studying for only a few of his classes.

Explaining the concept of compound growth is similar. Remember our example in Chapter 2 in which you take a penny and double it each day? Substitute the penny with a gumdrop and then have them do the math so they can see for themselves.

You can also try our family's "fact of the night" tradition, which my kids love. Every bedtime they ask for "the fact of the night," and I'll tell them something about a current event or the stock market—except for the evening I told them that the fact of the night was how proud I was of them. It's proved to be a terrific conversation starter.

From Kids to—er—Adults(?)

When it comes to teens and young adults, the right stuff still means being true to your values, sharing those values, and opening the lines of communication. In an age of triple-digit sneaker prices and single-digit teen responses, talking with teens can be trying at best. My friend Anna's brother-in-law reminds her that "the older your kids get, the more they cost and the less they talk to you." Of course if you've already survived that teen time, you know that some days the term *young adult* can seem like an oxymoron.

Fortunately for our purposes, mentioning money will probably elicit the attention of your fledgling adult. Do it the right way, and you may even get a mature response. But watch out. Advising your teenager about credit card abuses if you're drowning in debts yourself will likely backfire. You'll need to be a positive role model if you want to have any hope of influencing your teens and young adults.

TEEN TIME

Teenagers these days sure know how to spend money. According to Teenage Research Unlimited, of Northbrook, Illinois, America's teenage youth spent a mind-boggling $155 billion in the year 2000. That's as much as the gross national product of many foreign countries. No wonder so many ads are geared toward these wanna-be adults. But when it comes to knowing the basics about credit card

use, taxes, or even saving for college, most don't begin to know the
score. On average, high school seniors participating in a 2002
nationwide survey about basic personal finance sponsored by the
Jump$tart Coalition for Personal Financial Literacy, a national orga-
nization dedicated to improving the personal financial literacy of
young adults, answered just over half the questions correctly. In my
book, that's a failing grade.

DO YOUR KIDS KNOW THE SCORE?

How savvy are your kids when it comes to finances? Find out
how your teens score in personal financial literacy by having
them answer the following sample questions from the 2002
nationwide survey of high school seniors sponsored by the
Jump$tart Coalition. Any questions they can't answer correctly
will serve as terrific fodder for family discussions.

Note: The numbers next to each answer indicate the percentage of teens who gave that response. The asterisk indicates the correct answer.

1. If you had a savings account at a bank, which of the following would be correct concerning the interest that you
would earn on this account?

49.9% a) earnings from savings account interest may not be
taxed

16.1% b) sales tax may be charged on the interest that you
earn

*26.6% c) income tax may be charged on the interest if your
income is high enough

7.4% d) you cannot earn interest until you pass your eigh-
teenth birthday

2. Matthew and Alicia just had a baby. They received money
as baby gifts and want to put it away for the baby's education.

Which of the following is likely to have the highest growth over the next eighteen years?

- 37.5%   a) a savings account
- 3.6%   b) a checking account
- 40.2%   c) a U.S. government savings bond
- *18.7%   d) stocks

3. Many savings programs are protected by the federal government against loss. Which of the following is not?

- 9.3%   a) a U.S. savings bond
- 50.8%   b) a certificate of deposit at a bank
- 12.7%   c) a U.S. Treasury bond
- *27.1%   d) a bond issued by one of the 50 states

4. Inflation can cause difficulty in many ways. Which group would have the greatest problem during periods of high inflation?

- 10.1%   a) young couples with no children who both work
- 44.2%   b) young working couples with children
- 11.1%   c) older working couples saving for retirement
- *34.7%   d) older people living on fixed retirement income

5. Retirement income paid by a company is called

- 33.3%   a) Social Security
- 3.8%   b) rents and profits
- 27.7%   c) 401(k)
- *35.1%   d) pension

Used with permission of the Jump$tart Coalition for Personal Financial Literacy.

Although teenagers may not have all the answers yet (despite what they think), it's up to you to make sure they get them because there's a lot at stake. In fact, American adults under age thirty-five account for about one-third of the country's more than 1.5 million bankruptcies. As shocking as that figure is, it's not that surprising. If we don't teach our kids money-management skills, how can we expect them to understand or use those concepts?

The irony is that the only way for teens to learn about money management is to feel empowered. They need money that's unquestionably *theirs,* and they should never be made to feel stupid or foolish about how they use it. So ridicule is absolutely out. Similarly, you might as well throw criticism out the door as well, since that will also cause your teenager to shut down and shut you out.

So what's a parent to do? Go back to the basics of hands-on learning and lots of encouraging words. Start by opening a checking account for your teenagers. (If they're under eighteen, you'll probably have to cosign for the account.) Better yet, have them request information and account applications from several different banks. Then sit down together and compare account features and fees.

Once the account is open, don't assume your teens understand how it works. Explain that a check is a substitute for the cash they have in their account, and if they don't have enough cash in the account, they can't write a check. Show them how to record a check in the register and subtract the amount from the account balance. You'll also want to help them develop a system for recording ATM and debit-card transactions, encouraging them to keep all receipts so they can be reconciled against their monthly statement. Teach them to review that monthly statement and balance their checkbook. You'll probably need to help out with this more than once or twice. You might even want to introduce them to a software program such as Quicken or Microsoft Money.

If your teenagers' allowance never seems to stretch far enough, helping them figure out how to budget for movies, clothing, comic books, and the like will prove more valuable than simply giving them a raise. Having them jot down everything they buy during a two-to-four-week period can help them see where their money is going. And writing down their goals can help them plan and make conscious decisions. If they continue to try and tap your wallet, involving them in your family budget process may help. You may want to explain how much you pay for your mortgage or rent, property taxes, utilities, food, and so on. You might even want to consider outlining a new family budget together. Once you've come up with a plan, stick to the numbers you decided on together. This is the time to be consistent.

WORK FOR IT

When I was growing up, I didn't have any money to speak of unless I worked for it. So guess what? I worked as a teenager, every summer and part time during the year. Of course, the easiest place to find a job was within the family, which explains why I spent one summer working for my grandfather's development company as a "gofer" and the rest working for my dad as a kind of secretary's secretary. Don't think I was able to slack off just because it was all in the family. On the contrary, I think more was expected of me. And in some ways I probably had more to prove to them than I would have had I worked elsewhere.

Of course, work opportunities for teenagers are not limited to family businesses. Many teens are hired as fast-food-restaurant order-takers and grocery-baggers, and an increasing number of teenagers are entering the booming dog-walking business, which they can do before and after school. Creative teens can even sell what they make or bake at local and neighboring street fairs—or even to merchants around town.

Whatever their choice, walk your kids through the steps of negotiating a fair wage. First, make sure your child understands exactly what the job entails. Then help him get a sense of what he might be able to charge by asking around or checking the classifieds. Before he says a word, let his prospective boss suggest a fee or price. That way he won't underbid himself. If the offer is too low, advise him to review the demands of the job and counter with a number based on the facts you've dug up together.

Just as with allowances, what your child opts to do isn't really the point. What you want him to come away with is a strengthened sense of the value of work, as well as a sense of his own value and capabilities. Keep in mind, however, that frustration and failure are bound to hit at some point. That can help foster emotional resiliency, which, unfortunately, they can't get any other way.

And don't forget to talk to your teenager about her ultimate work or career aspirations. Encourage her to shoot for the moon.

INVEST IN AND WITH YOUR TEENS

With so much to contend with during those teenage years, fostering investing skills may not seem that critical, but I would beg to differ. According to our Harris poll, half of those adults who lack confidence when investing attribute their insecurity to their parents' lack of encouragement. Getting teenagers to start investing early—and then discussing their results—can make all the difference.

Just because minors can't legally open their own brokerage accounts doesn't mean that they can't actively participate in the market and invest part of their income with your help. Of course, you'll have to teach your children the basic concepts and stay involved. But you'll never have a more attentive or invested student than the one for whom you've just opened a custodial brokerage account.

If your teen is earning some money, one of the best things you can encourage her to do is to save a portion of her pay and let you open a custodial IRA for her. Teenagers and young adults who live for the moment may have a hard time accepting the wisdom of investing for so far in the future. But showing them the numbers and how compound growth works may help. Offering to match their contribution could help even more.

Roth IRAs may also make sense at this age, as most kids don't need tax deductions. Although the money is taxed before you invest it, you don't have to pay taxes on it—or what it earns—again if you don't withdraw it before you're 59½ (and have held the money for at least five years). That can really add up for those who start early. See Chapter 7 for more details on Roth IRAs and traditional IRAs.

One woman told me that she had grown up completely naïve about money and had to learn the hard way. When she realized that her teenage nieces' financial education was being as neglected as hers had been, she decided to open a custodial account for each of them. First she carefully laid out the value of long-term investing,

MATCH THIS!

Parents can encourage their young adult children to open an IRA by matching their contributions. Not sure you want to bother? I would urge you to reconsider by reminding you about the example of our twin sisters in Chapter 2. If you'll recall, the twin who invested during her twenties and then stopped after ten years wound up with more money than the one who started in her thirties and continued to invest for thirty-five years.

One friend of mine has decided that this is so important that she plans to match all contributions her children (now in their twenties) can manage to squirrel away. What better gift can you give your offspring (or yourself when it comes to peace of mind) than a secure future, so they never have to play catch-up? And what better way to instill good financial habits that will last—and bolster—a lifetime?

explaining (as we did in Chapter 2) the importance of time. Then she introduced the importance of diversification as a way to manage risk (also covered in Chapter 2).

Once the aunt had taught her nieces the basics, she turned them loose. Though she oversees and actually makes the investments, the girls do their homework and help her decide what to buy during their monthly phone conversations. The aunt has reserved veto power but hasn't needed to exercise it. Talk about an education!

Practice may not make perfect, but it does help build self-assurance. Add equal measures of fun and friendly competition, and you have a winning formula. Just ask Victoria Collins, Ph.D., CFP, author of several books about investing and financial planning, including *Best Intentions: Ensuring That Your Estate Plan Delivers Both Wealth and Wisdom* (Dearborn Financial, 2002). When she and her husband David married in 1985, Victoria had two children from a previous marriage and David had three—five children in all, ranging in age from seventeen to twenty-one.

Victoria and David's first goal was to bring the two families closer together. Their second goal was to teach their kids to be responsible about money and to know how to make rational investment decisions. So they set up a family-investing contest. Each child received $4,000 (in a custodial account for the two seventeen-year-olds) which, they were told, represented shares in Collins Family, Inc. "We're not just *giving* you four thousand dollars," they told their children. "Your goal is to increase shareholder value in this relationship."

Contest rules encouraged the kids to approach their parents or stockbrokers for advice, read books, and check in with one another. The requirements? The investments had to be easy to value in terms of profit and loss, and no loans could be made to friends.

The contest lasted for four years. At the end of every year, they held a family meeting in which the teens presented their results. "The person who had the highest returns and the best reasons for what they did or learned received $100 the first year, $200 the second year, and $300 the third year. The prize at the end of the fourth year was a trip around the world for two, paid for with frequent flier miles," says Victoria. "So there was good incentive." In addition, a bonus structure rewarded cooperation.

What happened? Two of the kids, Jennifer, twenty-one, and Nicole, seventeen, pooled their money and gave it to a broker who was a family friend. Two years later Jennifer announced that she couldn't understand why she had less than she'd started with even though the stock market had risen steadily. "What are you invested in, and how many trades are you making?" asked stepmom Victoria. That's when the girls figured out that they'd been socked with $1,400 in commissions on their $8,000 account. "Fine," her parents said. "That's a lesson."

Son David (Jr.), eighteen, invested all his money at another brokerage firm and proceeded to pump the brokers for information and ideas about mutual funds, calling at off-hours when he knew they'd have more time to talk. He made his own trades and tracked them on a spreadsheet complete with graphs. He took his investing very seriously and won every year.

With the help of his father, seventeen-year-old Todd invested in mutual funds, exhibiting neither a distinctive style nor any distinctive mistakes. Though he didn't win, his returns were consistently solid.

And finally, nineteen-year-old Kim kept her $4,000 in a money market account while she evaluated her choices. As the years went by, "she never took any action," says her mother. "But she talked a lot." A classic case of analysis paralysis!

The contest produced everything Victoria and her husband had hoped for. The kids bonded and gained invaluable financial experience and acumen. Sure, they made mistakes. "As parents, we didn't freak out when these things happened," says Victoria. "We listened, we understood, we empathized, but we didn't rescue or tell them they made a mistake and were stupid, because they learned. They really did learn."

DON'T TOUCH THAT!

All too often when parents talk to their kids about money, they impose their sense of the world without ever asking what the kids' sense of the world is, warns Deborah Tannen in her book *I Only Say This Because I Love You.* Like it or not, helping your children to fully realize their potential includes encouraging them to talk even when they're reticent, and then really listening to what they have to say. Of course, this applies to almost every subject you can think of, not just money issues.

Keep in mind that a dialogue is an exchange of ideas. If you have a teenager who seems reluctant to open her mouth, then you have to do what you can to elicit her reactions and thoughts. Otherwise, you've engaged in a dreaded monologue (also known as a harangue) or an interrogation, which certainly won't work with your teenager any better than it works with anyone else in your life.

You also want to make sure that you and your mate don't have cross-purpose agendas. When kids get caught in the middle, they may just clam up, which only gets you back to where you started.

Finally, just because you're not getting through doesn't mean that another adult (not a parent) might not fare better. Consider tapping friends and relatives to act as money mentors for your teen, suggests Joline Godfrey.

Leaving the Nest

As big, mature, and determinedly independent as your teenagers may be, you'll probably have to hold their hands once they get ready to fly off on their own. And you know what? They'll probably let you.

For all the educating that you may or may not have done, most college-bound teens still don't know how to budget their money. It's your job to teach them before they take off. After all, you didn't throw them into the pool and expect them to swim when they were little, did you? You made sure they wore their water wings, and then you kept them in the shallow water until they really developed their skills. Only then did they head to the deep end. Well, helping your kids figure out how to draw up a budget is no different.

Let's assume that all those talks about saving constituted the water-wings stage. Now it's time to teach the real skills and give your kids enough practice time so that they won't sink when they're on their own.

The summer before your teenager heads off to college, get him to draw up a budget and try to stick to it. Also encourage him to establish a savings reserve. A reasonable goal at this age is to have one to three months of living expenses stashed away.

Review the budget together after a couple of months to discuss how well it worked and how it might have worked better. Then draw up a new budget that will direct his spending during the first few months in college. Review it over the Thanksgiving break to see how he did, and discuss any problems or modifications that need to be made.

You may also want to consider signing your child up for a secured credit card, which is tied to the amount you deposit. For example, if you deposit $100, the credit limit might be $300 or $400. By definition, he won't be able to spend more than this limit, so you're safe. Yet he still builds his own positive credit history, as long as he pays on time. You'll also want to help him double-check the monthly statement by comparing charges listed with all the month's receipts. At the very least, he'll see how quickly plastic can make money vanish.

And finally, think about introducing your child to your banker or broker. This will show him that he can talk to these professionals, work with them, and even replace them if the service or performance isn't up to snuff. You might even attend an investment workshop together. The point is that your teen can feel empowered and be in a much better position to ultimately control his own finances.

Cutting the Ties

At some point you're going to need to let your kids swim in that deep end of the pool—or even in the ocean—without being buoyed by you or your financial support. Sure, you can continue to give and give and give forever, especially if your net worth and estate are sizable. But by doing so, you'll be depriving your children of one of the most important things they'll need to survive through thick and thin: the ability to take care of themselves.

How long should you provide financial support? That depends a lot on your particular child and family. Like many parents, you may opt to taper off the support slowly, perhaps setting your child up in an apartment after college. While that may be necessary, remember that you do children a disservice if you encourage them to grow accustomed to a life of luxury that they'll never be able to afford on their own. Some parents choose to let their kids find their own way by cutting them off cold turkey. That can be fine as long as their financial swimming skills are up to speed and they've entered the job market. Living in a dingy basement, or sharing an apartment with five others, never hurt anyone. What if they don't like it? Then they'll have that much more incentive to better their situation by bettering their salaries.

The Bottom Line

As we've seen, the key to raising money-savvy kids at any age amounts to initiating the active learning and ongoing conversation that will help shape their sense of financial initiative, confidence, and responsibility—and doing so as early as possible. The more people you include in these money lessons and discussions, the better. That can mean enlisting the help of grandparents, aunts, uncles, cousins, or friends. Realize, though, that you need to stay in close touch to make sure that everyone is on the same page.

Marie, a forty-something single mother in the process of starting a new career as a financial planner, needed some help motivating her twelve-year-old son Gabe. So she called her old friend Tina and asked her to help take Gabe in hand. First Tina suggested that if the boy washed her car, she'd give him $5. Then, as part of Gabe's math lesson, Tina asked him to calculate how many car washes it would take before he could afford to buy the PlayStation he wanted. "I'll even give you a letter of reference for the neighbors," she offered.

Together Tina and Gabe figured out that it would take thirty-nine car washes to earn the money he needed. Excitedly, Gabe started planning how he would drum up business. His mother was delighted. But all this fell flat when Gabe convinced his grandparents to buy him the PlayStation instead. It just seemed a whole lot easier.

That could have been the end of the motivation lesson. But Marie called the grandparents and explained the situation. Dismayed that they'd unintentionally undermined Marie and Tina's plan, the grandparents agreed that Gabe would have to be responsible for buying the PlayStation and set up a weekly payment schedule. In the meantime the PlayStation would stay at their house.

As a result, Gabe started doing odd jobs to make money. He gardened, he washed some more cars and helped a neighbor with chores. Every week he diligently handed his grandparents between $5 and $10—about half of what he earned—and returned home with an Excel spreadsheet charting his progress. On their end, his grandparents funneled all of Gabe's payments into a 529 college savings account (more on that in the next chapter).

See what talking can do?

Something to Talk About

• *Are you setting a good example for your kids?*

• *How can you best teach financial responsibility in an age of affluence, peer pressure, and media influence?*

• *Are you teaching—and talking to—your kids about money in age-appropriate ways? How can you make those experiences and discussions relevant and interesting?*

• *When it comes to money, do you talk to your daughter the same way you talk to your son?*

• *Do your kids have enough hands-on experiences with money?*

• *Are you paying your kids enough allowance so they can save a portion each week and donate regularly to charitable causes?*

• *If you have a blended family, how can you make sure that you're treating everyone fairly? Are there any underlying resentments you need to address?*

• *How can you motivate your children to earn their own money?*

• *How can you interest your kids in investing and encourage their efforts? Do they understand the concepts of compound growth and diversification? What activities can you engage in as a family to make finding out about finance fun?*

• *Do your teens understand how checking accounts and credit cards work? Have they been able to try them out for themselves?*

• *Have you reviewed budgets—your kids' and even your household's—together?*

• *How can you convince your teens and young adults to invest in a custodial Roth IRA—or a 401(k) once that opportunity presents itself?*

• *At what point do you want to cut the ties and stop supporting your kids?*

6

Investing in Your Children's Future

If you have kids or grandkids, you probably already know about the spiraling cost of a college education. It's faster than a speeding bullet. In fact, according to a 2002 survey conducted by the College Board, college costs are rising 9.6% per year at public schools and 5.8% at private schools, far outpacing inflation. That's pretty alarming, especially if you have more than one child. Still, if education is a priority in life, it simply must become a priority in your finances. Your values dictate not only how you scrape and save for your kids but how you help them have the future they want.

For most parents—or other intimately involved adults—this means financing all or part of your children's postsecondary education. Whether that takes the form of a musical career, a liberal arts degree, pre-med, pre-law, or vocational training, you'll need money to help him or her get there.

Fortunately, new tax-advantaged college savings plans make this a great time to put money aside. In this chapter we'll introduce you to the new 529 plans and to Coverdell education savings accounts, and we'll also review custodial accounts. For those of you who are getting a late start, we'll discuss financial aid and offer suggestions for how you might catch up.

Of course it's best to get started saving for college as early as possible. How early? Ideally, the day your child is born—or even before. Never again will you have such a great opportunity to put time on your side and reap the benefit of tax-free growth over a period of eighteen or more years.

Just three months into the pregnancy that would result in the birth of their first child, Roy and Carol, both in the investment business, invested $800 in a mutual fund for their unborn child. They continued to invest a set amount month in and month out, using the dollar-cost averaging strategy introduced in Chapter 2. "We started planting the seeds with the goal that the money would be there whenever the time comes that she decides to go to college," says Roy. "It was second nature, like breathing. It wasn't anything we had to think about." What a wonderful way to celebrate a pregnancy and upcoming birth!

How Much Will You Need?

According to the College Board, one year at a public college for the academic year 2002–03 costs an average of almost $13,000, and a year at a private college averages over $27,500. With expenses rising by more than 5% a year, it is estimated that for kids entering college in 2020, a four-year undergraduate education will cost more than $120,000 at a public school and more than $265,000 at a private school. And while many ambitious youngsters will wind up in graduate, law, or medical school also, for now we focus on how much money you'll need for four years of college. Table 6.1 provides estimated costs for four years of tuition, fees, books, room and board, and personal expenses at both a public and a private college.

Your first step in meeting this daunting task is to set a savings goal. To determine how much you'll need to set aside each month, find your child's age and select your college savings goal in Table 6.2. These amounts assume that your child will start college at age eighteen. They also assume an 8% after-tax return, although depending on what investment strategy you pursue, your actual returns may be higher or lower.

It Pays to Talk

Table 6.1
Future Four-Year Costs of College

Child's Age Now	Public College	Private College
Newborn	$123,614	$266,432
1	$117,727	$253,745
2	$112,121	$241,662
3	$106,782	$230,154
4	$101,697	$219,194
5	$96,854	$208,756
6	$92,242	$198,816
7	$87,850	$189,348
8	$83,667	$180,332
9	$79,682	$171,744
10	$75,888	$163,566
11	$72,274	$155,777
12	$68,833	$148,359
13	$65,555	$141,295
14	$62,433	$134,566
15	$59,460	$128,158
16	$56,629	$122,056
17	$53,932	$116,243
18	$51,364	$110,708

These amounts assume that college costs rise at an annual rate of 5%. Actual college costs may be higher or lower than the above figures.
Source: The College Board, 2002

Because there will always be conflicting demands on your money, a good strategy can be to have your monthly installment taken directly out of your bank account. That way there will be no room for discussion or conflict, and with time you'll likely find that you don't even notice the difference. Another suggestion for those of you in the corporate world fortunate enough to receive a periodic bonus: Contribute as much of it as possible to your child's college fund.

Table 6.2
Growth of Monthly Investing

Child's Age at Start	@ $100 Monthly	@ $200 Monthly	@ $300 Monthly	@ $400 Monthly	@ $500 Monthly
0–1	$46,918	$93,835	$140,753	$187,671	$234,588
1	$42,282	$84,565	$126,847	$169,129	$211,411
2	$37,990	$75,981	$113,971	$151,961	$189,951
3	$34,016	$68,032	$102,049	$136,065	$170,081
4	$30,336	$60,673	$91,009	$121,346	$151,682
5	$36,929	$53,859	$80,788	$107,717	$134,647
6	$23,775	$47,549	$71,324	$95,098	$118,873
7	$20,853	$41,707	$62,560	$83,414	$104,267
8	$18,149	$36,298	$54,446	$72,595	$90,744
9	$15,644	$31,289	$46,933	$62,578	$78,222
10	$13,326	$26,651	$39,977	$53,302	$66,628
11	$11,178	$22,357	$33,535	$44,714	$55,892
12	$9,190	$18,381	$27,571	$36,762	$45,952
13	$7,350	$14,699	$22,049	$29,399	$36,748
14	$5,645	$11,291	$16,936	$22,581	$28,226
15	$4,067	$8,134	$10,423	$16,268	$20,335
16	$2,606	$5,212	$7,817	$10,423	$13,029
17	$1,253	$2,506	$3,758	$5,011	$6,264

These amounts assume a hypothetical 8% after-tax return, which does not represent the performance of any specific investment. Your actual returns may be higher or lower.

Strategy Session

Although having the foresight and discipline to systematically save for your child's education is half the battle, the other essential part is investing that money wisely. Before you simply stash your hard-earned money in a CD or savings account, read on about three tax-advantaged education savings plans that can help you maximize your return: the Section 529 plan, the Coverdell education savings account (formerly known as an education IRA), and the custodial account. Each type of account has its pros and cons—and you may find that the best strategy for your family is to use the plans in combination. In this section we'll walk you through the features of each so you can discuss and choose what works best for you. We then provide a chart that gives you a bird's-eye view of how the plans compare.

THE 529 JUMBO JET

When it comes to saving for college, qualified state tuition 529 plans can get you off the ground in a hurry. Named for the section of the IRS Code that allows states to create tuition programs, 529 plans were originally set up to encourage parents to save for an in-state college education. Because of a ruling that the federal government couldn't tax money that was given to a state, these accounts gained in popularity and began to multiply. Today each state operates or is scheduled to begin operating a 529 plan, most of which are open to out-of-state as well as in-state residents. A few states offer more than one plan, providing even more choice. Cerulli Associates, a financial planning firm in Boston, predicts that 529 assets will grow to more than $140 billion by 2008, up from $20 billion at the end of 2002. Each plan has distinct differences as well as features in common, so once again—look before you leap.

Perhaps the biggest advantage of a 529 plan is the large amount you can contribute. Unlike the education savings account (which I'll discuss next and which tops out at contributions of $2,000 per year), parents, grandparents, or whoever else might be interested in helping finance your child's education can each invest $11,000 a year without triggering the federal gift tax. Families of significant wealth can also give a onetime gift of $55,000 in one year, provided they prorate it as five separate gifts of $11,000 (and make no additional contributions for five years). A couple can give $110,000 in the same way (combined gift of $22,000 per year prorated over five years). What a terrific way to launch an education account! In addition, this could fit in nicely with your overall estate plan. (For details on estate planning and gifting see Chapter 8.)

What is the total amount you can contribute over time to a single 529 account? That depends on the state plan you choose, and it is subject to change. Today it ranges from $100,000 to $300,000. Accounts of this size should be able to meet the college and graduate school aspirations of even the most ambitious child.

What if you have more than one child? You can—and should—open a 529 account for each. And what if one child decides not to go to college? The funds you've invested can be transferred to someone else in your family—provided you don't skip a generation, which could have gift-tax implications. Or if that doesn't pan out, you can even take the money back. In that case, you have to pay a 10% penalty and regular income tax on the earnings, but most of your portfolio will stay intact.

WHO CAN CONTRIBUTE TO A 529 PLAN?

One quirk of the 529 account is that although anyone can open one, only the official account owner (or owners) can contribute to it. So let's say that two parents have opened an account for their child (who is the beneficiary). They can cash the check Grandma sends Junior for his birthday and then deposit the proceeds into Junior's 529, but they can't deposit the check directly.

If she wants to, Grandma can open her own 529 for junior (as can others), but the total contribution for one beneficiary can't exceed the contribution limit for the plan selected.

The other advantages of a 529? Withdrawals for qualified expenses (those made for educational purposes including tuition, books, and educationally required equipment) are not federally taxed. Although the plans vary state by state, there are no income limitations or age restrictions on when the money must be used. You can even set up a plan for yourself if you're thinking about going back to school. The savings can be used to finance any kind of post-secondary education, from beauty to medical school, and everything in between, as long as the school is accredited and is in the United States.

Many financial institutions offer these plans, and some states sell them directly to the public. You should be aware that none of the 529 plans will allow you to direct your own investments, and there are significant differences from state to state in how the plans are administered. Variables include initial investment selection, investment strategy, fees, investment performance, and potential state tax benefits such as tax deductions or matching contributions (assuming your home state offers a 529 account). For example, one of the plans that Schwab distributes (which is managed for the state of Kansas by American Century Investment Management under the name Learning Quest) lets you choose among three portfolios: conservative, moderate, and aggressive. Layered into each one is a secondary track determined by when you'll need the money. In each case, the closer your child gets to entering college and withdrawing the money, the more the portfolio shifts from riskier (and potentially higher-yielding) stocks to less volatile investments like bonds and cash. Again, you don't direct the day-to-day investments, but with recent tax law changes, you have the ability to reevaluate your initial investment choice and change it once a year.

Also note that some states allow residents to deduct their 529 contributions from their taxable income and others provide a tax credit. Most allow state-tax-free withdrawals for qualified expenses. Therefore, as you compare plans, don't overlook this potential saving in state taxes. Also realize that you can open more than one 529 account. For example, you can contribute the state-tax-deductible limit to your own state's plan and also contribute to another plan that may have other features you're looking for.

Perhaps the easiest way to compare plans is to log onto www. savingforcollege.com. This terrific website evaluates each state's program and allows you to compare and contrast them based on the criteria you consider most important.

Also realize that 529 plans come in two distinct types. So far we've been describing the savings type of 529, which is by far the most versatile and is typically recommended for most families. But there are also 529 prepaid-tuition plans that allow you to buy units of tuition from your state university system, thereby locking in tuition costs. For example, if you've decided that your child should go to the University of Washington, just as you and the rest of your family did, the $1,000 you pay into Washington's 529 prepaid-tuition plan will buy you a specified number of college units. The price of those units is determined by the year when your child will be attending.

The upside of this alternative is that you're buying a sure thing, no matter what the stock market or inflation does. (Do you remember those double-digit inflation days? They could happen again.) And the downside? The most obvious is that your child may not want to attend the school you choose, or he may not be accepted by that school. To anticipate this problem, most prepaid programs allow you to convert your units into tuition at another school. But the value of that dollar of tuition you invested may be more or less depending on your child's school of choice. And although you can transfer the benefits to another family member or even request a refund if your child doesn't attend college, the value of your investment is limited to the contractual arrangement in your plan.

RIDING THE COVERDELL EDUCATION SAVINGS ACCOUNT EXPRESS

If the 529 plan is a jumbo jet, you can think of a Coverdell education savings account, or ESA (formerly known as an education IRA and now renamed after the late Georgia senator), as a commuter train that is reliable but can only take you so far. Unlike the 529, though, which allows savings only for postsecondary education, recent changes in the tax laws allow you to apply ESA money toward primary and secondary education as well. If you're planning to send your child to a private elementary or high school, this is a great bonus.

Your annual contribution to an ESA (recently raised from $500 to an annual maximum of $2,000) is made after taxes. Most likely this amount will not be enough to finance an entire education, but with tax-free withdrawals for qualified expenses, it can be a good start. In addition, when your child withdraws the money, provided he or she spends it on qualified education expenses such as tuition, books, or room and board, those withdrawals are tax-free.

Another limitation of an ESA is its income cap. If you earn more than $110,000 as an individual or $220,000 as a couple, this plan is off-limits (although other qualified relatives or friends could open an account for your child). Phaseouts begin at $95,000 for an individual and $190,000 for a couple. For those of you who do qualify, however, an ESA can be a great part of your overall education savings strategy. Unlike the 529 plan, you can direct the investments in any way you see fit—individual stocks, bonds, cash, stock mutual funds, or a mix. Do note, however, that contributions can

CHOOSE YOUR INVESTMENTS WISELY

If your child won't be entering college for at least five to ten years, we recommend that you invest at least part of your college fund in a well-diversified mix of stocks or stock mutual funds. Then, as that date gets closer, gradually move into less volatile investments, such as CDs or money market funds.

Another good way to invest your child's college fund, especially in a high-interest environment, is a zero-coupon bond issued by either the U.S. government or your state or local municipality. (Higher-interest corporate zeros are also available, although they carry higher risk.) You purchase zeros at a deeply discounted rate. Instead of getting an annual income, you get the total face value of the bond when it matures (which you can time to coincide with the year your child is entering college). In this way, if you hold them to maturity, zeros can be a great way to provide a predictable return. A caveat, though: Zeros tend to fluctuate in value more than coupon bonds; if you're forced to sell before maturity, you may lose a substantial amount of your investment. Also, you do pay income tax annually on the income even though you don't receive it until maturity.

no longer be made once the beneficiary has turned eighteen, and unless he or she is disabled or has special needs, the money must be used by age thirty.

Before we leave ESAs, it's important to realize that the assets are considered to belong to the child when it comes to eligibility for financial aid. By contrast, unless a 529 savings plan is set up as a custodial account, those assets currently are not.

DRIVING THOSE CUSTODIAL ACCOUNTS

Continuing with our transportation analogy, if 529 plans are jumbo jets and education savings plans are commuter trains, then custodial accounts are automobiles—and they range from economy models to sports cars. You can put in as much money as you'd like (although amounts over $11,000 a year, or $22,000 for a couple, will incur gift taxes). And, yes, you get to drive the investments in the accounts, as long as you invest the money responsibly. You can use the funds to pay for anything—from private school to a car— as long as the withdrawals are for the sole benefit of the child.

Tax advantages for custodial accounts aren't as significant as those for a 529 or an education savings account. When your child is less than fourteen years old, the first $750 of earnings is tax-free, and the next $750 is taxed at your child's income tax rate. Additional earnings are taxed at your rate. As soon as your child hits fourteen, all gains are taxed at his rate.

But the biggest danger of a custodial account is that once your child reaches the age of majority, the money becomes his to do with what he will. (This is either eighteen or twenty-one, depending on your state, although in UTMA states, you can designate up to age twenty-five.) This is definitely worth talking about, because at that point you have no control over how he spends it. So he can essentially drive that custodial account to school and finance his education, or to the coast for a surfing safari. Of course, sharing your sense of why education is so important with your children may help you sidestep the latter fate and enable you to take advantage of the tax benefits of a custodial account.

One final consideration: Like an education savings account (but unlike a 529), a custodial account is owned by your child, and therefore a larger percentage is allocated in figuring out financial aid eligibility.

THE FINE PRINT

Depending on the state where you live, your child's custodial account will be governed by either the Uniform Gifts to Minors Act (UGMA) or the Uniform Transfers to Minors Act (UTMA). Although the basic principles are the same, there are slight variations from state to state. For example, a custodial account may terminate at age eighteen in one state and up to age twenty-one in another.

• UGMA, which was first adopted in 1956, allows you to give gifts to minors in the form of money and securities.

• UTMA, which is a bit more flexible and allows you to give both of the above, plus real estate, royalties, patents, and art, was adopted in 1986. Almost all states have adopted UTMA. Note that in UTMA states, custodians can designate that they maintain control of the account until the beneficiary reaches up to age twenty-five.

MIX AND MATCH

The fact is that you really don't have to choose among these plans or settle for a single account. If you're saving exclusively for college, a 529 is almost always your best bet: it's flexible, has great tax advantages, and allows for large contributions. But if you're planning to send your child to private school and then to college, you could put $2,000 a year into an ESA and invest the college money in a 529 savings plan. If you're able to save even more, you could put additional funds into a custodial account.

When choosing between 529 plans, it is wise to first check your state's plan so that you can capture any potential savings in state taxes. After that you will want to compare and contrast the fees and features of other plans to find the plan or combination of plans that makes the most sense.

If you already have money invested in a custodial account, you also have the ability to transfer it into a custodial 529. But depending on the age of your child and the size of the account, your best bet may be to leave it where it is and to direct new contributions to a 529 plan. First, when you make the transfer, you have to liquidate the assets and pay taxes on the gains. In addition, the funds will remain segregated as the property of your child, and she will gain control of the money once she reaches the age of majority. But the younger your child and the larger the account, the more you may benefit from the tax-free growth of a 529.

Table 6.3 gives an overview of these three plans so that you can quickly compare their features.

Playing Catch-up

If your child is only a few years away from college and your savings haven't kept pace, the first thing to realize is that you're in very good company. As members of the "sandwich generation," many parents today are trying to pay for expensive educations at the same time that they are caring for aging parents and saving for their own retirement. Competing demands for money, especially among the growing number of single parents, have made it increasingly difficult for parents to keep college savings accounts on track.

Of course, catching up is never easy. The most obvious place to start is by pulling back on what you're spending every month and investing the difference. One important note: As with funding 401(k)s, starting late is certainly better than not starting at all. Another alternative is to focus on your state schools. Public universities offer excellent educations for about half the cost of private colleges. Community colleges also offer great value and can be the perfect launching pad for a college education.

Also realize that you don't have to shoulder the load by yourself. Many families get support from their extended families. Many oth-

Table 6.3
Comparison of College Savings Accounts

	529 College Savings Plan	Coverdell Education Savings Account
Ownership		
Who owns the account?	Donor, unless it is a custodial 529.	Child.
Who has authority over the account?	Account owner, or responsible individual if owned by child.	Parent or guardian until child reaches set age.
Can I change the beneficiary?	Yes; can transfer to another member of beneficiary's family without penalty anytime, but only once a year.	Yes; can transfer to another member of beneficiary's family if new beneficiary is under 30.
Withdrawals		
How can I use the money?	Qualified expenses at an eligible postsecondary institution.	Qualified education expenses, including primary and secondary school; must be used before age 30 (unless child is disabled or has special needs) to avoid penalty.
Contributions		
Does it affect my child's eligibility for financial aid?	Possibly.	Yes.

What are contribution limits?	Determined by state; currently ranging up to $300,000.	$2,000 per year.
Does my income limit my contributions?	No. In some states, your contribution to a state plan may be deductible from state taxes.	Yes. Eligibility begins to phase out at $95,000 for an individual and $190,000 for a couple. Ineligible after $110,000 for an individual and $220,000 for a couple.
Taxes		
How are earnings taxed?	On federal level, not taxed until withdrawn; then taxed only if *not* used for qualified expenses. States can vary.	On federal level, not taxed until withdrawn; then taxed only if used for qualified expenses. States can vary.
How are qualified withdrawals taxed?	Exempt from federal tax. States can vary.	Exempt from federal tax.
How are gift taxes handled?	No federal gift tax on contributions for each student up to $55,000 per contributor ($110,000 per couple) in one year if gift prorated over five years.	N/A
What are penalties for nonqualified use?	Earnings taxed as ordinary income and subject to 10% penalty.	Earnings taxed as ordinary income and subject to 10% penalty.

Source: IRS Publication 590 and www.savingforcollege.com

ers receive financial aid in the form of grants, scholarships, loans, or work-study programs. One word of caution, however: No matter how much you're tempted, be very careful about dipping into your retirement savings.

Max (whom we met in Chapter 4) recalls, "My father was very proud and very determined to provide for the family so none of us would want for anything, including private school and college. But when his law firm experienced a downturn after my brother and I had already graduated, he and my mom started talking about how to make some money on the side. They kept the details quiet. Whenever I asked, they always said everything was fine. Then one day I opened the trunk of their car and found all these Amway products. They finally admitted that they'd spent all their retirement savings putting us through college."

Of course Max's parents had acted out of generosity and love. But what they didn't realize was that there were other ways for them to pay for their children's education. They didn't have to jeopardize their retirement.

TAX RELIEF

Tuition support comes in two flavors of tax relief: deductions and credits.

Deductions reduce the amount of your income that is taxed, thereby lowering your tax bill. Credits, on the other hand, are subtracted directly from the amount of taxes you owe. You have to choose, though, because you can't take both. You simply have to do the math to see which will save you more money overall.

Tuition deduction. If as a single filer you earn less than $65,000 per year (or $130,000 for a couple), you can deduct up to $4,000 a year in college expenses. (Note: Although this deduction is currently scheduled to expire in 2006, Congress may renew it. Stay tuned.) Also note that this deduction applies only for your legal dependents, so if you contribute to the education of a niece or nephew or another child, you won't be able to take the tuition deduction. You also can't deduct tuition paid for with 529 earnings or Coverdell money.

Tuition credits. If your income is less than $41,000 as a single filer (or $82,000 as a couple), and your child is enrolled in a certified school, the HOPE Scholarship tax credit allows you to subtract from your tax bill 100% of the first $1,000 you spend on tuition and fees and 50% of the second $1,000 (if you earn up to $51,000 as an individual or $102,000 as a couple, this benefit is gradually phased out). This applies only to the first two years of postsecondary education and not at all to graduate or professional programs. Also note that these income levels were for 2002. They will increase by $1,000 increments in the future to keep up with inflation.

The Lifetime Learning tax credit steps in where the HOPE leaves off. This program, which every year helps several million juniors, seniors, and graduate students, allows you to subtract 20% of the first $10,000 you spend on tuition and fees. Qualifying income levels are the same as for HOPE.

Recent changes in the tax law allow you to receive the HOPE or Lifetime Learning credit as well as use 529 or ESA withdrawals to pay for other college expenses. Prior to this change, you had to choose one or the other.

Getting Help Shouldering the Load

Our society has gotten increasingly insular, to the point where many of us focus only on our immediate family. We may get together with our parents and siblings for holidays and special occasions, but for most of us those encounters aren't a part of our everyday lives. Today's economic pressures, however, are causing us to rely on our extended families more and more. And that, in turn, connects us and brings us closer.

What form would that help from your extended family take? Anyone at all, including nonrelatives, can gift up to $11,000 a year to various savings accounts (subject to specific contribution limits) tax-free and can pay unlimited tuition expenses free of gift tax when that payment is made directly to the school. For those who can afford it, this is a terrific way to leave their mark on future generations.

If your family hasn't approached you about helping with your child's college fund, you might think about taking that first step yourself and opening the door. If this idea makes you uncomfortable, think about whether your family even knows that you would welcome help. Maybe they live far away. Maybe you haven't been all that close. Maybe they just aren't that observant. Whatever the reason, consider allowing them to assist you.

I'm not necessarily suggesting that you ask straight out, although some of you may have the kind of candid and direct relationship that allows for that. But when your relatives ask you what present they should get the kids, you could respond that you're desperately trying to save for their college education and that a small check that your child could split between an inexpensive toy and his college savings plan would be welcome.

You might also share your concern about the high cost of education and ask for your family's advice. Though the conversation could be difficult, especially at first, this could be something your relatives already have been contemplating. Besides, most people like to feel needed and appreciated, and asking for their help could bring you closer. I've heard of several individuals who didn't have children—either because they're single, in a same-sex relationship, or simply offspring-free—who've enjoyed helping to support the education of their siblings' or friends' children.

One very close colleague of mine has started a college fund for her niece because she knows her brother will have a tough time putting her through school. "As someone who values education, I wanted to make sure she would be able to attend the college of her choice," says Elizabeth. "So I sat down with my financial planner and we set up a fund. Every month five hundred dollars is automatically deducted from my salary and deposited into that account."

Times have gotten harder since Elizabeth established her ten-year-old niece's college fund. "I'm watching my pennies because the money's just not coming in right now," Elizabeth admits. "That extra could make life a whole lot easier right now." Still, she faithfully socks away that $500 every month and refuses to touch a penny of the money she's saved so far, no matter how tempted. "I don't have children of my own," she explains. "This is the child I'm choosing to invest in."

To give is better than to receive, they say. When my father offered to help Gary and me with tuition for our three children, at first we had a difficult time accepting his offer. But when I thought back to the stories of my grandparents and great-grandparents always helping out the next generation, I realized that this was my father's way of putting his values into action. Besides, like so many other grandparents, helping out with our educational bills has made my father feel more involved in the lives of his grandchildren. In a sense, it's been just as important for him as it is for them.

NOTE TO GRANDPARENTS: FUNDING YOUR GRANDCHILDREN'S FUTURES

If you've got the money to spare, you can make no better investment than financing your grandchildren's private school or college education. At least that's how my father feels. To him, education is the bedrock upon which lives are founded and futures built. So helping to ensure that his grandkids get the best is as much a privilege as it is a responsibility.

How to know if this financial assistance will be welcome? If you don't feel comfortable asking, Jane Adams, author of *I'm Still Your Mother: How to Get Along with Your Grown-Up Children for the Rest of Your Life* (Delta Trade Paperbacks, 1994), suggests the following rule of thumb: "If it's something [the parents] would do themselves if they could, do it. If it's not, don't."

Of course, grandparents and other extended family members can step up in other ways as well. Gifts of time, especially in the form of child care, can allow you and your children to funnel more savings into a college savings account.

Chuck's Two Cents:
Helping Your Kids or Grandkids Financially

As a parent and a grandparent, I've received great joy and satisfaction in helping my kids and grandkids out financially, whether that means contributing to their higher education, or to a business, or to a first home. In particular, I've found contributing toward my grandkids' education very rewarding because I see that as an investment in their future. And while you can certainly contribute through a will or estate plan, I have to say that it's very gratifying to help out while you're alive and to see the fruits of your labor.

If you do decide to offer financial help, I encourage you to initiate the conversation and to let the recipient know of your intentions early on. If your child or grandchild needs help, it's far easier to accept an offer than to go asking for help. By offering your help in advance, your child or grandchild won't lose face by asking. The conversation might be as brief as you telling him or her, "If you need help, call me." Just that much can pave the way later on and make things that much easier for the person you want to help.

One of the best stories I've heard about family giving comes from my colleague, Lynn. When she was in college, Lynn's grandmother, Josephine, used to send her money she'd saved from Social Security almost every month. They had an agreement that if Josephine ever needed the money, Lynn would give it back. When Lynn graduated with her M.B.A. from the University of California at Davis, her grandmother was the one to "hood" her during the ceremony. Since then, Josephine has moved into a nursing home. True to her promise, Lynn put a phone in her room and regularly pays her grandmother's monthly phone bills.

One of my clients realized that his grandchildren would need his help in paying for their education. Ever the egalitarian, he devised a formula for giving so that his grandchildren, then ages seven and eleven, would wind up with roughly the same amount by the time they were ready for college. As a result, he deposits more into the account of the older child, reasoning that the assets of the younger one will grow larger with the extra time.

GET YOUR KIDS IN ON THE ACT

Just as your extended family may be able to lend a hand, so too can your children. Being responsible for a portion of their education can not only help them appreciate its value, it also can give them a goal to shoot for.

Before you can convince your children to get involved, you need to share with them your sense of how important education really is, which means you'll need to talk about it—a lot. Again, I said *talk*, not preach. Encourage your children to indulge in dreams of what they might want to be when they grow up—whether that be a ballet dancer or president—and then discuss what that means in terms of schooling.

It's never too early to start these conversations. Even young children can understand why college is so critical. One extraordinary story stands out. After winning a school poetry contest, life for seven-year-old Travis—then a homeless boy with a drug-addicted mother and a missing father—changed. A local Phoenix newspaper covered his story, which inspired a local resident to take him into her home. Shortly thereafter the youngster published a book of poetry, whose first printing quickly sold out. Although you'd think that a young boy might squander this windfall, Travis proved wise beyond his years. He already knew that education was his highest priority, and he decided to save the money for college. "I'm keeping it in the stocks, and I'm putting it in my bank account," says Travis, whose new guardian Julie Hall is responsible for piquing his marked interest in the stock market. "Julie told me all about it, and after that I got really interested," he says. Does he worry that the market is down? "No. When the whole economy is bad, you shouldn't be worried about any of your stocks going down, only if it's doing bad alone," he told the *Today Show*.

Naturally, you'll want to discuss your family's financial situation with teens and young adults and let them know how much financial support they can expect in college and graduate school. That way they can start considering their own potential contributions as well as financial aid. Remind them that costs extend well past tuition and room and board and include everything from books and supplies to sports equipment and entertainment.

Even if you do plan to pay for 100% of your children's postsecondary education, making them an active part of the college-saving process will not only help them appreciate it more, it will also help teach them about personal finance and money management. When the bank or brokerage statement arrives each month, show it to your children and talk about how their accounts are doing. If you need to make adjustments, include them in the discussion. Simple yet practical exercises like this can help prepare them for the day they manage their finances.

The Business of Financial Aid

No matter what your situation, don't overlook the possibility of financial aid. According to the U.S. Department of Education, more than $60 billion (yes, that's spelled with a *b*) in scholarships, grants, and loans is awarded yearly, with millions more unused simply because no one applied for the money. Although most financial aid packages are based at least partially on need, others are open to all applicants. Indeed, with one out of every two applicants winding up with something, the odds are definitely with you.

According to Ben Kaplan, Harvard graduate and author of *How to Go to College Almost for Free* (HarperCollins, 2001), the more your kids apply, the better their chances of succeeding, no matter what their grades. "The common link among all scholarship winners [is that] they apply. You need to apply again and again."

His advice? Your children should unearth as many scholarship possibilities as they can by looking in the binders high schools keep and staying current with online databases such as www.college scholarships.com, www.fastweb.com, and www.salliemae.com.

Robert went on the scholarship hunt in 1979 after being accepted to the University of Southern California. Although his parents were determined to pay for his schooling, Robert knew that it would seriously stretch their resources. His solution? After visiting the USC admissions office and learning what he could about financial aid opportunities, he tenaciously applied for absolutely anything and everything he qualified for. He filled out volumes of paperwork and wrote what felt like nonstop essays tailored to the Rotary Club and the Ebell Club of Los Angeles, as well as religious, fraternal, and professional organizations. Once in school, he kept applying, with increasing success. By his final year Robert had garnered a total of two dozen different financial awards, ranging from $500 to $1,000. Each individual award may not have been huge, but together they paid for his entire college education as well as four years of room and board.

When you're thinking about applying for financial aid, whether a grant or a loan, one of your first steps should be to fill out the Department of Education's Free Application for Federal Student Aid, or the FAFSA, which is available online at www.fafsa.ed.gov. A lot of federal and private financial aid is granted on a first-come first-served basis, so this is not a time to procrastinate.

As soon as you submit your FAFSA, the government will calculate your EFC, or *expected family contribution,* which is based on your family's income, investments, and savings. Although public schools mostly stick to a strict formula, private schools use a lot more discretion in appropriating their financial aid. Most schools, however, award some portion of their aid for merit rather than need. If you're a National Merit Finalist, you'll probably be in the enviable position of choosing among multiple scholarship offers.

A typical financial aid package will contain several elements, including grants, work-study opportunities, and possibly loans. When you're comparing offers, clearly you should lean toward the package with the most grants (such as a federal Pell Grant, a Supplemental Education Opportunity Grant, or a direct grant from the college), which don't have to be repaid, as opposed to a package that consists mostly of loans.

If you're still coming up short, don't give up. The government offers subsidized loans that can keep college within reach. In fact, almost half of all college students take out some type of student loan. Your first line of defense can be a Stafford Loan, which is subsidized by the government and which the students borrow themselves. PLUS (Parent Loans for Undergraduate Students) are also subsidized by the government, but they are for parents (for their children) rather than for students. In general Stafford Loans are a better choice because the interest rates are lower than those for PLUS, and the interest payments can be deferred. With the recent tax law changes, up to $2,500 per year in student loan interest is tax-deductible (as opposed to just the first five years' worth of interest as previously stipulated), assuming your income falls below $65,000 for an individual (or $130,000 for a couple). This too is an improvement, since income phaseout amounts used to be $55,000 for an individual (or $75,000 for a couple). Also check out www.salliemae.com for an online comparison of the best rates and terms for college financing.

COLLEGE SAVINGS TIMETABLE

Eighteen years before college:

• Figure out how much you'll need to save for both a public and a private school.

• Open a college savings account, preferably a 529 savings plan or an education savings account.

• Contribute as much money as possible on a regular basis.

• Approach investments with an eye toward accepting higher risk if you can while your child is young, and move toward a more conservative course as he or she gets closer to college.

Eight to ten years before college:

• Reassess how much you'll need to save for both a public and a private school.

• If you haven't already, open a 529 college savings plan. With fewer years to benefit from compound growth, this plan will allow you to contribute up to $11,000 per year without incurring the gift tax (or $55,000 if you prorate it over five years) and will help you make up for lost time. Custodial accounts also allow for large contributions, but they lack the tax benefits, and the impact on financial aid may be greater.

• Make regular contributions, and put in extra money whenever possible.

• Whenever you receive a bonus or raise, try to allocate some of the funds to your kids' education.

One to two years before college:

• Estimate how much your family will be expected to pay, perhaps using an online expected-family-contribution calculator such as the one offered by the College Board and located at www.collegeboard.org.

• Explore financial aid choices, including scholarships, grants, and work-study programs.

• Find the best loan programs for your family: federal Stafford Loans (for students) and PLUS loans (for parents) are two possibilities.

Something to Talk About

• *If your first child was just born, have you thought about how you can start saving for college?*

• *Have you estimated how much college will cost for your child? Have you established appropriate savings goals?*

• *If you're facing significant college costs in the next several years, how can you balance saving for retirement with saving for college?*

• *Have you reviewed the pros and cons of the various college savings accounts?*

• *If you decide to open a 529 plan, which variation will work best—the savings plan or the prepaid-tuition plan? Which state's system do you want to use?*

• *If you're investing in an ESA, have you factored in your child's age when choosing investments? Are you properly diversified?*

• *Before you invest a significant amount of your education fund in a custodial account, have you thought about the fact that it will become your child's own property when he or she reaches the age of majority? If you live in an UTMA state, do you want to specify that the funds will remain under your control until your child is twenty-five?*

• *If your child will enter college in just a few years and you need to play catch-up, where can you cut back in order to speed the savings process?*

• *Have you looked into state schools and financial aid?*

• *What kinds of financial aid options should you explore?*

• *How can you gather support from your extended family without feeling embarrassed or seeming too demanding?*

• *How can your kids contribute to this college-savings effort?*

• *Do you want to provide your children with nest eggs once they've graduated from college?*

7

Investing for the Second Half

As a rule, we Americans are simply not saving enough for retirement. Some of us don't like to think about growing old. Others, especially those who are raising children or caring for aging parents, feel that they have a hard enough time paying today's bills, let alone saving for the future. Others assume that someone else—such as a mate—will take care of everything. And still others simply underestimate how much they will need.

About a year ago, a thirty-five-year-old doctor came to see Theresa, a broker in our San Francisco offices. Right away the doctor announced that he wanted to retire at fifty with a million dollars so he could support his current standard of living exclusively with the interest it generated.

"If I give you five thousand dollars a month, will that be enough?" he asked.

Now, he could put $5,000 a month in a shoe box, and he'd have close to $1 million in fifteen years. So that part was obvious. The problem was that a million dollars, even though it sounded like an awful lot, would never be enough for the retirement he had in mind.

When Theresa asked the doctor how much he lived on now, he answered that he and his wife currently spend $100,000 a year for their fixed expenses such as their mortgage, car payments, insurance, utilities, and taxes, and another $50,000 a year on discretionary items such as clothing, restaurants, and vacations.

"Taking into account the effect of inflation over the next fifteen years, and assuming that you will be spending at the same level, you'll need about $250,000 a year by the time you're fifty," Theresa told him as gently as possible. "Your retirement could last for forty years. In order to make sure that you don't outlive your money, you're going to need approximately five million, not one million."

But this young doctor was actually ahead of the game because he had at least taken that important first step—he had started to plan. According to the national 2003 Retirement Confidence Survey conducted by the Employee Benefit Research Institute, the American Savings Education Council, and Mathew Greenwald & Associates, only 46% of Americans have tried to compute how much money they will need in retirement (and only 37% of Americans have completed a detailed analysis—up from 32% in 2002).

Unfortunately, the blunt truth is that you can either save now or pay later—with your quality of life. It's actually a kind of double-hit: Just when most of us are living longer, more active (read: more expensive) lives, most companies have moved away from the traditional pension plans upon which previous generations have depended. Now, instead of receiving a guaranteed retirement benefit for life, most of us are enrolled in a defined contribution plan such as a 401(k)—and are responsible for creating our own retirement nest egg. Compounding this situation, as the years roll by we may receive less from government assistance like Social Security.

It's a challenging situation, to be sure, but not an insurmountable one. In this chapter we'll start out by exploring what constitutes a satisfactory retirement and address how retirement has changed over the past forty or fifty years. These days those golden years don't consist of just golf and bridge games but are more likely to include second careers, international travel, education, and more. The second part of the chapter will provide you with the financial nuts and bolts of retirement. Central to the discussion are several worksheets that walk you through the necessary calculations. Before you decide that this step isn't necessary, think again. The Retirement Confidence Survey also reveals that the people who actually go to the trouble of crunching the numbers do a better job of preparing for retirement than those who do not. According to Don Blandin, president of the American Savings Education Council, "The mere act of calculating your numbers gives you a goal and makes you a more disciplined saver."

If you're getting a late start, we'll also offer suggestions for catching up. Although sooner is certainly better than later, it is never too late to start planning for your retirement. Throughout the chapter we'll again encourage you to keep the lines of communication open. Retirement can be a tough issue for many people, so we'll give you suggestions for talking it out with the people closest to you. Just one more thing before we begin. This chapter covers all the basics for planning your retirement and is a great place to start. But if you'd like to delve into the topic in more detail, my father's book *You're Fifty—Now What?* provides a much more in-depth look at the issues crucial to retirement planning and investing.

What's Your Vision for the Future?

Before you embark on a discussion of dollars and cents, it's essential to think about your dreams and aspirations, your vision of what you want the second half of your life to be. And it can be anything. As my father points out, "Eleanor Roosevelt was appointed as the U.S. delegate to the United Nations when she was seventy-seven, and Frank Lloyd Wright completed the Guggenheim Museum when he was eighty-nine. When you hit fifty, the first half of your life is known. But what you find in the second half, well, that's up to you."

How much will you—and your parents—need for retirement? Certainly the whole concept of retirement is changing, with more and more Americans choosing to continue working well past the traditional retirement age of sixty-two, either full time or part-time. Consider my family and friends. My father, who's in his sixties, has no plans to quit or scale back work anytime soon. My grandfather is eighty-eight and still goes to the office. As a young woman, my friend Anna assumed she'd retire at sixty. Now fifty-two, she says she's not close to wanting to retire. In fact, according to research conducted by AARP, "Eighty percent of baby boomers 45 and over expect to continue working past the age of 65—either for the money or for the fun of it." For myself, I can't imagine a life without work. I simply get too much satisfaction and sense of identity from my career.

Chuck's Two Cents: A New View of Retirement

As a society, we are redefining "retirement." Thanks to the fact that we're living longer and that we're healthier, "retirement" no longer means a few years of leisure at the end of your life; it can instead mean thirty years or more of travel, leisure, or even a second career. More than anything, "retirement" is coming to mean choice. And to me, that's as good a reason as I can think of to put some effort into financial planning: You're doing some work today so that you'll have more choices tomorrow.

Maybe you have a pretty good idea of what you want your retirement to be like; maybe you've known it for years. Or perhaps you have no idea, or you can't even imagine not going to your current job every day. In fact, maybe you don't plan on ever retiring, in the old sense of the word. You just want to keep at it. If so, you and I are similar. I love what I do and have no plans to give it up. Whatever your situation— even if you want to continue working—you'll need to do some planning for your future. The steps in that process can seem daunting, but I urge you to do whatever it takes to sit down and do it. Write it on the calendar, make a date with your spouse, and stick to your word.

The good news is that the kind of planning I'm talking about isn't difficult; it just takes a little time to develop a road map of where you are and where you're going. Like any worthwhile endeavor, the process takes commitment and focus. But it can be done. And when it is, you'll have the satisfaction of knowing you've done all you can to secure the future you want.

Others do stop work—but only to reinvent themselves through new careers. Engineers and doctors become actors and writers. Accountants and teachers return to graduate school to study marine biology or to practice psychotherapy. Advance planning is what makes achieving these sorts of dreams possible.

Even if you don't know what you're going to want later in life, a healthy retirement fund will give you choices. Beatrice didn't want an ordinary retirement community, so in January 2000, at the age of eighty, she boarded the *Queen Elizabeth 2* and took up full-time residence. She'd fallen in love with the ship and cruising when she and her husband, Robert, then a retired engineer, first tried it in 1995. Thereafter the couple returned to the *QE2* for four months out of each year. Upon Robert's death in 1999, Beatrice decided to sell the houses they owned in New Jersey and Maine and take to the seas full time. And why not? The staff loves her, so she has a built-in community. By definition, everything she needs—from restaurants and shops to a beauty salon and the ship's doctor—is in walking distance. There's nonstop entertainment on board (including nightly dancing), as well as day trips in ports of call ranging from Hong Kong to the Seychelles. The cost? About $5,000 a month, which she's well prepared to pay.

Do you want to stop working completely? Maybe you do. If, on the other hand, that doesn't feel quite right, you can always consider the notion of "gradual retirement," during which you work part-time. That's what one of my colleagues' parents, John, sixty-three, and Emily, age sixty-two, chose to do. When John, an insurance broker, decided to retire at sixty-two, his wife, Emily, an X-ray technician who had always worked part-time, made a change as well. Knowing that they'd need some income, but fed up with all the mergers and consolidations that were changing the way he was able to do business, John decided to strike out on his own. These days he works the equivalent of two to three days a week. And although he left the corporate world a good three years before he'd planned to, that part-time income—along with effective planning—affords them exactly the life they want. They've bought a brand-new house in a retirement community they absolutely adore, replaced all of their old furniture, and established an active social life. John's new goal is to find a consulting position that will offer him employee benefits as part of his compensation. Then he'll feel completely set.

Like John and Emily, many people in their fifties through seventies view this period as a transition instead of an end. Accordingly, they use the second half of their lives to reinvent themselves. And then there are couples like my clients Beth and Martin, who revamped their careers to serve those in need.

Several years ago a medical scare prompted this couple to begin the vigorous retirement they'd planned much earlier than anticipated. Martin and Beth knew they wouldn't have as much money as they would have if they'd delayed their quasi-retirement, but they weren't willing to wait. Wanting to retire while they were still healthy enough to enjoy it, Beth, a fifty-three-year-old physician, gave one year's notice before quitting her family practice outright. Her fifty-five-year-old ob/gyn husband also gave a year's notice but didn't actually leave. Instead, he committed to covering his partners during their vacations and other times off.

Beth and Martin knew what they wanted to do: travel around the world. They just didn't quite agree on how they wanted to do it. Martin wanted to set up a travel-work situation, providing health care in third world countries. Beth, however, didn't want to work at all. She wanted to see the world's sights and enjoy herself.

After much discussion Beth and Martin came up with a compromise that satisfied both. Beth would figure out what the first year would look like, and Martin would determine the next. Thereafter they would alternate. So the first year they traveled through Europe for several months, returned for Christmas, then headed out across the United States in their RV. While they were away, they let their house to help pay for the trips. As planned, they returned home so Martin could work over the summer.

Then it was Martin's turn to call the shots. They wound up in Ecuador, in part because both wanted to learn Spanish. There they did volunteer medical work for four months. Living conditions were spartan and the hours long, but both enjoyed being immersed in the local culture. Before returning home, they met friends in Chile for a monthlong vacation. "We figured we could splurge since we had lived fairly inexpensively in Ecuador," says Beth. At $7 a day per person for room and board in Ecuador, I'd say that's a fair statement.

Beth and Martin have continued to discuss and fine-tune their plan. Since Martin really didn't like moving around from hotel to hotel and country to country during that first year, they've agreed that they'll rent a house or apartment as a home base next time they travel for fun. That way they can really get to know one area (Martin's preference), while still indulging Beth's yen to visit new places. Beth, who has now become fluent in Spanish, realizes that she enjoys the volunteer work more than she thought she would and is enthusiastic about the next assignment. They've also realized that they can't hold to a strict schedule, as Martin wants to take advantage of home-based moneymaking work opportunities as they arise. "We continue to discuss our plans—it's an ongoing process," says Beth. And those conversations—along with having diligently saved 15% to 20% of their income for the last twenty years—are what make all of this possible.

Beth and Martin's version of retirement may be a far cry from anything you'd want to do. But Martin in particular has wanted to practice medicine in underdeveloped countries since before he started medical school. That didn't happen. "You get married, you have a family, life changes, and you can't do these things so easily," he says. "Now I'm getting a second shot to realize that long-held dream."

What do *you* want the second half of your life to look like? A smart plan, devised early and managed intelligently, will let you imagine and plan for anything. In short, proper preparation for your retirement means giving yourself the ability to do the things you've always dreamed of.

Breaking the Silence with Your Parents

There's no question that talking to your parents about their retirement can seem awkward. As young adults, many of us separate from our parents as part of our natural move toward independence, and reversing that practice isn't easy. Some of us may also feel that we're engaging in a bit of role reversal—suddenly we feel more like the parent than the child. That can be difficult, but I encourage you to forge ahead.

The most obvious reason to talk to your parents is to find out if they're okay: Do they have enough money set aside to live on? How is that money invested? Are they properly insured (more on that in Chapter 9)?

You might find yourself pleasantly surprised. According to Elderplan's 1997 study, 31% of adult children assumed their parents would need their financial assistance, but only 18% of their parents felt that they would need help. In addition, a 1989 study conducted by researchers in Albany, New York, showed that "parents are twice as likely to be helping their adult children as they are to be receiving help from them!" writes author Susan C. Richards, CFP, in *Protect Your Parents and Their Financial Health . . . Talk with Them Before It's Too Late* (Dearborn Financial, 1999).

On the other hand, don't just assume from appearances—as my colleague Rich did—that your parents are fine. As the son of an immigrant who had made his living selling fruits and vegetables from a horse-drawn cart, and the youngest of nine children, Rich's father not only attended college but also became the vice president and eventual owner of a food brokerage business. According to Rich, "None of us knew anything about his financial condition, because even though he was more 'modern' than many in his family, he was king of the household and was never questioned." Growing up, Rich and his family lived in a large home, always had nice cars, owned several boats, and took great family vacations. So, according to Rich, "even though we didn't know that much about his affairs, we didn't worry too much."

It wasn't until after his father's death that Rich and his eldest sister discovered the truth, which Rich describes as "one of the saddest things in my memory." As Rich came to realize, his presumably well-to-do parents had been living on their Social Security income for the last several years. To help make ends meet, Rich's dad had taken out a home equity loan that carried exorbitant fees. He used that money to pay off a credit card and a bank overdraft. To make matters worse, Rich found that his dad had been sending money to a company that promised large prizes. "Instead he was receiving cheap, worthless jewelry. The mail we found from that one company filled a large trash bag." Like so many other elderly people, not only had Rich's father struggled financially, he had become a target for unethical companies. Rich now says with a great deal of regret, "If we had just taken the right steps, or at least tried, we might have been able to make his last years better."

At what point should you become involved with your parents' financial life? There are no easy answers here, but certainly the more you know about their finances—from their retirement plan to their insurance coverage to their estate plan—the better prepared you will be for helping them in the future. If your parents aren't on track for their retirement, you may be able to steer them in the right direction. If they're going to need your financial assistance—the sooner you know, the better you'll be able to manage.

In fact, you may find that breaking open this conversational dam proves as much of a relief to your parents as it is to you. "Discussing the future . . . helps prepare your family emotionally for what may come. If your father is encouraged now to explore the possibility of moving out of his house, it will be easier for him to make the move if it becomes necessary," writes Virginia Morris in *How to Care for Aging Parents* (Workman, 1996). "These talks give your parents and family members a chance to air their worries and anxieties, to reassure one another, and to learn the truth about any haunting questions."

How to start?

You might ask how your parents envision their lives upon retirement and share what you've been thinking about for yourself. Then you can steer the conversation toward money.

You might even want to ask for advice about your own retirement plans, perhaps bringing along any financial documents as a springboard for the discussion. "I'm trying to figure out how to best fund my retirement," you can say. "How did you do it?" You may well learn something. And at the very least, you've gotten everyone talking.

As always, the news can supply plenty of nonthreatening openings. Falling or rising interest rates. Tax law changes, like the one that recently increased IRA and 401(k) contribution limits. And then there's the fall of Enron. As I write, thousands of ex-Enron employees have lost their retirement savings. Your conversation angle? The importance of diversification.

However you initiate the discussion, remember that you're not engaging in an interrogation. Your parents have as much right to their privacy as you do. Furthermore, they probably come from an era when polite people simply didn't talk about money. By initiating the conversation in a nonthreatening way, however, you may very well get them to open up.

Just a few words of caution: Although your parents may welcome talking to you about their financial situation, they may also resist. Losing their privacy may feel like a first step in losing control over their lives. Add some insecurity about money management, and they could even become hostile. "Although it's tempting, don't take it personally, don't strike back, don't give in, and don't break off the conversation," advises Susan Richards in *Protect Your Parents and Their Financial Health.*

The key is to avoid unproductive communication patterns, no matter what your parents say. Keep in mind that although your parents may initially lash out at you, their reaction is more likely a reflection of their fears rather than an indication of a lack of love or trust. In addition, as Richards points out, feelings are fact to whomever is experiencing them, and you can't argue about facts.

DON'T TOUCH THAT!

As tough as the conversation with your parents may be, it will eventually pay off. The following tips, culled largely from Morris's *How to Care for Aging Parents,* can help you avoid pitfalls along the way:

• Your parents may harbor some degree of Depression-era mentality that makes it hard for them to spend money, even if it will save them money in the long run. This could include everything from hiring a financial planner to installing insulated windows to reduce heating bills. Openly acknowledging this attitude, rather than passing judgment on it, should help keep the conversation rolling. The flip side of their thrift is that your parents are probably better at budgeting than you are. You just might wind up with a few helpful tips.

• Instead of offering your own opinion right away, "listen to [your parent's] views about his situation—his sense of what his problems are, his priorities, and his solutions," recommends Morris.

• Don't take offense if your parents decide that they'd feel more comfortable talking about their finances with a non–family member. Simply give them the name and number of a good financial planner, and then ask if they'd like you to make an appointment for them.

• If your parents refuse to engage in the conversation, ask them to think about whatever you wanted to discuss, and don't press the issue. If the matter can't wait, push—but delicately and with love. You might even share your own feelings of anxiety.

• Should your parents require money to tide them over, treating it strictly as a business deal can help prevent conflict down the road. "You might give your mother a loan that will be paid off at her death, or buy a share of her house and let her remain in it as a renter," writes Morris. "Write up a contract that clearly defines the terms and the penalties, and have it signed by both parties."

Whatever you do, avoid sending what Deborah Tannen calls metamessages: those unspoken and often unintentional messages that can stymie communication. Simply telling your mother that you want her to see a lawyer or a financial planner may send her the metamessage that you think she is incompetent or that you're disappointed in her. Rephrasing

your request and focusing on a positive outcome—such as fulfilling a retirement dream—will get you off to a much better
start.

And finally, always remember that your goal is to have a
dialogue. You're not the expert, you're the caring child.
Implying that you know best or that your parents have erred
won't help. So keep both the judgment and the condescension
at bay. It's time to solve problems, not create them.

What Will It Take?

Will you and your parents be able to follow your dreams? That
depends on two things: how much those dreams will cost, and what
you can afford to spend. Filling in your estimated expenses in
Worksheet 7.1 will give you a good sense of the first question and
help you quantify the life you foresee for yourself and your family.
Later in the chapter we'll address the second question of how much
you can afford, walking you through the steps of adding up your
investment and noninvestment income.

As you fill out Worksheet 7.1, be realistic. For now, use today's
dollars; we'll factor in inflation later. Also, although some or all of
your income will likely be taxed, don't worry about that for now
either. We'll deal with taxes in later calculations.

Note: Throughout this section we use the hypothetical example
of a couple who are both forty-five years old and who hope to retire
at sixty-five and live to eighty-five. They plan to have paid off their
mortgage by the time they retire.

Also, before you begin to fill out the worksheets in this chapter,
you may want to photocopy extra copies. That way you can test a
few scenarios: best case, worst case, and maybe something in
between. Yes, you'll have to crunch the numbers two or more times.
On the other hand, you can factor in higher inflation rates, a longer
life, or any other variations that might apply. By exploring those various "what if" situations, you can determine a plan that best meets
your goals and expectations.

And finally, having financial records on hand—including your most recent bank, brokerage, pension, and IRA statements, as well as a tally of your monthly expenses—will also help. But this isn't the time or the place to sweat the minute details, so just provide your best estimates.

Worksheet 7.1
Estimating Your Retirement Expenses

	Your Information		Example
	Monthly	Annual	Annual
1. Housing (mortgage or rent)	$____	$____	$
2. Property taxes	$____	$____	$4,500
3. Travel and entertainment	$____	$____	$8,000
4. Utilities	$____	$____	$4,500
5. Insurance (life, health, home, auto, long-term care)	$____	$____	$10,000
6. Transportation (public transit, gas, parking, auto upkeep)	$____	$____	$4,000
7. Durable goods (e.g., furniture, art, home remodels, appliances)	$____	$____	$4,000
8. Health care expenses (not covered by insurance)	$____	$____	$2,500
9. Education	$____	$____	$1,000
10. Food	$____	$____	$6,500
11. Clothing	$____	$____	$4,000
12. Personal care	$____	$____	$1,000
13. Alimony/child support	$____	$____	
14. Other	$____	$____	$10,000
15. Total estimated expenses (in today's dollars and not including taxes)	$____	$____	$60,000

Just a few things to think about as you go: My father and I disagree with those who predict that expenses during retirement will diminish by 25%. For starters, today's retirees live longer and are more active than they used to be. They travel, indulge their hobbies, return to school, and launch new careers and businesses. All this costs.

The savings so often touted don't compute either. Although the common assumption is that retired people will save money on commuting or work clothes, most Americans say they plan to continue working part-time during retirement. Savings in 401(k) contributions or Social Security taxes are usually offset by increased spending for travel, entertainment, and other discretionary expenses.

And regrettably, more active, healthier lifestyles don't guarantee us—or our loved ones—health. Even with Medicare, there are plenty of out-of-pocket medical expenses, including prescription drugs, dental care, hearing aids, and eye care that can mount up in a hurry. Eventually, many elderly people who live independently end up having to hire people to help with household maintenance—or even with basics like grocery shopping or meal preparation. Those who can't manage on their own might also face the expense of nursing care, at home or in a facility. (See Chapter 9 for a discussion of insurance needs.)

In short, even if you've retired your mortgage, along with any other debts, your expenses during the latter years of your life aren't likely to be substantially less than they are now. So unless you plan to live on a sailboat docked in an underdeveloped country, you're probably going to need about the same amount of purchasing power as before.

As you run your numbers, don't forget to talk openly with the people who know and love you and get their input. You might want to talk about the paths that other people have chosen and explore whether those would work for you. Or if you've ever had a dream—or even a notion—that you've squelched because it just didn't seem practical, this is the time to explore it. Use this opportunity to engage in flights of fancy and soul-searching. Just to get the conversation started, you might want to ask yourself the following questions:

• Do you want to move closer to your grandkids—or even help care for them?

- Do you want to turn a favorite hobby into a part-time job?
- How about scuba diving or another new sport?
- Would you prefer to simply relax and enjoy your friends and your home?

The answers you come up with may change down the line, and that's okay. As Beth and Martin found out, this is a process. What's important here is stretching your imagination and considering all the possibilities, so you begin to have some sense of the basic shape of life to come. Once you've done that, you can start to estimate how much that life will cost.

Where Do You Stand Now?

Now that you have a vision of your retirement and a sense of how much it will cost, how close are you to accomplishing your goal? I think of retirement savings as a three-legged stool made up of:

- Pensions and Social Security
- Tax-advantaged accounts
- Taxable accounts

We'll include all three of these as we walk through the calculations in Worksheets 7.2–7.7.

CAN YOU COUNT ON SOCIAL SECURITY?

With 75 million baby boomers approaching retirement age in the next thirty years, the system is sure to be strained if not broken. Certainly the most conservative approach is to think of Social Security as a potential windfall more than as a guarantee. Regardless, you should be aware of your potential benefits.

You can begin collecting your Social Security benefits at age sixty-two, but you won't receive full benefits until you reach what the Social Security Administration defines as "full retirement age." Depending on the year you were born, that varies from sixty-five to sixty-seven. If you begin collecting Social Security benefits at sixty-two, your payments will be reduced by 20% to 30% for life—to compensate for that longer period of time you receive them. Similarly, your benefits will go up if you hold off until a later age to start receiving them.

Social Security benefits also vary according to the amount of money you made during your working years. In 2003 the maximum monthly benefit is $1,741 for an individual retiring at age sixty-five and $2,612 for a couple, assuming that one of the spouses isn't eligible on his or her own.

A word of caution for retirees under sixty-five: If you have more than about $11,500 of earned income a year ($11,520 in 2003), your monthly benefits will be reduced. Once you reach sixty-five, you can earn unlimited income and receive your maximum Social Security benefit.

Every worker over twenty-five should receive an annual benefit report from the Social Security Administration. Make sure you review yours carefully and report any errors. If your update doesn't arrive, you can order a copy at www.ssa.gov or by phoning 1-800-772-1213.

Chuck's Two Cents: On Social Security

I've noticed an odd phenomenon: When the topic of Social Security comes up, the fearmongers out there become pretty vocal. I have a two-part message for them.

First: It's my belief that despite all the fears in the world, there will always be Social Security. It may be a struggle to make that happen, but it's my feeling it will.

Second: But—and it's a big but—the amount you receive will probably never be more than the present amount, adjusted for inflation. So, if you retired in the year 2002, the maximum amount you'd receive would be $1,660. If you retired in 2003, that maximum would be $1,741. The amount will probably rise at a rate of 2.5% to 3%, which means that $1,660 might reach $2,000 in, say, the year 2012. Keep in mind that such an increase is tied to inflation, so it doesn't have any more purchasing power.

So while the good news is that you'll have Social Security, the bad news is that it probably won't be very much. It may cover 25% or so of your expenses. And as always, you have to remember that that amount is fully taxable.

ADDING IT ALL UP

Now it's time to add up the income you know you can count on, such as from a pension plan, Social Security, or rental property, in Worksheet 7.2. Although you may well want to include Social Security in your calculation, our hypothetical couple has chosen to be conservative and *not* include it in their expectations. Also realize that up until now we haven't accounted for taxes. However, even though you may be in a lower tax bracket when you retire, your income will be taxed. Our couple anticipates having $1,000 of after-tax monthly income from real estate they own and $1,000 of after-tax salary from a part-time job.

Worksheet 7.2
Estimating Your After-Tax Noninvestment Income

	Your Information (Monthly)	Example (Monthly)
1. Social Security	$_____	
2. Annuities	$_____	
3. Pension	$_____	
4. Real estate	$_____	$1,000
5. Salary	$_____	$1,000
6. Other	$_____	
7. Total	$_____	$2,000

Now turn to Worksheet 7.3. Here you compare your total noninvestment income from Worksheet 7.2 with the estimated monthly expense figure that you came up with in Worksheet 7.1. The difference is the amount of additional investment income you will likely need. Because withdrawals from a traditional IRA, 401(k), and most other accounts are usually subject to income taxes at ordinary income rates, we need to calculate how big a bite taxes will take (of course, withdrawals from your taxable accounts will be taxed at the lower capital gains rate). Therefore, in line 5 of Worksheet 7.3, you'll convert your monthly income goal to the amount of money you'll need before taxes.

Worksheet 7.3
Estimating Your Monthly Retirement Income Needs

	Your Information	Example
1. Monthly retirement expenses (from Worksheet 7.1)	$_____	$5,000
2. Monthly after-tax income from noninvestment sources (from Worksheet 7.2)	$_____	$2,000
3. Net needed from investments (line 1 minus line 2)	$_____	$3,000
4. Income tax factor*	_____	0.70
5. Total pretax monthly income needed from investments (divide line 3 by line 4)	$_____	$4,286

*The formula for calculating your income tax factor is: 1 − [(federal tax rate + state tax rate) − (federal tax rate × state tax rate)]. This example assumes a 25% federal tax rate and a 7% state rate. The calculation in this example is 1 − [(.25 + .07) − (.25 × .07)], which equals 1 − (.32 − .02) = (1 − .30) = .70.

The next thing we have to think about is inflation. Remember the young doctor who wanted to save a million dollars? He forgot to factor in inflation and how it diminishes purchasing power. In fact, inflation is probably the number-one enemy facing your retirement plan.

To convert today's dollars to the amount of inflation-adjusted money you will likely need when you retire, turn to Worksheet 7.4 and Table 7.1. As you can see, depending on the number of years until your retirement, the effect of inflation could mean that you will need two or three times as much money as the amount you came up with in Worksheet 7.3. Continuing with the example we have been using, and assuming that our couple won't retire for another twenty years, the $4,412 of monthly income in Worksheet 7.3 doubles to almost $9,000.

Worksheet 7.4
Estimating the Effect of Inflation

	Your Information	Example
1. Monthly income needed from investments (from line 5 of Worksheet 7.3)	$_____	$4,412
2. At what age do you plan to retire?	_____	65
3. How old are you now?	_____	45
4. Years until retirement?	_____	20
5. Inflation-adjustment factor (from Table 7.1)	_____	2.0
6. Estimated inflation-adjusted income needed (multiply line 1 by line 5)	$_____	$8,824

Table 7.1
Inflation-Adjustment Factor

Years Until Retirement							
	1	5	10	15	20	25	30	35
Inflation Factor	1.0	1.2	1.4	1.7	2.0	2.4	2.8	3.3

Note: This inflation-adjustment factor calculates the future value of $1 based on a 3.5% rate of inflation over different time periods. In any given time period, inflation may exceed or fall below this level.

HAVE YOU SAVED ENOUGH?

Now that you know how much inflation-adjusted pretax investment income you will need each month, you can use Worksheet 7.5 to estimate how close you are to achieving your goal. Although this calculation would normally be complex, the data in Table 7.2— which are provided by the Schwab Center for Investment Research and are based on thousands of simulations using historical stock market performance figures—will greatly simplify the process.

Just a few things to point out: Table 7.2 gives you an estimate of the amount of money you will need to have saved by the time you retire in order for your income to last for your entire retirement. In other words, it's a figure that is designed to prevent you from outliving your money. The figures are based on increments of $1,000 of monthly income.

Second, the figures in Table 7.2 are based both on the number of years you plan to be in retirement and on the way you invest your money. Historical data reveal that your asset allocation strategy (from conservative to aggressive) not only affects your return but sometimes does it in ways that seem counterintuitive. For example, a more aggressive allocation seems to work in your favor when you are anticipating a forty-year retirement, but it may not be as effective if you expect a shorter retirement. Later in this chapter we'll revisit some investing principles that may be helpful as you make your investing decisions. For now, you can simply enter the number of years you plan to be in retirement as well as your projected asset allocation into Worksheet 7.5 to arrive at an estimate of how much you will need.

Worksheet 7.5
Calculating Your Monthly Inflation-Adjusted Retirement Income

	Your Information	Example
1. Your life expectancy	____	85
2. Age when you plan to retire	____	65
3. Number of years you plan to be in retirement	____	20
4. Monthly inflation-adjusted income goal (line 6 from Worksheet 7.4; round up)	$_____	$9,000
5. Asset allocation strategy (from conservative to aggressive)	____	moderate
6. Amount of money you need to save for every $1,000 of monthly retirement income (from Table 7.2)	$_____	$240,000
7. Divide line 4 by $1,000	____	9
8. Amount of assets needed (line 6 multiplied by line 7)	$_____	$2,160,000

Table 7.2
Amount of Assets You Need for Each $1,000
of Monthly Income

Years in Retirement	Asset Allocation		
	Conservative	Moderately Conservative	Moderate
20	$220,000	$230,000	$240,000
30	$300,000	$300,000	$300,000
40	$370,000	$350,000	$360,000

Source: Schwab Center for Investment Research

Third, it is important to realize that the figures in Table 7.2 factor in inflation *from the date of your retirement onward.* No matter what year you retire, you will need the number of dollars specified in Table 7.2 *when you retire.* Once you are *in retirement,* your monthly expenses (and the amount you withdraw) will continue to increase with inflation.

For example, our hypothetical couple has a moderate asset allocation strategy of 60% equities, 30% bonds, and 10% cash, and is planning a twenty-year retirement. When they retire (no matter what year that is), they will need approximately $240,000 of assets for every $1,000 of monthly income. After they are retired, that $1,000 will increase with inflation.

Continuing with this example, and assuming that our couple will need approximately $9,000 (and increasing) a month to obtain the quality of life they want during retirement, they will need to have approximately $2,160,000 invested when they retire in twenty years.

One final piece of advice: When in doubt, my father's and my advice is to err on the side of being conservative. You will probably spend more than you think, and you may not garner the return on investments you anticipate. Or inflation could creep up to 5% or 6%. You may want to copy this worksheet before you start, and then work through it twice, delineating best- and worst-case scenarios. Afterward you'll have a very good idea of where you stand.

THE FINAL CALCULATION

Now that you have a good idea of what you will need, your next step in Worksheet 7.6 is to add up the value of your current investment assets, estimate the additional contributions you'll be making prior to retirement, and compare this total to the figures you came up with in Worksheet 7.5. In order to express the totals in retirement-year dollars (not today's dollars), you also need to factor in your expected annual rates of return using Tables 7.3 and 7.4. Keep in mind that your annual rate of return (and your risk) will depend to a large extent on how aggressively or conservatively you invest. If you are between years or unsure of your rate of return, I suggest you use a conservative estimate.

In our example, our couple is assuming a conservative 8% annual return for the twenty years until they retire. Therefore, the compound growth factor of their current balance (per Table 7.3) is 4.7. The compound growth factor for their future contributions (per Table 7.4) is 45.8.

Worksheet 7.6
Tallying Your Current and Future Investments

	Your Information	Example
Estimating Your Current Financial Investment Balances		
1. IRA accounts	$_____	$50,000
2. Employer-sponsored plans (e.g., 401[k], 403[b], SEP-IRA)	$_____	$95,000
3. Other accounts (e.g., regular brokerage, money market)	$_____	$75,000
4. Total current balance (sum of lines 1–3)	$_____	$220,000
5. Compound growth (of your current balance; insert factor from Table 7.3)	____	4.7
6. Estimated value at retirement (multiply line 4 by line 5)	$_____	$1,034,000

Estimating Your Additional Annual Contributions

7. IRA accounts	$_____	—
8. Employer-sponsored plans (e.g., 401[k], 403[b], SEP-IRA)	$_____	$13,000
9. Other accounts (e.g., regular brokerage, money market)	$_____	$10,000
10. Total annual contributions (in today's dollars; sum of lines 7–9)	$_____	$23,000
11. Compound growth (of your annual contributions; insert factor from Table 7.4)	____	45.8
12. Estimated value at retirement (multiply line 10 by line 11)	$_____	$1,053,400

Total Retirement Portfolio

13. Estimated assets at retirement (sum of lines 6 and 12)	$_____	$2,087,400

Table 7.3
Compound Growth of Your Current Balance

Years Until Retirement	Expected Annual Investment Rate of Return Prior to Retirement									
	5%	6%	7%	8%	9%	10%	11%	12%	13%	14%
1	1.1	1.1	1.1	1.1	1.1	1.1	1.1	1.1	1.1	1.1
2	1.1	1.1	1.1	1.2	1.2	1.2	1.2	1.3	1.3	1.3
3	1.2	1.2	1.2	1.3	1.3	1.3	1.4	1.4	1.4	1.5
4	1.2	1.3	1.3	1.4	1.4	1.5	1.5	1.6	1.6	1.7
5	1.3	1.3	1.4	1.5	1.5	1.6	1.7	1.8	1.8	1.9
10	1.6	1.8	2.0	2.2	2.4	2.6	2.8	3.1	3.4	3.7
15	2.1	2.4	2.8	3.2	3.6	4.2	4.8	5.5	6.3	7.1
20	2.7	3.2	3.9	4.7	5.6	6.7	8.1	9.6	11.5	13.7
25	3.4	4.3	5.4	6.8	8.6	10.8	13.6	17.0	21.2	26.5
30	4.3	5.7	7.6	10.1	13.3	17.4	22.9	30.0	39.1	51.0
35	5.5	7.7	10.7	14.8	20.4	28.1	38.6	52.8	72.1	98.1

Table 7.4
Compound Growth of Your Annual Contributions
Prior to Retirement

		Expected Annual Investment Rate of Return Prior to Retirement								
		5%	6%	7%	8%	9%	10%	11%	12%	13%	14%
Years Until Retirement	1	1.0	1.0	1.0	1.0	1.0	1.0	1.0	1.0	1.0	1.0
	2	2.1	2.1	2.1	2.1	2.1	2.1	2.1	2.1	2.1	2.1
	3	3.2	3.2	3.2	3.2	3.3	3.3	3.3	3.4	3.4	3.4
	4	4.3	4.4	4.4	4.5	4.6	4.6	4.7	4.8	4.8	4.9
	5	5.5	5.6	5.8	5.9	6.0	6.1	6.2	6.4	6.5	6.6
	10	12.6	13.2	13.8	14.5	15.2	15.9	16.7	17.5	18.4	19.3
	15	21.6	23.3	25.1	27.2	29.4	31.8	34.4	37.3	40.4	43.8
	20	33.1	36.8	41.0	45.8	51.2	57.3	64.2	72.1	80.9	91.0
	25	47.7	54.9	63.2	73.1	84.7	98.3	114.4	133.3	155.6	181.9
	30	66.4	79.1	94.5	113.3	136.3	164.5	199.0	241.3	293.2	356.8
	35	90.3	111.4	138.2	172.3	215.7	271.0	341.6	431.7	546.7	693.6

Here comes the final step. In Worksheet 7.7 compare your figures from Worksheets 7.5 and 7.6. This will give you a clearer picture of whether you have already saved enough or whether you have to accelerate your contributions. As you can see, provided that they maintain the discipline of continuing to invest over the next twenty years, our hypothetical couple has an excellent chance of meeting their goal.

Worksheet 7.7
Estimating Your Retirement Surplus or Shortfall

	Your Information	Example
1. Retirement asset goal (line 8 from Worksheet 7.5)	$_____	$2,160,000
2. Estimated assets at retirement (line 13 from Worksheet 7.6)	$_____	$2,087,000
3. Potential retirement surplus or shortfall (line 1 minus line 2)	$_____	-$73,000

Doing It Right

Now that you have a good sense of where you stand relative to your ultimate retirement goal, let's discuss the best ways for you to realize your dreams. After all is said and done, maximizing your retirement savings boils down to three essential steps:

1. Start saving as soon as possible. As we discussed in Chapter 3, time in the market—rather than timing the market—is a key factor in investing success.

2. Contribute the maximum amount allowed each and every year to *all* of the tax-advantaged retirement plans that are available to you. If you have a 401(k), a 403(b), or a Keogh plan, you should contribute the maximum to it—and also contribute the maximum to an individual retirement account (IRA). With fewer and fewer Americans receiving guaranteed pensions, it's up to us to make sure that our retirement accounts are adequately funded.

One of the best parts of the Tax Relief Act of 2001 was an increase in the amount of money we can contribute to our 401(k)s and IRAs—with extra catch-up provisions for those who are fifty or over (see Table 7.5 on page 244 for details). I encourage everyone to take advantage of this exceptional opportunity.

Chuck's Two Cents:
On the Importance of Maxing Out Your 401(k)

Contributing the maximum amount allowed to your 401(k) is one of the smartest investment moves you can make, even if it means tightening your belt a little. Chances are you'll need to supplement your retirement investments with additional funds in other accounts, but maxing out your 401(k) is a great start—and a smart one. Over time, those contributions can translate into growth and dividends and move you toward the financial independence you want later in life.

Also realize that if you're hesitating to invest in your retirement plan, you can take early withdrawals penalty-free to pay for qualified higher education expenses, to make a down payment on your first home ($10,000 lifetime limit here), to support your family while you're disabled, or to pay for certain medical expenses in excess of 7.5% of your adjusted gross income. If you've lost your job, you can even withdraw money from your IRA to cover medical insurance without incurring any penalties. Of course, your best choice by far is to make sure that you have a cash emergency fund that will cover you for at least two to three months of expenses. That way you can be fairly confident that you won't have to touch your IRA or 401(k) until retirement.

3. Save even more. Depending on when you want to retire, how long—and how lavishly—you expect to live, and whether you can count on any supplemental income during that time, investing the maximum in your IRA, 401(k), or other retirement plans may well not be enough. That's right. Even if you've been diligently investing in your tax-deferred accounts, it is likely that you will need to supplement your retirement savings in your taxable accounts.

HOW MUCH IS ENOUGH? A CASE STUDY

Our hypothetical investor is thirty-five years old, earning $100,000 a year, and is ready to start saving. (So far he hasn't managed to save anything.) His goal is to retire at age sixty-five with the equivalent of a $65,000 income in today's dollars (which is roughly equivalent to his after-tax income today). Every year until retirement, he plans to make the maximum contribution to his 401(k) ($13,000 in 2004 and increasing) and IRA ($3,000 in 2004 and increasing). After consulting with his investment advisor, he chooses a moderate asset allocation (60% stocks, 30% bonds, and 10% cash). He knows that if he switches jobs, he won't cash out but will move his money into a rollover IRA, so that it can continue to grow tax-deferred. Since he also knows that life spans continue to stretch longer and longer, he assumes that he'll live to the age of ninety. If he does stop working at age sixty-five, that means twenty-five years in retirement.

Sounds pretty reasonable, doesn't it? Unfortunately not. When the Schwab Center for Investment Research simulated how this investor's portfolio might perform under thousands of different market scenarios, using historical market data from as far back as 1926, they found that his estimated probability of reaching his goal is only 37%! But if he supplements his original plan with an extra $1,000 a month in a regular brokerage account, he meets or exceeds his goal 77% of the time.

A Plan for Everyone

We've already stressed how important it is to invest the maximum in all of your retirement accounts. This section will review the most common plans, which fall into three basic categories: individual retirement plans (IRAs), employer-sponsored plans, and plans for the self-employed and small business owners. Each plan is governed by specific IRS regulations concerning eligibility, taxation, maximum contributions, and required withdrawals. In addition, matching and vesting schedules vary from employer to employer. We'll hit on the highlights, but as you piece together your strategy, pay attention to the details. You may also want to consult your financial advisor or accountant about your particular situation and changes in tax law. That kind of careful scrutiny is the only way to figure out which plan or combination of plans will maximize your ability to save.

Before we jump in, just a few preliminaries. First, depending on the plan as well as your individual circumstances, you may be able to *deduct* your contribution from your income. By investing *pretax* dollars, you not only reduce your income tax bill for that year but also supplement your contribution with money that would have otherwise gone to the IRS. In other words, the money you invest—all of it—can benefit from compound growth. By not paying taxes on the money until your retirement, you get the benefit derived

RETIREMENT PLANS AT A GLANCE

Individual-Sponsored Plans

- Roth IRA
- Traditional IRA

Contribute to an IRA, even if you have an employer-sponsored plan such as a 401(k) or 403(b), and even if you can't deduct your contribution.

Employer-Sponsored Plans

- 401(k)
- 403(b)
- 457

If your employer offers one of these plans, with or without matching, you should contribute the maximum and also make an IRA contribution.

Plans for the Self-Employed and Small Business Owners

- SIMPLE IRA   Employer matches employee's contribution.
- SEP-IRA   Employer contributes for self and employee.
- Keogh   Employer contributes for self and employee.

Note: In addition to your self-employed plan, you can contribute to an IRA.

from investing all that extra income you've delayed paying the government.

For all tax-deferred accounts, you don't pay taxes until you withdraw your money—at which time it will be taxed as ordinary income. If your income is lower at that stage, you'll be taxed at a lower rate. (Note that when you invest in a taxable account, your earnings may be taxed at the capital gains rate, which is currently 15%, or 5% for investors in the 10% or 15% tax bracket.)

For all of the following plans except the Roth IRA (and the 457 under certain circumstances), if you withdraw your money before age 59½, you may have to pay a 10% federal tax penalty in addition to ordinary income tax (and you may have to pay a state penalty and taxes as well). On the other end, there are also minimum amounts you *must* withdraw starting at age 70½. More on this later in the chapter.

Individual Retirement Accounts (IRAs)

TRADITIONAL IRA

Edging up on its thirtieth anniversary, the traditional IRA has become an important part of many Americans' retirement savings. In a nutshell, it offers anyone with $3,000 of earned income (and his or her spouse, even if that spouse doesn't have earned income) the opportunity to invest $3,000 a year (with that amount increasing to $5,000 by 2008; see Table 7.5 on page 244) in a self-managed, tax-deferred account.

One important caveat, though: If you (or your spouse) are covered by an employer-sponsored retirement plan (if you are an "active participant" in IRS lingo), and if in 2004 your adjusted gross income exceeds $75,000 for a couple or $55,000 for a single person (with these amounts gradually increasing to $100,000 by 2007 for a couple and $60,000 for a single person by 2005), you will not be able to deduct your contribution from your income taxes. If you are not covered by an employer-sponsored plan, you can deduct your IRA contribution regardless of your income. Also, if only one spouse is an "active participant," the income limit for deducting your contribution is $160,000.

However, even if you aren't eligible for the tax deduction, you should still contribute the maximum to your IRA every year so that you can have the opportunity for tax-deferred growth. In this case, you might qualify for a Roth IRA (see below).

ROTH IRA

For those who qualify, a relative newcomer—the Roth IRA—can prove a great boon to your retirement nest egg. Here's how it works: You can't deduct your contribution from your taxes (you contribute after-tax dollars), *but* once you've paid taxes on this initial amount, you won't pay taxes on this money again. It doesn't matter if your money grows by 5%, 10%, or 25% each and every year. When you start taking that money out once you hit retirement age, those withdrawals are tax-free.

Just a bit of fine print: You can withdraw your *contributions* (but not your *earnings*) tax-free at any time. The earnings must stay invested until you turn 59½, and they must have been held in the account for a minimum of five years; otherwise you will have to pay taxes as well as a penalty on your withdrawal.

Like a traditional IRA, a Roth IRA also has income cutoff points. A married couple that makes up to $150,000 a year or a single person who makes up to $95,000 a year can contribute the maximum ($3,000, or $3,500 if you're fifty or older in 2004, increasing to $5,000, or $6,000 if you're fifty or older in 2008; see Table 7.5). If as a single person you earn between $95,000 and $110,000, or as a couple you make between $150,000 and $160,000, you can make a partial contribution. After that you are not eligible for a Roth IRA.

SHOULD YOU CONVERT?

When the Roth IRA was first introduced in 1997, many owners of traditional IRAs were anxious to capture the new tax-free withdrawal benefits of a Roth IRA—hence the birth of the Roth conversion.

Does a Roth conversion make sense for you? First you need to qualify. No matter if you're single or a couple, you can't earn more than $100,000 in the year you make the conversion. Still interested? Provided you qualify, you'll pay ordinary income taxes on the money you convert. (You don't have to convert your entire account.)

After that, it's a matter of doing the math. In general, the longer you anticipate keeping your money invested (and thus the greater the value of your eventual tax-free withdrawal), the more sense it makes. Next, think about what you expect your tax bracket to be when you retire. The higher the bracket, the greater your eventual savings. If you believe that your tax bracket will decrease, a Roth conversion probably isn't a good choice. And finally, you should only convert if you can pay your taxes from your taxable account—that is, if you don't use funds from the IRA itself to pay the tax bill.

Employer-Sponsored Plans

401(K) AND 403(B)

September 4, 2001, marked the twentieth anniversary for the 401(k) plan. With more than 40 million participants and $2 trillion in tax-deferred assets, it has become the cornerstone of many retirement plans. At the latest count 6 million investors were participating in the nonprofit world's less well known variation, the 403(b) plan.

401(k) and 403(b) plans may not provide the security of the old-fashioned pension plan, but they're still a great way to save for retirement. In fact, not taking advantage of them potentially amounts to walking past hundreds—or thousands—of dollars on the ground each and every year and not stopping to pick them up. Why? First, because you contribute pretax dollars. Second, many employers will match a percentage—or even all—of your contributions. And third, your money has the opportunity to grow tax-deferred until you withdraw it at retirement age.

Here's an example of how all of this works: Let's say you're in the 25% tax bracket. Because you don't pay income taxes on your contribution until you withdraw it, you are essentially deferring the payment of 25 cents for every dollar you contribute (or even more, if you count the state taxes you'll save). If your employer matches part of your contribution, say 50 cents on the dollar, you now have $1.50. Then add a hypothetical 8% tax-deferred annual rate of return on that $1.50, and your contribution grows to $1.62. Still need convincing?

Another great benefit of both 401(k) and 403(b) plans is that they're automatically deducted from your paychecks. Talk about easy—you can just dollar-cost average away!

As we mentioned earlier, with both a 401(k) and a 403(b) you must depend on yourself, not your company, to invest your money wisely. You're in the driver's seat, which can be a benefit but also a responsibility. In 2001 many Enron employees lost their nest eggs because they had invested too heavily in their company's stock. Others lose out on opportunities for growth by investing far too conservatively. As we've stressed so many times, having the appropriate asset allocation and adequate diversification is key. More on this later in the chapter.

ROLLOVER, IRA

In the true spirit of instant gratification, almost three-quarters of people who leave their jobs take cash withdrawals from their tax-deferred accounts. For this I have just two words: Bad idea!

When you leave a job, your best bet—without a doubt—is to transfer your old 401(k) or 403(b) funds into what is known as a *rollover IRA.* This way your money has an opportunity for tax-deferred growth until you withdraw it. Otherwise, not only do you lose this opportunity *forever,* but if you're younger than $59\frac{1}{2}$ when you withdraw your money, you'll be hit with a 10% early-withdrawal penalty on top of your tax bill.

The simplest strategy is to transfer your funds directly from your ex-employer into a rollover IRA. Otherwise, if you take possession of the funds yourself, you only have sixty days from the day the check is cut to complete the transfer—or else pay taxes on the entire amount as well as paying the penalty. And even if you do roll the money over within the sixty-day window, there's a mandatory 20% federal tax withholding that you'll have to pay. (Hint: The best way to orchestrate a seamless transfer is to open your rollover IRA first—which you can do at any major financial institution—and then give your account number to your former employer. Your former employer can then write a check directly to the financial institution that is holding your account.) In most cases, your former employer will liquidate your holdings and transfer it in cash. It is then up to you to reinvest it.

A major advantage of a rollover IRA is that you have complete control over how you invest your money and a wide range of investment choices available to you. Also, there's no limit to the amount of money you can roll over. Even Bill Gates could transfer his entire account.

457 PLAN

This relatively obscure plan (with about two million participants) is primarily offered by nonprofit organizations or state or local governments. Like the 401(k), it provides pretax contributions and the opportunity for tax-deferred growth. Unlike the 401(k), though, the money you invest is not separately protected from the nonprofit's finances. So if the organization you work for goes belly-up, your retirement funds are in jeopardy. In addition, employers rarely match 457 contributions. And finally, in the past you were not allowed to transfer your 457 money to a rollover IRA when you changed jobs. (But to offset this there was no penalty if you withdrew your money prior to age 59½.) With the tax law changes of 2001, you are now able to move your funds, but there may be certain restrictions. Despite these limitations, if a 457 is your only employer-sponsored plan, you should take full advantage of it.

TAKE IT TO THE MAX

The Tax Relief Act of 2001 raised contribution limits for both IRAs and employer-sponsored plans. The amounts will go up every year until 2006 and then be indexed to inflation in $500 increments. Note that if you're age fifty or above, you can contribute even more. See Table 7.5 on the next page.

Table 7.5
Maximum Contributions to Retirement Plans
IRAs (Traditional and Roth)

	2004	2005	2006	2007	2008
Up to Age 50	$3,000	$4,000	$4,000	$4,000	$5,000
Age 50 and Above	$3,500	$4,500	$5,000	$5,000	$6,000

401(k), 403(b), and 457 Plans

	2004	2005	2006	2007	2008
Up to Age 50	$13,000	$14,000	$15,000	$15,000	$15,000
Age 50 and Above	$16,000	$18,000	$20,000	$20,000	$20,000

Simple IRAs

	2004	2005	2006	2007	2008
Up to Age 50	$9,000	$10,000	$10,000	$10,000	$10,000
Age 50 and Above	$10,500	$12,000	$12,500	$12,500	$12,500

Plans for the Self-Employed and Small Business Owners

SIMPLE IRAS AND SIMPLE 401(K)S

Short for Savings Incentive Matching Plan for Employees, SIMPLE IRAs and SIMPLE 401(k)s are available to businesses with fewer than one hundred employees. Most of the time, though, it's the really small businesses (with fewer than ten employees) that use them. SIMPLE plans are attractive to small businesses because they carry very low administrative costs, they're easy to understand, and in most cases the employee participants take care of their own investments. Although the contribution limits are lower than those for a 401(k) (a maximum $9,000 in 2004, moving to $10,000 in 2005), SIMPLE plans offer the same advantages of tax-deductible contributions and tax-deferred growth.

As the name implies, both employer and employee can contribute to a SIMPLE plan. They can be funded in one of two ways:

• The employer provides a dollar-for-dollar match of up to 3% of the employee's salary. The employer must maintain this level three out of every five years. (With a SIMPLE 401[k], employers aren't free to reduce their contribution below 3%.)

• The employer contributes 2% of the employee's salary regardless of whether the employee participates or not.

Note that participating in a SIMPLE IRA or SIMPLE 401(k) doesn't prevent you from contributing to a traditional or Roth IRA in addition. In order to maximize your tax-advantaged savings, I highly recommend that you do both!

SIMPLIFIED EMPLOYEE PENSION IRA (SEP-IRA)

If you work for yourself or own a small business with fewer than a hundred employees, a simplified employee pension plan, or SEP, is a straightforward, no-hassle retirement plan. In essence, it's an IRA with higher contribution limits. Each participant can open his or her account in whatever brokerage house, bank, or other financial institution he or she chooses, then manage his or her own account.

Unlike a SIMPLE IRA, with a SEP-IRA only the employer makes contributions—which can be as high as 25% of compensation or $40,000 per year, whichever is less. As an employer, you're required to contribute the same percentage for your employees as you contribute for yourself. But you're also free to reduce that percentage any year you want, or even decide not to contribute at all.

Of course, the biggest advantage for you as an investor is that like other retirement plans, you can enjoy the benefit of tax-deferred growth until the money is withdrawn. At that point, you're taxed at your ordinary income tax rate. Like other retirement plans, you'll have to pay a 10% penalty if you withdraw funds before the age of 59½.

In addition, because a SEP-IRA is an employer-sponsored plan, you can still contribute to an individual IRA as well. But your IRA contribution may not be deductible, depending on your modified adjusted gross income and whether your spouse is covered by an employer-sponsored retirement plan.

KEOGHS

Keogh plans are as complex as SEPs are easy. They generally require more paperwork and may have additional funding requirements. Like a SEP, deductible contributions are limited to 25% of compensation or $40,000, whichever is less. However, to make things a bit more complicated, as a result of new tax laws you may be able to contribute as much as 100% of compensation, not to exceed $40,000 (although only 25% of compensation would be deductible). Because of the complex nature of a Keogh plan and potential additional tax-filing requirements, if you are contemplating setting up one of these plans, you should definitely consult a CPA or other tax specialist.

In general, there are two types of Keogh plans. In both cases the business must include workers who are age twenty-one and over and who have a minimum of two years of service.

• In a *profit-sharing* plan the employer decides on the contribution amount each year, which cannot exceed the limits mentioned above. A contribution is not required.

• In a *money purchase* plan the employer makes a fixed contribution commitment and must fulfill that obligation in order to maintain the tax-qualified status of the retirement plan. Again, contributions are limited as above.

An employer may also combine the two plans (into what is called a *paired plan*) to get the flexibility of the profit-sharing plan and the discipline of the money purchase plan. In this case, the total contributions still can't exceed the limits above.

When comparing a SEP-IRA to a Keogh, note that there are differences in ownership. Because the employee owns his or her SEP-IRA, he or she can immediately withdraw the funds (and pay any appropriate penalties and taxes). The assets in a Keogh, on the other hand, are controlled by the employer and are subject to more restrictive distribution rules. Many Keogh plans also allow employee participants to obtain loans against their available assets—which is prohibited in a SEP.

Investing Your Retirement Nest Egg

Like so much else in life, figuring out how to invest your retirement nest egg is a process that changes and evolves with time. According to Fred Taylor, U.S. Trust vice chairman and chief investment officer, "Portfolio building is an ongoing, dynamic process. We need to be aware of and respond to a constantly changing environment, not to mention our own evolving needs and risk tolerance."

What does this mean for you, as you try to carve out the best combination of investments to secure your retirement? At Schwab we always stress investing for the long term. Certainly as you approach retirement your definition of *long term* will change—but it's still key to stay focused on your ultimate goals. As you talk to your family and think about your future together, go back and revisit the Investor Profile you filled out in Chapter 3. Think about your resources, your time frame, and how much risk is appropriate for your circumstances. All the basic investing principles that we described in Chapters 2 and 3 apply.

Also realize that even though we tend to think in terms of an average return (perhaps 8%), you're probably not going to get 8% each and every year. In some years you may do better, in other years worse. If that decline hits early, your losses will be less significant simply because you have less money to lose and more time to make it back. Thirty or forty years down the line, when your portfolio's assets have grown, bad returns can mean the loss of tens of thousands of dollars. That can constitute a substantial portion of your retirement savings, right at the time in your life when you have less time to recover from the loss.

Your best protection against this possibility? Yes, you guessed it: appropriate asset allocation coupled with diversification within asset classes. You need to find the correct balance between risk and return for every stage of your life.

EXPERT ADVICE FROM THE SCHWAB CENTER FOR INVESTMENT RESEARCH

Diversifying Your 401(k) Plan

As you're probably aware by now, we cannot overemphasize the need to diversify your investments. And as 401(k) plans are many people's biggest chunk of retirement savings, the diversification message is even more important here. Yet when you ask the average person if his or her 401(k) plan is diversified, the response more often than not is a shrug of the shoulders and a mumbled, "I guess so."

Our advice is to check. Review your holdings—all of them, including individual equities and bonds, as well as the mutual funds in your 401(k). If you're holding individual equities, for example, make sure that these stocks aren't also in the mutual funds in your 401(k). And don't forget about your employee stock options. No matter how much you want to support your company, you'd be wiser to think of protecting yourself first; having a concentrated position in one company is not being good to yourself.

You only have to look back to 2001 to see more than $1 billion in Enron employees' 401(k) plans going up in smoke. Even though they didn't have the choice of trading their stock near the end, you probably do. Don't be afraid to do so.

While in the past companies have been restricted from giving investment advice to employees for their 401(k) plans, 401(k) regulations are easing in this regard, and providers now can employ an independent professional to offer advice. Another new tool, called a targeted asset allocation plan, relies on computer programs to design individualized asset allocation plans.

While there are no guarantees how any one investment will turn out, history repeatedly reminds us that the best way to create wealth in the financial markets over the long term is to hold a broadly diversified portfolio. And if there is ever a place where you want to create wealth, it's in your retirement plan.

Note: If your company isn't offering a broad array of funds from which to choose, ask about adding some new ones. It can't hurt.

INVEST FOR GROWTH OR PLAY IT SAFE?

At one extreme, far too many investors simply keep their entire 401(k) invested in the default money market account. This doesn't make long-term sense if you're fifty, and it certainly doesn't make sense if you're twenty-five. At the other extreme, it's just as dangerous to fall into the "casino mentality" and put money you can't afford to lose at high risk. That doesn't make sense at any age.

Traditional investing wisdom says that the older you get, the more conservatively you should invest. And I agree—to a point. Certainly the closer you are to retirement and to actually drawing on that money, the more you're going to want to preserve it. You're probably not going to want any money you'll need in three years or less to be in stocks. But the way my father and I see it, even the most cautious approach has to include some stocks. Let's face it: In order to finance a retirement that could last thirty to forty years or even more, you simply must stay at least partially invested for growth.

Research conducted by the Schwab Center for Investment Research shows that when you're twenty or thirty years away from retirement, a moderate investment plan (60% stocks, 30% bonds, 10% cash) improves your chances of reaching your retirement goals by an estimated 25% over a conservative plan with 20% stocks, 55% bonds, and 25% cash. Oddly, a moderately aggressive plan of 80% stocks, 15% bonds, and 5% cash only improves your chances ever so slightly while opening you up to greater risk. You just don't get the same kind of big bang for your buck. According to this research, a moderate investment plan may be the sweet spot on the curve, like hitting a tennis ball smack in the middle of the racket and seeing it zing across the net.

As you move closer to your retirement, the figures shift a bit toward a more conservative allocation, but only slightly. This suggests that if you have had a moderately aggressive allocation, you may want to choose a moderate allocation as you close in on your ten-year mark.

AND DON'T FORGET . . .

It may seem obvious, but when you're choosing an investment for one of your retirement accounts, don't forget that you already have built-in tax deferral. Unfortunately, investors forget this basic principle all too frequently. If you have a 401(k) or 403(b), your investment choices are already determined by your employer. But if you have more freedom of choice, don't make the mistake of putting muni bonds or annuities in your IRA. Their tax-advantaged status, which comes at the expense of lower returns, is a waste in an account that is already tax-deferred.

As a final note, if you're part of a couple, you should do your retirement planning together even though your accounts are held separately. It's important to be diversified across your entire portfolio. At one extreme, you don't want your investments to overlap, since that doubles your vulnerability in those areas. At the other end of the spectrum, don't fall into the trap of one client couple who had opposite investing philosophies. The husband, an attorney, invested only in cash-equivalents like Treasury bills. His wife, a social worker, disagreed vehemently: Only stocks would provide the growth they needed for their retirement, she argued. Their solution was for each of them to do their own thing; they hoped that their portfolios could simply balance each other out. The problem was that if something ever happened to either one of them—or to the relationship—each could end up in real trouble. Swayed by this reasoning, the couple worked out a compromise that both could tolerate.

WHAT ABOUT ANNUITIES?

Annuities, which come in several varieties, can provide tax-deferred growth, flexibility to move among investments without taxation, and the chance to receive income for life. Kind of a cross between a mutual fund and an insurance policy, they can be a useful supplement to your other tax-advantaged retirement accounts. But because annuities come in so many forms, you have to do your homework—and know what you're buying—before you write that check.

Here's how they work. In the *accumulation phase,* you invest a lump sum or make installment payments into an account that accumulates on a tax-deferred basis. Unlike your IRA or 401(k), there is no IRS limit to how much you can contribute. There are two types of annuities: *fixed,* which grow at a specified rate of return, and *variable,* which include a choice of mutual fund–like investments and therefore provide a variable return. The sponsoring insurance company (not the investor) assumes the investment risk for fixed annuities, so they are considered to be an insurance product, not a security.

In order to decide between a fixed and a variable annuity, think about your time horizon as well as your tolerance for risk. If you are a conservative investor and you don't have long until retirement, you might want to choose a fixed annuity. A fixed annuity is also more attractive in a high-interest-rate environment because you're likely to get a higher fixed rate of return. On the other hand, if you're a more aggressive investor with lots of time until retirement, you might benefit from the many choices and the growth potential of a variable annuity. Your asset allocation decisions are similar to those for your 401(k) or other retirement plan assets. At a younger age, you might start with more aggressive investments, then gradually move your money to more conservative investments as you near retirement.

When you are ready to take money out of your account, you have reached what is called the *distribution phase*. Your payments can be either immediate or deferred. An *immediate annuity* is purchased at retirement, and as the name implies, payments begin right away. The benefit? In a fixed immediate annuity the insurance company typically guarantees you a payment stream throughout your lifetime. If you choose a *life-only annuity,* payments stop at death regardless of how long they have been made. If you choose a *life annuity with period certain,* not only will payments cover your life, but if you die, it will continue to pay your beneficiary for a specified minimum period. A *joint and last survivor* annuity will continue for the life of another person as well (in effect covering two life spans). You may also wish to choose an inflation factor, in which case your payments may start out smaller but will keep pace with inflation over time.

If you invest in a variable deferred or immediate annuity, your payments will change based on the performance of the investment choices that you selected.

How do you decide among all of these products? If you want an income stream you know you can count on, a fixed annuity is more appropriate. Similarly, if the annuity is your sole or major source of retirement income, you may not be able to afford the risk of a fluctuating payment stream. But if the annuity is one of several sources of retirement income and you are willing to assume some risk, you could choose a variable payout and structure the asset allocation to fit your personal risk profile. For example, one hypothetical investor, age forty-five, has about fifteen years until retirement and is in the accumulation phase. She has maxed out her 401(k) contribution and her IRA. She receives a large sales bonus and decides to invest part of it for retirement. Given her desire for a tax-deferred investment, time to retirement, and her aggressive investing style, she chooses a variable annuity and selects several stock funds that reflect the asset allocation in her 401(k) plan. On the other hand, another hypothetical investor is in the distribution phase. He owns two fixed immediate annuities to balance out his other more aggressive growth-oriented investments. He derives peace of mind from knowing that he has a stable and consistent stream of income that is unaffected by market fluctuations and that he won't outlive.

The pros? Annuities provide tax-deferred (not tax-deductible) growth, have no income limitations, no tax implications when trading among investment choices, and no contribution limits. They can offer a guaranteed income stream for life, and some offer a death benefit during accumulation. Taken together, these features can provide peace of mind during your second half.

The cons? The insurance component of annuities can carry a significant fee, eroding your bottom line. In addition, if you choose a fixed annuity, inflation is likely to take its toll (although fixed annuities consistently pay higher rates than CDs). Many new annuities offer bells and whistles of questionable value. Purely as an investment, you can probably do better.

The bottom line? Annuities can be a useful supplement to your retirement savings (especially if you're concerned about a guaranteed income stream), but not a substitute for first investing fully in your 401(k), IRA, and other retirement accounts. If you decide that the tax-deferral and other features are right for you, be sure to shop for no-load, low-cost annuities (variable annuities with insurance fees that are less than 1%). According to an analysis done by the Schwab Center for Investment Research, if you are trying to decide between investing in a mutual fund and investing in a variable annuity, you generally need to have an investment horizon of at least five to fifteen years for the advantages of tax-deferred growth to outweigh the extra costs associated with variable annuities. In addition, if you are stuck with a high-cost variable annuity, talk to your advisor about a tax-free exchange to a lower-cost product.

Latecomers, Take Heart (and Heed)

Age forty-five seems to be the time when denial ebbs and awareness kicks in for many of us. Of course, the earlier you start, the more choices you'll have. But don't panic if you've delayed investing for your retirement longer than you should. Bridging this retirement gap isn't rocket science. Once you've double-checked all your numbers, from projected monthly expenses to projected rates of return on your investments, you've got several solid possibilities to think about. You can:

• Consider a career shift if it means getting—or improving—your retirement benefits. "When I hit my forties, a lightbulb suddenly went off," says one client, then a restaurateur-turned-realtor. "I realized that I wasn't prepared for retirement, which was suddenly looking a whole lot closer than it ever had." So even though she made quite a healthy amount of money peddling dirt, as they say, she switched careers yet again, opting for a well-paid nine-to-five job that offered terrific retirement investment benefits.

• Reframe your expectations about the length of your working life. Instead of retiring at sixty, you may want to wait until sixty-five. Instead of fully retiring, you may want to work part-time, either in your current profession like John, the insurance broker who now works on his own part-time, or Martin, who fills in for his vacationing medical partners, or in something completely new. Talking out the alternatives with your loved ones may give you ideas you might never have considered otherwise, so take the plunge and raise the topic. Then be open to any new ideas that surface. All too often we respond with an automatic *no* to new ideas without considering their value simply because they're different.

• Pay down any debts you may have accumulated as efficiently and quickly as possible, and don't accumulate new ones.

• Cut down on your current expenses, and instead save and invest in every which way you can. Lynn and her husband, for example, opted to scale back their kitchen remodel rather than cut into their retirement contributions. They know that they can always put in a new refrigerator and cabinetry later on. But an opportunity to invest in one's retirement, once missed, is gone forever—right along with the compound growth that that money might have engendered. If you're coming up short vis-à-vis your retirement goals, reevaluate your investment strategy. You may be missing some important opportunities.

• Take advantage of what you have and may not be using. Remember physicians Beth and Martin? They rent out their home to help finance their lengthy trips and have even converted their basement into a downstairs apartment, which they lease full time. In addition to covering the mortgage and related house expenses, the rental income covers most of their travel costs. "It's more expensive to stay home than to leave," says Martin.

• In a pinch, you can always redefine your dream for retirement. Just because you always envisioned yourself traveling the country and playing every golf course in sight doesn't mean that a part-time job wouldn't actually make you happier.

Whatever you do, don't turn a blind eye to the whole affair just because you don't like what you see. One client, Mary Ellen, age sixty-two, had her heart set on retiring. Four days before she was planning to retire, she stopped in to consult with a retirement specialist, just to make sure she had all her ducks in a row. "I'm fine, aren't I?" she asked, proudly showing the $125,000 she'd saved. The broker she spoke with didn't even need to run the numbers to know that Mary Ellen would soon run out of money. After breaking the bad news, she showed the would-be retiree how those funds would grow if she simply worked another two years—or better yet, until she was sixty-five. But that wasn't what Mary Ellen wanted to hear. So she quit anyway. And unless she wins the lottery, she's going to find herself job-hunting when she's seventy or seventy-five.

Chuck's Two Cents: Deciding Whether to Pay Off a Mortgage

For many people, paying off a mortgage is a dream come true. For some people it can be a very wise move—but it's not a given. Here are the pros and cons:

First, the advantages. The main one is obvious: Because a mortgage payment is likely one of your largest single expenses, by paying it off, you significantly reduce your monthly expenses. This fact can become increasingly important as you approach retirement. Second, there's no denying the psychological appeal of paying off a mortgage. The feeling of owning your home free and clear can be attractive at any age.

I can certainly understand that, and I think that the idea of eliminating debt can be wise—especially as you get older. While borrowing money at thirty-four is, generally speaking, pretty safe, borrowing at sixty-four is something altogether different for the simple reason that you don't have as much time, or as many opportunities, to pay off the loan.

In terms of the disadvantages of paying off a mortgage, there are two. First, by paying off the mortgage, you lose the opportunity to invest that money. My feeling is that the people who advise paying off a mortgage are disregarding what you can earn by investing that money. Second, you lose a significant tax break. The IRS allows you to deduct the interest paid on your mortgage from your current income. If you pay off the mortgage, you lose that deduction.

So how do you decide? There are three questions to ask:

• First, given the interest deduction, what is the after-tax rate you're paying for your mortgage? For example, suppose that the interest rate on your mortgage is 6% and you're in the 25% tax

bracket. Once you deduct the interest from your income, what you're really paying in terms of interest is around 4.5%.

   • *Second, comparing that tax-adjusted figure to the performance of the stock market, what's the best use of your money? If it's lower than what your investments are earning, you're probably better off keeping the mortgage. If the interest rate on your mortgage is higher than what your investments are earning after tax, it may be worth paying it off. I should add that there is, of course, some uncertainty here. We can't predict the future; no one knows how their investments will be doing in a year, let alone ten or twenty years. All you can do is make the best decision you can, based on what you now know.*

   • *And finally, how many more years are left on the mortgage? Because the tax benefits decrease the longer you hold your mortgage, it's often wise to pay off your mortgage as it nears the end of its term—say, when it has only five years left. If it's more than five years, you'll likely do better investing the money for that length of time.*

   So, to net things out, I think paying off a mortgage is a wise move if the after-tax interest rate you're paying on your mortgage is higher than the rate of return on your investments, and if you have less than five years to go on the mortgage.

PLAYING CATCH-UP

According to a recent analysis in the *Wall Street Journal,* many investors fail to appreciate how big a difference a serious effort to save and invest can make in the five years prior to retirement. But instead of ramping up the savings, many are ramping up their lifestyle. If this sounds familiar, read on.

   If you or your loved ones are in the position of playing catch-up, the recent changes in the tax laws make this an especially good time to do so. The IRA contribution limit, which held at $2,000 for so many years, is increasing in increments to $5,000 by 2008. Contribution limits for 401(k)s, 403(b)s, and other plans are increasing as well (see Table 7.5 on page 244). And if you're fifty or older, you can contribute even more. This is a terrific opportunity

you simply don't want to miss. Why? Because compounding will
work for you no matter what your age. Let's walk it through.

You're about to turn fifty and you haven't saved a thing. You wake
up on your birthday morning and finally see the light. Starting that
day, you begin to contribute the maximum amount to both your
401(k) and a traditional IRA—but at the under-fifty 2004 rates
($13,000 plus $3,000 for a total of $16,000). Assuming a 5% annual
return, at age sixty-five, when you're ready to retire, you've saved
just a little over $378,515. But let's say that on your birthday morn-
ing your conscience prevails and you instead invest at the new
increasing rates, taking advantage of your over-fifty status. This
means that in 2004 you contribute $19,500; in 2005, $22,500; in
2006, $24,500; and so on. The sum total by age sixty-five (again
with a 5% return): almost $540,000!

FOR WOMEN ONLY

I have a distant relative in her sixties who, when she was divorced
at age forty-four, was unprepared to take care of her own finances.
She didn't even set up an IRA for herself until she was fifty-four,
when I finally took her by the hand and forced the issue. Since her
lawyer hadn't advised her to include her husband's retirement benefits in her divorce settlement, she has almost nothing set aside for
retirement. So she has no choices. She has to continue working for
her $35,000-a-year wage, because, in essence, that paycheck is her
pension. "Carrie, I never thought at sixty years old, I'd have to be
doing this," she tells me. It breaks my heart that basic sustenance
will shape the rest of her days, and that the future she envisioned
will probably never come to pass.

Unfortunately, my relative's story isn't unique. According to the
New York Times, "hundreds of thousands of women in their
60's . . . are finding themselves forced to stay in the workforce
because they lack sufficient money to retire. Wages, in effect, are
becoming their pensions."

In fact, retirement planning is particularly vital for women, who
wind up increasingly disadvantaged as the years go by. Since women
tend to outlive men, they need more money to see them through their

retirement. But as a result of less time in the workforce (often because of raising families) at lower pay, their retirement savings are usually smaller. Add to that the fact that women often fare worse then men in divorce situations, and you wind up with the following statistics:

• According to the U.S. Census Bureau, women make up about two-thirds of the elderly poor.

• According to the Social Security Administration, more than half of women over age sixty-five rely on Social Security for 71% of their retirement income; one out of four relies on Social Security for her entire retirement income.

If you're married and are planning to work in rather than out of the home, one way to counteract this situation is to have your spouse set up a spousal IRA. Although regular IRAs require the contributor to be employed, up to $3,000 a year can be contributed to a spousal IRA for a stay-at-home spouse (or $3,500 if he or she is over fifty), even if he or she doesn't have income—as long as combined compensation is at least equal to the amount con-tributed to both IRAs and you file a joint return. Started early, this can grow to a significant amount once retirement rolls around.

If you're a divorced older woman who must rely exclusively on your own financial resources, you probably will want to work just as long as you possibly can if those resources aren't large enough, advises Cindy Hounsell, executive director of the Women's Institute for a Secure Retirement. You won't be alone in this. According to a 1999 poll conducted by AARP, 23% of Americans are planning to work during retirement to supplement their incomes. Another 40% will be working just for the sheer interest or enjoyment of it, while 17% plan to start their own businesses. Indeed, only 16% plan to stop work entirely after age sixty-five.

Take the Money and Run?

After all this talk about putting money away, we finally get to the good part: taking it out. But before you do that, there are several considerations that will affect not only how much you can with-draw—and when—but also which accounts you should draw from first. In a nutshell, your challenge is to be able to withdraw enough money to support the life you want and at the same time feel rea-sonably secure that you won't run out of resources. Unfortunately, this isn't as simple as it might seem. Because your retirement funds are probably spread out over a number of different accounts, some tax-deferred and others not, when and from where you withdraw the money can make a big difference. You have to think about income taxes, estate taxes, and government-imposed minimum withdrawals. In this section I'll give you an overview of how all of these factors weigh in and provide you with some broad guidelines. To get the maximum bang out of your hard-earned buck, though, I highly recommend that you consult a financial advisor about your particular situation. The analysis can get quite complicated, and it's far too easy to make a costly mistake.

With that caveat, let's tackle the first question first: How much can you safely withdraw without risking running out down the line? Thanks again to the Schwab Center for Investment Research, Table 7.6 gives some pretty precise figures for the percentage of your port-folio's value at retirement that you should be able to withdraw each year (i.e., with a low chance that you will run out of money before you die), depending on how long you expect your retirement to last. But be sure to keep in mind that these figures are not absolute—they're really just the statistical likelihoods, based on historical returns for a well-diversified moderate risk portfolio (60% stocks, 30% bonds, and 10% cash).

Clearly, the shorter you anticipate your retirement to last, the more you'll be able to withdraw each year—perhaps almost as much as 10%. But if you're just launching your retirement, you shouldn't deplete those funds by more than 3% to 5% a year. (Once a year, or once a quarter if you prefer smaller installments, you can transfer 3% to 5% of the value of your portfolio to your money mar-ket account. That, plus any other income you manage to bring in, is what you'll live on.) Taking out any more than that just leaves you too vulnerable if you live to a ripe old age. I don't know about you, but I'd rather bank on the positive possibility than on any other.

Table 7.6
Percentage You Can Safely Withdraw from
Your Retirement Account Each Year

Number of Years in Retirement	Withdrawal Rate (per year)
10 years or fewer	9.4%
11–15 years	6.5%
16–20 years	5.2%
21–25 years	4.4%
26–30 years	4.2%
31–35 years	3.8%
36–40 years	3.6%

Source: Schwab Center for Investment Research

Before we move on, just a couple more notes about Table 7.6. First, the withdrawal percentages are based on *the date of your retirement* and remain constant. For example, suppose you retire with $1 million and you anticipate having twenty years in retirement. According to the table, you can withdraw $52,000 (or 5.2%) every year for twenty years *regardless of market fluctuations.* It doesn't matter if your portfolio value goes up or down, you still withdraw the equivalent of $52,000. But the actual amount you withdraw *will increase* over time due to inflation. So in ten years, if the compound inflation rate has been 3%, you can now withdraw $69,884.

Now that you know how much you can withdraw, where should this money come from? First you have to pay attention to government regulations. Basically, there are two important ages that affect withdrawals from tax-deferred retirement accounts: 59½ and 70½. Get out your party hats for the former, because that's the age you're entitled to take a withdrawal without penalty. (But because of the benefits of tax-deferred growth, my father and I usually recommend that you wait to withdraw it if you can.) But at 70½ (unless you are still working), you are *required* to take a minimum withdrawal from all of your retirement plans *except a Roth IRA.* That's right, you *must* remove this minimum from every traditional IRA, rollover IRA, SEP-IRA, SIMPLE-IRA, Keogh, 401(k), or 403(b)—whether you want to or not. In fact, you're subject to a 50% (!) penalty on the amount not withdrawn.

Fortunately, though, new regulations that went into effect in January 2001 have greatly simplified (and relaxed) required minimum withdrawal calculations. If you think they're complicated or overly strict now, you should have tried to work through the formulas in 2000! Here's a quick run-through.

First, refer to Table 7.7 to find your *life expectancy factor.* Then divide the value of your account (as of December 31 of the previous year) by the factor that corresponds to your age.

Let's say you're seventy-five and your IRA is worth $150,000. Using the Uniform Life Expectancy Table, your life expectancy factor is 22.9. Your required minimum withdrawal is thus $150,000 divided by 22.9 or $6,550 a year, or roughly 4.4% of your account's value. This amount will be included as income for tax purposes.

Just as an aside, the Uniform Life Expectancy Table assumes that your beneficiary is no more than ten years younger than you are. If, in fact, your spouse is your beneficiary and he or she is more than ten years your junior, you should consult the IRS's Joint Life Expectancy Table, which will result in an even smaller required minimum withdrawal.

If you have more than one IRA, you can calculate your required minimum withdrawal based on their combined value. You can then take a distribution from any single account or any combination of accounts that you choose. In the case of qualified plans (e.g., 401[k]s and 403[b]s), the specific required minimum withdrawal must be taken from each account.

Now that that part (and it may well be the lion's share) of the amount you need to live on is spoken for, it's time to figure out how best to withdraw the rest so that it will stretch as far as possible—not only for you but for your heirs as well. Taking the most simplified perspective, the standard advice is to withdraw your funds in the following order:

1. Taxable accounts
2. Nondeductible IRA

3. Traditional IRA or other qualified retirement plan

4. Roth IRA

Caution, though: This is an area that can get very complicated, very fast. The above sequence doesn't take into consideration a host of variables that include your life expectancy, the tax status of your

Table 7.7
Uniform Life Expectancy Table

Age of IRA Holder	Life Expectancy Factor	Age of IRA Holder	Life Expectancy Factor
70	27.4	93	9.6
71	26.5	94	9.1
72	25.6	95	8.6
73	24.7	96	8.1
74	23.8	97	7.6
75	22.9	98	7.1
76	22.0	99	6.7
77	21.2	100	6.3
78	20.3	101	5.9
79	19.5	102	5.5
80	18.7	103	5.2
81	17.9	104	4.9
82	17.1	105	4.5
83	16.3	106	4.2
84	15.5	107	3.9
85	14.8	108	3.7
86	14.1	109	3.4
87	13.4	110	3.1
88	12.7	111	2.9
89	12.0	112	2.6
90	11.4	113	2.4
91	10.8	114	2.1
92	10.2	115 and older	1.9

Source: IRS Publication 590

estate, your income tax rate, the tax rate of your beneficiaries, and the particulars of your portfolio. Consider, for example, the following:

• Capital gains on your investments in a taxable account are taxed at a lower rate (currently 15%, but 5% if you're in the 10% or 15% tax bracket; both rates are subject to change).

•Investments in your taxable accounts receive a stepped-up cost basis at your death (see Chapter 8 for more on this point). As you age, this benefit to your beneficiaries may outweigh the advantages of pretax compound growth in your retirement accounts.

• If you hold tax-efficient investments in your taxable accounts, even long-term investors may be better off leaving them alone.

• If your beneficiary has a lower tax rate than you have, you may want to withdraw funds from your Roth IRA (tax-free) first and leave your other accounts (and the associated tax burden) for your heirs.

• If you're anticipating estate taxes, you should realize that your beneficiaries may face a "double tax" (estate tax plus income tax) on the entire balance of a traditional IRA or a qualified retirement plan. But in a nondeductible IRA only the investment returns are double-taxed. In this case, you may want to withdraw from your traditional IRAs and qualified retirement plans prior to withdrawing from the nondeductible IRA.

Not only do all these factors come into play differently for different people, they will also affect you differently at different stages of your retirement. For this reason, it's wise to review the particulars of your situation with a financial planner or tax advisor not only as you approach retirement but again every two to three years.

As you can see, all this has plenty of estate-planning ramifications, which gives me the perfect transition to the next chapter. I know that reading about—much less actually considering—your own demise or that of your loved ones is hard to deal with. But the last thing you want to leave your heirs is a problem instead of an inheritance. Besides, that inheritance can be so much more with some proper planning. Isn't your life's work worth at least that much?

Something to Talk About

• *Have you started saving for retirement? If not, why not?*

• *What's your vision for the future? Do you want to stop work altogether? Continue to work part- or full time? Explore a new career? Open a business?*

• *How much are you spending on your hobbies today? Do you plan to spend more once you have more time to enjoy them?*

• *If you and your spouse have different ideas about what you want to do in retirement, can you reach a compromise that will satisfy you both?*

• *Considering that you'll need to have a minimum of $220,000 banked for every $1,000 of monthly income you want in your retirement, are you saving enough?*

• *Are you better off saving for retirement or paying off your mortgage?*

• *Are you taking advantage of all your tax-deferred savings opportunities? Have you considered opening a supplemental taxable retirement savings account?*

• *Do you have appropriate asset allocation for your age and risk tolerance?*

• *Do you still have some of your retirement assets invested for growth?*

• *Can your parents realize their retirement dreams? Do they have enough to live on now?*

• *What was the lesson you took away the last time you had a hard conversation with your parents? Can you use this reflection to initiate another?*

• *If you—or your parents—are starting late, what adjustments can you make in terms of earning, saving, spending, and investing, as well as expectations for the future?*

• *If you decide to invest your latest bonus rather than take a vacation, what will that money be worth in five or ten years?*

• *How can you encourage your adult children to start saving for retirement now? Have you thought about matching their savings, at least when they're young and just getting started?*

8

Estate Planning for You and Your Parents

If there's one thing we hate to talk about more than money, it's death, whether our own or that of a loved one. Combine the two, and it's no wonder we avoid making plans for the very capital we've worked so hard all our lives to amass.

The highly technical nature of estate planning, which is rife with legal details and arcane language, presents another obstacle. But once you get past these obstacles, estate planning is very much about human issues. After all, the whole point is for you to decide how you want to provide for the people and causes you care about most. If you allow yourself to think about the unthinkable, you soon realize that your estate plan is all about your legacy—something you can come to feel very good about. By taking the time now to craft a plan that reflects your wishes, you can make sure that you safeguard the money, material goods, and property you leave from unnecessary taxes and fees, while ensuring that the fruit of your life's work winds up where you'd like it to be.

Some of you may be thinking that this topic doesn't apply to you. And you may be right. If you're young and healthy and you have no children or assets, you may be off the hook—for now. But everyone else should read on. Depending on your circumstances, an appropriate estate plan can range from a simple will to a foray into the world of trusts and other contractual devices. Your age and your wealth certainly come into play. But more than that, it's your family makeup that affects your planning. "It's not necessarily the rich who have complicated estates, it's people with complicated families who have complicated estates," says Michael Ferguson, an estate planning attorney and adjunct professor at the University of California's Boalt Hall. If you're single and have few assets, or if you and your spouse have no children, your estate plan may be very simple. But as soon as you add a marriage, children, remarriage, or stepchildren into the equation, you've got a lot more to plan for.

I know this may seem like a nasty business that you don't want to think about. I don't blame you—I don't either. But when I find myself avoiding the topic, thinking about the potential misunderstandings or misappropriations that might result, it forces my hand.

While it's tough enough to get your own affairs in order, making sure your parents have appropriately handled their estate planning is even trickier. Still, by addressing the issue now and helping your parents craft a smart plan, they can make sure that their legacy is passed on and their wishes honored.

Appropriately, it all gets back to exactly what you started with—your dreams. Some people think of this as their last hurrah, the final chance to make a difference, to leave their mark on the world. So when you consider your estate, you again need to ask yourself what's important to you. The same values that dictate your life (and all your financial plans) can shape your estate plan, thereby making it a proper exclamation point to a life well lived.

Just one more thought before we jump in. Despite the proliferation of do-it-yourself estate-planning books and software packages, estate planning is not a task you should tackle on your own. The goal of this chapter is to help you get through the language and technical barriers and give you a good grasp of the basics. Then we strongly suggest that you find an experienced estate-planning attorney and work together to create the best plan for you and your family.

Do You Really Need All This?

Every year it's estimated that seven out of ten Americans die without a will. Contrary to commonly accepted wisdom, that doesn't mean that their estates automatically go to the state. The fact is that each one of us has a will whether we draw one up or not. When you die *intestate,* or without having drawn up a will, your state's law dictates the distribution of your estate. Putting aside the cost and inconvenience, dying intestate simply means that you don't get to apportion your wealth and property yourself. By not drawing up a will, you're basically allowing the state to dictate what happens to everything you have. A judge will appoint a *personal representative* or administrator, as well as a guardian for your minor children.

Virtually all the intestate laws in the United States split up what's left of the estate after probate (court) costs and estate taxes between your spouse and your children, regardless of how estranged from them you might have been. "You might as well say: 'I want half my estate to go to my spouse, even if we are estranged and haven't been living together for fourteen years, and the rest to go to my children, even though three of them haven't talked to me since they left home,'" says one attorney.

If you've neglected to spell out arrangements in a will or trust, then your assets will likely go first to your spouse and then to your descendants—your kids or grandkids. Depending on your state, if you don't have any descendants, your assets will likely go to your parents if they're alive, then to your brothers and sisters, and then to your nieces and nephews. If you don't have any of those, your estate goes over to your grandparents and starts working down their line (i.e., aunts, uncles, cousins, second cousins, and so on). That's where the term *laughing heirs* comes from: The money winds up so far removed from you that the heirs (who knew you slightly if at all) wind up laughing all the way to the bank.

Now there *are* some people who don't actually need to worry about all this estate-planning business. A significant number of people in our country have what is known as a *negative net worth*. They don't need a will because there will be no assets to distribute upon their death. A simple letter detailing who's to get which personal effects will do the job. (Legally speaking, *assets* are money and property; *personal effects* are anything that you can pick up and move around—and that doesn't have registered title—such as jewelry, furniture, and art.) Young single people who don't have many assets and who don't mind if those few assets revert to their parents, or their siblings, don't need to worry about an estate plan either. Remember that if you want to leave money to a charity, a school, or a special niece or a nephew, no matter how small the amount, you need a will.

Of course, the moment you have children, no matter what your assets, you absolutely *must* draw up a will that specifies a guardian for them in case something happens to you and their other parent. Once your kids are of legal age and can take care of themselves, the guardian issue becomes moot. By then, however, your assets will probably make an estate plan essential. Indeed, the older you are, and the more money you have, the more likely it is that you should set up a trust or a combination of trusts.

In addition, if you're in a committed nonmarital relationship, you absolutely must have a will or trust should you want to provide for your partner. Most states don't recognize either common-law or same-sex marriages. This means that if you die without a will or trust, your estate will be distributed according to your state's intestate laws and your partner will get nothing. If you're in such a relationship and haven't made the appropriate provisions to protect your partner, you have no time to lose. Pick up the phone and make an appointment with an estate-planning attorney today.

Earlier we talked about your estate plan as your legacy. Unfortunately, by not spelling out your wishes in a proper legal document, the legacy you leave could be family divisiveness and bitterness. When money, property, or family heirlooms are concerned, things can get nasty in a hurry. And when turmoil leads to a legal fight, "the attorneys usually make out like bandits, and everybody gets less than they would have if they hadn't fought in the first place," says

Michael Ferguson, the California estate-planning attorney and law professor.

Never Assume

No matter how organized your parents, in-laws, siblings, or closest friends may seem, don't assume that they've taken care of their estate planning. Marcus, the Schwab broker whom we met in Chapter 5, recalls that his dad, an investment banker, told him early on that when it comes to handling taxes and estate planning, it is very important to work with the best people you can afford. "Don't try to be cute or cut corners; it's not worth it," he said. Between that warning and his father's superior organizational skills, Marcus assumed that his father had everything under control. Later, when his father's health was taking a turn for the worse, Marcus asked if everything was in order, and his father assured him everything would be fine. But after his father passed away, Marcus was amazed to find that although his father had established a trust, many of his investment assets remained in certificate form in a safe-deposit box. In the end, Marcus was able to get most of his father's affairs in order, but not without some last-minute scrambling, a fair amount of family dissension, and considerable anxiety.

Compare that to the legacy that my colleague Louise's father, a tax and estate-planning attorney, left upon his death. As soon as Edward began accumulating property, he put together what he called his Black Book, a compilation of data that would be needed if he were to pass away or have a disabling illness. In those fourteen pages and in a supplemental letter that he wrote to his wife about a year before his death, Edward provided the full history and context behind each of his assets.

Edward first listed the house he and his wife shared. After noting the address and how the title was registered, he specified when they had purchased it, the original cost, and the adjusted cost after improvements. He wrote that he had been careful about paying the taxes and that canceled checks could be found among his records.

Then he proceeded to note everything of value—from the antique phone system to the old railway lantern in the entryway—that the family should take with them upon selling the house.

In addition to covering his various real estate holdings, Edward also chronicled his own work-related history, even specifying the lawyer who handled the dissolution of the professional corporation he'd founded in 1978. He then reviewed the family's finances, including IRAs; checking, savings, and brokerage accounts; major possessions including cars; insurance policies; and more. Everything was organized by section and completely spelled out.

He also listed the names and contact information of his trusted professional advisors, including his financial planner, accountant, lawyer, and insurance broker. He had, he said, been through the terrible process of losing a good friend, which had caused him to think of what would happen if he died. Then he told his wife to whom she should turn for each part of the financial puzzle.

When Edward passed away in 2000, several decades after he had first prepared the Black Book, his wife and children were able to pick up and keep going in terms of the day-to-day details. His care and attention enabled his family to continue on with a solid emotional and financial base.

Remember, estate planning is all about specifying what you—or a loved one—wants. You need to do what it takes to make sure those wishes are honored.

Talking About Tough Issues in Families

Here's a conundrum: How do you bring up an unmentionable subject with the people you love most? Let's face it, the elements that lie just under the surface of this discussion—dependency, incapacity, and death—are difficult topics under even the best of circumstances. Add a history of conflict or resentments (most of us have a little bit of that tucked away in our family history), and you could be looking at a positively chilly reception.

Unfortunately, there are no hard-and-fast rules to facilitate—or even initiate—this important discussion, since circumstances and personalities vary so much from family to family. We hope, however, that these basic tips will help make these potentially tough talks a little easier.

• Find your moment. There's a season for everything, and if the time is right, you talk about it. Of course, sometimes we need to make the time. In that case, everything from the death of someone close to you to a calamitous world event can serve as a catalyst. You might even use this book to initiate a conversation.

• Use any excuse, including asking for company at an upcoming estate-planning seminar, to broach the topic. If you fear your questions could be misinterpreted as interference or worse, ask for advice about your own plan.

• Come prepared with an opening line such as:

"We need to draw up a will or establish a trust. How did you do yours?"

"What if something awful like [fill in with a recent event] had happened to us? Where would we stand?"

"The estate tax law has changed. Let's figure out how that affects us."

"Did you hear that _____ unexpectedly passed away? That makes me wonder whether our affairs are in order."

• Make it plain that you're not looking for details about who's being left what. State clearly that you just want to make sure that everything's been covered. That should quell any doubts about your motive.

The Preliminaries

Before we launch into wills, trusts, and other ways to organize your estate, we need to spend a little time reviewing how estates are processed and taxed. This information and these definitions will help you to prepare yourself and understand the basics, which can save you and your family a lot of time, money, and grief.

PROBATE

Probate is the court-supervised process of wrapping up a person's financial affairs after he or she dies: collecting the assets, submitting the will to the court for approval, paying the bills and taxes, dealing with any issues that come up, and distributing the estate according to the terms of the will. Probate is generally required when assets are registered only in the name of the person who has died.

Proponents of the probate system will tell you that probate guarantees that your assets wind up in the right hands. That may be so, but it's also true that probate is an expensive, inefficient system that can stretch on for months and months and seriously erode the value of your estate. Depending on your state, probate can easily take up to a year (or more) and can cost anywhere from 2% to 2.5% of the value of your estate for attorney's fees alone. If your executor gets a fee as well, the cost to your estate can double. And remember that separate probate proceedings are required for each state in which you own real property. Finally, bear in mind that probate documents are public records, which means that family privacy can be compromised.

Sound like something you want to avoid? Absolutely! In fact, a good portion of estate planning is about how best to avoid probate. We'll get into that later in the chapter.

ESTATE TAXES

If you own property in the United States, you are subject to federal estate taxes, whether or not your estate goes through probate. (Depending on where you live, you may have to pay an additional state death tax.) A common misperception is that if you avoid probate, you'll also avoid estate taxes. This simply isn't so. Your taxable estate includes *everything* you own, whether it goes through probate or not. With the proper estate planning it's fairly easy to avoid probate, but you may still have to pay estate taxes.

In reality, less than 2% of the population has an estate large enough to be affected by estate taxes. But before you automatically disqualify yourself from that group, realize that you could be worth more than you think. Your total assets are calculated based on:

- Your cash
- The current market value of any property you own
- The current value of your investment portfolio
- The total value of all your IRAs, 401(k)s, and pensions
- The value of any life insurance policy you hold (as long as you have what's called an *incident of ownership,* which allows you the right to name beneficiaries or borrow against it)

In other words, the value of your estate can mount up more quickly than you think. If you have $75,000 in the bank or in cash-equivalents, a house now worth $500,000 (no matter what you paid for it), $200,000 worth of stocks and bonds, $300,000 in retirement plan savings, and a $250,000 cash value life insurance policy (see Chapter 9), you're already across that estate tax line.

MARITAL PROPERTY

If you're single, property ownership is quite straightforward. Unless you own property in a partnership or under some other shared-ownership agreement, you're free to leave your property to whomever you please.

Marital property is more complex. Most states (as well as Washington, D.C.) use the common-law system derived from English law. That system generally granted all ownership rights to the husband. Today, under common law, property is owned by whoever's name is listed on the title or other ownership document.

Eight states (Arizona, California, Idaho, New Mexico, Nevada, Texas, Washington, and Wisconsin) use a "community property" system instead, in which all property acquired or earned during a marriage is owned equally by both spouses. (It is community property.) Any property that was owned by one spouse prior to marriage remains separate property unless it is commingled with other marital assets. Likewise, property received as a gift or an inheritance is separate property so long as the recipient maintains title in his or her name alone and the property is controlled solely by that spouse. (However, the growth and return on separate property in community-property states can be treated differently in different jurisdictions.)

In community-property states, each spouse is free to leave his or her half of the community property to whomever he or she chooses. There's no requirement to leave it to a surviving spouse. In common-law states, laws prevent one spouse from completely disinheriting the other even though one spouse may own all the property. Depending on the state, the surviving spouse is generally entitled to anywhere from one-third to one-half of the deceased spouse's property.

On the positive side, the Tax Relief Act of 2001, which is being phased in over the next ten years, not only raises the amount of your estate that is exempt from taxes but also decreases the estate tax rate (see Table 8.1).

What this means is that if you die in 2004 and your estate has a value of less than $1.5 million, you will owe no estate taxes. Or if you die in 2009, you will owe no taxes unless your estate is worth more than $3.5 million. But if you come in above these amounts, the toll can be significant. Prudent estate planning can help you minimize this tax bill to Uncle Sam.

You should also realize that the tax rates in Table 8.1 are the maximum, but in reality the rates are progressive. In other words, the larger your estate, the greater the percentage of your estate that you'll pay in taxes. Despite this apparent similarity to income taxes, however, estate taxes are calculated differently. This is how it works: Let's say you die in 2003, leaving a taxable estate of $1 million. Using Table 8.2, you can see that your tax is $448,300. From this you *subtract* your credit of $345,800 (per Table 8.1), leaving you a tax bill of $102,500.

Table 8.1
Scheduled Changes in the Estate Tax

Year	Applicable Exclusion Amount	Highest Estate Tax Rate	Applicable Credit Amount
2003	$1 million	49%	$345,800
2004	$1.5 million	48%	$555,800
2005	$1.5 million	47%	$555,800
2006	$2 million	46%	$780,800
2007	$2 million	45%	$780,800
2008	$2 million	45%	$1,455,800
2009	$3.5 million	45%	$1,455,800
2010	Estate Tax Repealed	0%	N/A
BUT! 2011	$1 million unless repeal is extended	55% unless repeal is extended	$345,800 unless repeal is extended

Source: Internal Revenue Service

If your taxable estate is instead $1.5 million, you still subtract the credit of $345,800 from your tax (in this case, $555,800) to arrive at a tax bill of $210,000. In other words, regardless of the size of your estate, you first figure your tax and then subtract your credit (which in 2003 is always $345,800, but increases in future years per Table 8.1).

Note that the estate tax is currently scheduled to vanish in 2010 and then reappear in 2011. When this was first announced, the rather ghoulish joke being circulated was that if you were going to die, you should do it at 11:59 P.M. on December 31, 2010, to take advantage of that one year without taxes. Of course, the more likely scenario is that somewhere around 2006, 2007, or so, Congress will cap the exemption at $2 or $3 million and the top tax rate at 45%.

Before we leave the subject of estate taxes, there are three important estate tax deductions that you should be aware of. First is the *unlimited marital deduction,* which allows all spouses who are U.S. citizens to transfer unlimited assets to their spouses—

Table 8.2
2003 Federal Estate Tax Rates

Value of Estate	Tax Rate
Over $1,000,000, but not over $1,250,000	$345,800, plus 41% of excess over $1,000,000
Over $1,250,000, but not over $1,500,000	$448,300, plus 43% of excess over $1,250,000
Over $1,500,000, but not over $2,000,000	$555,800, plus 45% of excess over $1,500,000
Over $2,000,000	$780,800, plus 49% of excess over $2,000,000

Source: Internal Revenue Service

both during their life and at death—free of estate tax. (If your spouse is not a U.S. citizen, you can use what is known as a QDOT; see the "Rules for Noncitizen Spouses" box for details.) Second, the *charitable deduction* exempts all property left to a qualified charity from estate taxes. And third, if your family owns

RULES FOR NONCITIZEN SPOUSES

If you are married to a noncitizen, you may not be able to transfer your estate to your spouse tax-free. (Interestingly, though, a U.S. citizen is entitled to the unlimited marital deduction when he or she receives property from a noncitizen spouse.)

There are, however, a few ways to compensate. First, gift tax laws allow a citizen spouse to give his or her noncitizen spouse up to $110,000 per year without paying gift taxes. Combine this over several years with your personal estate tax

> exemption ($1 million in 2003 and increasing per Table 8.1 after that), and you may well not have to pay any taxes.
>
> If your estate exceeds these limits, you can also set up what is known as a *qualified domestic trust (QDOT)*, which postpones payment of estate taxes until after your noncitizen spouse dies. Clearly, this is necessary only if your estate exceeds the estate tax threshold.

a small business, you may be entitled to a special estate tax exemption when one of you dies.

The most unusual use of the marital deduction I've heard about involved a wealthy ninety-one-year-old woman who had never been married. After many years of being cared for by a friend's seventy-something son, she decided she wanted to leave her entire $5 million estate to him. "I'm going to make an outrageous suggestion," her estate attorney told the two when they came to him to revise her estate plan. "If you got married, it would save $2.5 million in taxes." The white-haired woman, who had never been married, cracked up. Her companion turned green. After many questions and lengthy discussions, however, they finally did tie the knot. For the honeymoon, the groom returned the bride to the rest home where she lived.

A NOTE ABOUT STATE DEATH TAXES

Depending on your state, you may be liable for what are known as state death taxes in addition to federal estate taxes. State death taxes can be either estate or inheritance taxes. Although both types of tax are due on your death, there is a fundamental difference in the way they are structured.

Estate taxes are based on the total value of your estate, no matter who receives it. Inheritance taxes, on the other hand, are imposed on the transfer of assets to each particular beneficiary. Inheritance tax rates vary depending not only on the amount being transferred, but also on the relationship between the deceased and the beneficiary. In most states, the closer your relationship, the lower the rate: A spouse will pay the least; a minor child will pay more; an adult child or parent will pay still more; a brother, sister, or cousin will pay more yet; and all others (including nonrelatives) will pay the most.

Until recently, most people didn't concern themselves with state death taxes, for a couple of reasons. First, fewer than half of the states had them. Second, even if your state has death taxes, prior to 2002 the federal government gave you an almost dollar-for-dollar credit against your state tax bill. In other words, part of what you paid to the federal government actually went to your state—at no extra charge to you.

All of this is changing. With the increase in the estate tax personal exemption and the decline in the federal estate tax rate starting in 2002, the federal government began to gradually phase out the credit for state death taxes. To compensate for this loss of revenue, some states are in the process of imposing or reimposing death taxes. The eventual result may well be an increase in your combined federal-state tax bill.

GIFT TAXES

The close cousin to estate tax is the *gift tax*. In essence, what the government is telling you is that you can't just give your estate away unrestricted during your lifetime and thereby avoid estate taxes at your death. For that reason, the *taxable* gifts that you make during your lifetime are taxed at the same rate as the property you transfer at death. Notice that we used the word *taxable*. Under current law, several types of gifts are not subject to gift taxes, including: gifts to your spouse (the unlimited marital deduction), tuition or medical expenses paid on behalf of another person (provided you pay the school or medical provider directly), gifts to political organizations (within certain limits and defined by state or federal laws), and gifts to charities.

In addition to these types of transfers that can be made free of gift tax, each individual is allowed to give a tax-free gift of up to $11,000 to as many people as he or she chooses. You can give $10,000, $100,000, or $1 million without gift taxes as long as no one person receives more than $11,000 in any one year. This also means that a married couple can give up to $22,000 to an individual each year. Let's say, for example, that you want to give your daughter a gift of $18,000. You can stay under the $11,000 limit by splitting the gift between you and your spouse.

ANNUAL TAX-FREE LIMIT

Note that the maximum size for a tax-free gift is periodically adjusted for inflation. In 2002 the amount you can give per year free of tax to any one individual was increased from $10,000 to $11,000. This amount is subject to change in the future.

LIFETIME GIFT TAX EXEMPTION

Everyone has a lifetime gift tax exemption that's currently set (and scheduled to remain) at $1 million. This is how it works: If you give more than $11,000 to an individual in any given year, the amount over $11,000 is subtracted from your lifetime exemption until the exemption is used up. For example, if you give your son $25,000 in 2004 and don't split the gift with your spouse, the amount over $11,000—in this case $14,000—will be subtracted from your life-time gift tax exemption of $1 million (you don't pay taxes on this $14,000, but you must report it to the IRS). Your remaining exemption is $986,000. If you exhaust your lifetime exemption limit, any subsequent gifts (over the $11,000 limit) will be subject to gift taxes, which until 2009 are charged at the same rate as estate taxes (as high as 48% in 2004; see Table 8.1). After 2009 they will be taxed at the then-existing highest personal income tax rate. And to make things more complicated, any amount of your gift tax exemption that you use up (in the previous example, $14,000) will also be deducted from your estate tax deduction.

Bear in mind that for a gift to qualify for the $11,000 annual exclusion from gift tax, it must be a *gift of a present interest*. This means that the person receiving the gift must immediately be able to receive benefit from it. A gift of cash is a clear example of a gift of present interest. But if enjoyment of the gift is post-poned to some point in the future, such as a gift made by cer-tain types of trusts, the gift does not qualify for the $11,000 exclusion.

Another way to qualify for the annual gift tax exclusion is to set up a trust with *Crummey provisions*. Named after the case that decided it, the beneficiary of a Crummey trust must have a speci-fied amount of time to withdraw the annual gift from the trust. A common example is a life insurance trust. Let's say you have five children, and you put $10,000 for each (a total of $50,000) in a Crummey trust to pay the premiums. Each child has the right to withdraw their annual gift within thirty days (and they must receive written notice of this fact), but they also understand that if they do take it out, the premiums won't be paid, and they won't get the life insurance proceeds. But simply having the right to withdraw the money qualifies the gift as present interest, and you get the annual gift tax exclusion.

STEP RIGHT UP

Up until now we've been focusing on the tax liability of the person who's giving the gift or passing on an estate. It's also important to think about the tax consequences for the recipient. Here's an exam-ple that will illustrate why.

Let's say you give your daughter two hundred shares of XYZ stock that's worth $50 per share on the day you give the gift, but for which you paid only $40 per share. The total value of the gift is $10,000 ($50 multiplied by 200 shares). But for *her* tax purposes, your daughter will assume your *cost basis* of $8,000 (the price you origi-nally paid). This means that if your daughter sells the stock for $50 per share, she will owe capital gains tax on the $2,000 of profit ($10,000 value minus $8,000 cost basis equals $2,000).

However, if you instead keep the stock as part of your estate, and your daughter eventually inherits it, she will not inherit your cost basis but will obtain a new *stepped-up cost basis* equal to its value at the date of your death (or at an alternate valuation date, which can be six months after death or at a time determined by the executor). It doesn't matter who inherits your property or what you give (it can be stock, real estate, or any other property), the stepped-up basis will wipe out any capital gain. As one estate planner has quipped, "The stepped-up basis is the only advantage of dying."

However, despite this apparent advantage, it's important to realize that even though capital gains may be erased, estate taxes may still be due. Therefore, before you decide to defer your gift until after your death, thereby avoiding capital gains taxes, be sure to consider your potential estate tax bill and how that might erode the value of your gift. This is especially important for large estates.

Looking at this from another vantage point, suppose you plan to give away property that you expect will appreciate in the future. In this case, again depending on the size of your estate, you may want to make that gift now. This way you not only remove that asset from your estate but you also remove the potential appreciation on that asset that would otherwise be taxed at the much higher estate tax rates.

Caveat: All of this is scheduled to change in extremely complicated ways after 2010. Be sure to check with your tax advisor.

STEPPED-UP COMMUNITY PROPERTY

If you live in one of the eight community-property states (Arizona, California, Idaho, New Mexico, Nevada, Texas, Washington, Wisconsin—and Alaska if agreed to by husband and wife), the value of a stepped-up cost basis for community property is multiplied by two! Here's how it works.

Let's say you live in California and your wife predeceases you and leaves you her share of stock that you bought together several years ago for $100,000. At the time of her death the stock is worth $500,000. Had you sold it prior to her death, you would have had to pay capital gains taxes on the $400,000 gain. Upon her death, however, the basis of the stock is "stepped up" to its current value of $500,000, avoiding all that capital gain. When you eventually sell the stock, your capital gain will be calculated based on that reassessed value. So assuming the stock is finally worth $600,000 when you decide to cash out, you will pay capital gains tax on only $100,000.

If, on the other hand, you live in a non-community-property state, that stepped-up basis would be applied only to your wife's interest. So instead of eventually paying capital gains tax on just $100,000 (assuming we keep all the same numbers), you'd also have to pay the capital gains tax on your share of that pre-death $400,000 capital gain. Clearly, married couples in community-property states enjoy a major advantage over those in common-law states.

Getting Down to Business

It used to be that before you died, you drew up a will that specified your final wishes and that was that. Like everything else, dying is a little more complicated these days, so you'll need to make a few more plans if you want your beneficiaries to get the most out of your assets. In this section we introduce wills, trusts, and various contractual devices, the building blocks of estate planning. Table 8.3 provides a quick look at how their various features compare.

All of those items will take care of the money part of things. But these days, as many of us are living longer due to advancements in medical technology, we also need to make provisions for illness or incapacity. Therefore, in addition to a will or trust, everyone should fill out a *durable power of attorney for finances* as well as a *durable power of attorney for health care*. Once you've taken these additional steps, you can feel confident that you have truly provided for all

Table 8.3
Estate-Planning Vehicles at a Glance

	Avoids Probate?	Pros	Cons
Will	No	• Easy to prepare • Appoints guardian • Backup to trust	• Probate
Revocable Living Trust	Yes	• Flexible • Maintains control over property • Provides for incapacity	• Can be more expensive than a will • More difficult to set up and maintain
Joint Tenancy	Yes	• Simple	• Joint tenant can take over other's interest; subject to creditors' claims; might defeat tax planning
Pay-on-Death Bank Account	Yes	• Easy to create	• Limited to bank accounts and government securities (and TOD on brokerage accounts in 37 states)
Beneficiary Designation on Retirement Account	Yes	• Easy to do	• Can get outdated; easy to overlook

eventualities. Later in this chapter we'll walk you through these steps.

WILLS

As we've already discussed, anyone who doesn't want his or her assets distributed according to their state's intestate laws, or who has children, needs a will. And if you're young and have an uncomplicated estate, that may be all you need.

The biggest advantage of wills is that they're usually relatively inexpensive to prepare and can be a straightforward way to distribute your assets. Also, in most states, a will is also the only way to appoint a legal guardian for your minor children.

The biggest downside of having only a will is that your estate will probably have to go through probate. Some states have simplified probate proceedings for small estates (for example, in California up to $100,000 can be transferred without probate), but if you don't qualify for such an exclusion, not only is the probate process time-consuming and expensive but the documents are public.

"I have nothing to hide," I hear you thinking. But do you really want all your finances to be made public? The lack of privacy inherent in wills can be a serious drawback to using them as your primary estate-planning vehicle.

HOW TO PREPARE A WILL

There are several ways to prepare a will, but to make sure that your will is legal and binding, you should have it prepared or at least reviewed by an attorney who specializes in trusts and estates. The legal requirements vary from state to state but in general are as follows:

• You must be of sound mind and legal age (eighteen in all states except Wyoming, where you must be nineteen).

• Your will should be typewritten. Although handwritten, or *holographic,* wills have been prepared in a number of unusual formats, they are not legal in all states. (And in states where they are recognized, they will certainly be subject to considerable scrutiny.)

• You should appoint an executor to manage your estate, to deal with probate court, and to collect and distribute your assets according to your directions.

• Your will must have precise text that indicates how you want your assets to be distributed.

• You must sign and date the will, or if you are physically unable to sign, you must have an authorized person sign for you.

• Your will must be witnessed and signed by two or more disinterested individuals, meaning people who are not beneficiaries. (But a holographic will does not have to be witnessed.)

One question that many people ask is "If I have set up a trust, do I still need a will?" Absolutely. In most cases, you and your attorney will set up what is known as a *pour-over will* as a companion to your trust. This way you can cover all eventualities such as transferring property that's either best left out of a trust (such as your car or other personal property), that you've just haven't gotten around to placing in your trust, or that you don't currently own but expect to receive. Even if you win the lottery and keel over in excitement, your winnings will be covered by your pour-over will. And of course if you have minor children, you will use your will to name a guardian.

THE HOLOGRAPHIC HALL OF FAME

Although I certainly don't recommend a holographic will as a reliable way to pass on your assets, history is filled with examples of interesting and unusual handwritten documents. In 1948, W. J. Burns wrote "Every-thing-I-possess-at-time-of-death/I will-to-my-son . . ." on the bottom of a chest of drawers. The piece of wood was sawed out and admitted to probate in Los Angeles County. In 1953, Stella Meehan inscribed on her purse, "In case of my Death, there is only one article in the Bag that is of any Interest to anyone except my Bank Book and Insurance. I want the Bureau of Public Assistance to have any money Left. Destroy all papers." Other noteworthy examples

> include a will written in lipstick on a mirror and one written on the cardboard insert from a panty hose package. In all cases the court upheld the documents.

TRUSTS

Today, more and more people are using trusts as a key component of their estate plan. Speaking in the broadest terms, trusts can be set up either under the provisions of your will (called a *testamentary trust*) or as a separate legal entity while you are alive (known as a *living trust*). Since a testamentary trust isn't created until after you've died, it's *irrevocable,* which means it can't be changed. A living trust, on the other hand, becomes effective the moment you sign the document and fund the trust. As a result, a living trust can be either irrevocable or *revocable,* which means that you can change or cancel it while you are alive and thereby retain complete control of your assets. But note that when you die, a revocable trust usually becomes irrevocable (unless the trust specifically provides otherwise).

Depending on your circumstances, your attorney may recommend that you use a combination of these different types of trusts to fit your specific needs. For many, a revocable living trust is the best choice. Later in this chapter we'll get into the details of how revocable living trusts work, but in the meantime, suffice it to say that although a trust costs more and takes more time to set up than a will, it has several significant advantages. First and foremost, it spares your beneficiaries the time and expense (and lack of privacy) of probate. Second, it provides for your potential incapacity. And finally, when combined with other irrevocable trusts that we'll talk about later (primarily a bypass trust), it can significantly reduce your estate tax bill.

In addition to a revocable living trust, you may want to set up an irrevocable trust that provides for a child or someone with a physical or mental disability, a life insurance trust, or a charitable trust that can ensure that your money is used in a way that reflects your values. We discuss charitable trusts more at the end of the chapter.

PROPERTY TITLING AND CONTRACTUAL DEVICES

As we've said, a revocable living trust is a great way to avoid probate. But it isn't the only way. In addition, there are three categories of contractual arrangements that allow you—while you're alive—to arrange to transfer your property at your death. As a result, these methods also sidestep the probate process (although, as we pointed out earlier, *not* estate taxes). As usual, each method has its pros and cons, but used judiciously (and often in combination with a revocable living trust), they can be important components of your estate plan.

1. *Joint tenancy* is a form of ownership that says that if one party in the joint tenancy dies, the entire property—whether it's real estate, a brokerage account, a bank account, a car, or anything else for which you can hold title—goes to the surviving joint tenant. Watch out, though. Although joint tenancy can work smoothly in many cases, it also can open the door to some potentially serious problems. For example, let's say a mother is seventy and her children are in their forties. By putting property in joint tenancy with her children, Mom figures she can avoid probate. But as soon as the children's names are added to the deed, they have immediate access to it. This means they could theoretically take it for themselves and wipe Mom out if they wanted. That tends not to happen if the mother is fifty and the children are twenty-five, but when Mom is ninety and her children, now sixty-five, think she's becoming incompetent, the children can close down the account and transfer the property to their own names.

The other problem with joint tenancy is that if one of the parties gets in trouble, creditors often will try to take what the party owed from an account that shows both names. Suppose that happens in the joint tenancy between the mother and her children: One of the child's creditors comes after the account. Mom can usually get that money back, but not without a great deal of bother. Finally, let's say she puts her eldest son on the account with the expectation that he'll share it with his siblings. When she dies, however, the son has other plans and decides to keep the money for himself. The siblings can file a suit claiming that their mother's intention was to share the property, but the burden is on them to prove it. Since the paperwork includes only the son's name, the other siblings are fighting an uphill battle. So joint tenancy can create plenty of family strife. Be aware of that as you make decisions.

2. Another way we commonly avoid probate is by *designating beneficiaries* on documents ranging from retirement accounts to life insurance policies. No matter what you've specified in your will or trust, these accounts will go to whomever is listed as the beneficiary. As a result, it's vitally important to make sure you know whom you've chosen and to keep those designations updated as your life circumstances change.

3. A third way to avoid probate is to set up *pay-on-death accounts* for bank accounts and certain government securities like U.S. savings bonds. This simply specifies that when you die, the money in your account goes to the person you designate. A similar arrangement, known as transfer on death, or TOD, is available in thirty-seven states for brokerage accounts.

If all your assets pass contractually—whether by joint tenancy, beneficiary designation, or a pay-on-death account—your estate planning may actually be taken care of without your even having to bother with a will (if you don't have underage kids), let alone a trust. But double-check with an attorney to make sure.

BY DESIGN, NOT DEFAULT

Amazingly, most people don't even know whom they've designated on all those forms that ask for beneficiaries. As a result, it's not unheard of for those assets to wind up in the hands of ex-spouses or old girl- or boyfriends. If you've neglected to designate a beneficiary, the assets revert to your estate, which means that they'll be subjected to the time and cost of the probate process.

To make sure that your assets go where you want them to, double-check who's on record as your joint tenant or beneficiary (and when necessary complete a change-of-beneficiary form) for the following:

- Government entitlements (including Social Security)
- Retirement accounts: pension plans, 401(k) or 403(b) plans, IRAs, Keoghs
- Credit union plan accounts
- Disability and life insurance policies (potentially job-related benefits you may have forgotten you even have)
- Bank accounts
- Annuities

To be safe, always name a backup to the primary beneficiary.

POWERS OF ATTORNEY

Because a will doesn't go into effect until your death, it makes no provisions if you become ill or incapacitated. Therefore it's critical for every estate plan to include a *durable power of attorney for finances* as well as a *durable power of attorney for health care* in addition to a will.

A power of attorney gives the person you have appointed (known as your *attorney-in-fact*—but no law degree is required!) the right to conduct broad financial and legal affairs on your behalf. This way, provided of course that you have discussed your wishes ahead of time, you can feel confident that your financial intentions will be carried out. A power of attorney for health care will allow your spouse or other trusted family member or friend to make medical decisions for you, including decisions about life-prolonging care. If you become incapacitated and haven't appointed an attorney-in-fact, the court will appoint a conservator for you, and your wishes may not be honored. Note that it's especially important for same-sex couples to appoint an attorney-in-fact, as a partner may otherwise not be able to act on your behalf.

LIVING WILLS

Not really a will at all, a *living will* is a document in which you can state your wishes about receiving life-sustaining medical treatment if you are terminally ill. Also known as a "directive to physicians," it's frequently incorporated into a durable power of attorney for health care.

In general, a standard power of attorney expires when you become incapacitated. Therefore, if you want your attorney-in-fact (for your finances or for your health care) to retain power when you can no longer act on your own behalf, you'll need to make sure your power of attorney is "durable." (And as an aside, make sure that your durable power of attorney specifically provides for any assets—such as your retirement accounts—that remain outside of your trust.) Also, a durable power of attorney for finances can go into effect immediately or not until you become incapacitated. In the latter case, this is known as a *springing* durable power of attorney.

My Personal Estate-Planning Journey

Now that you've read about many of the basic estate-planning concepts, I'd like to put a more human face on it all by sharing my own recent estate-planning experience. Of course no two estate plans will be exactly alike, but by showing you how the pieces can fit together, I hope to give you a better idea of some of the issues you should talk about among yourselves and with your attorney.

At the time Gary and I moved from Georgia to the Bay Area in 2001, all our estate-planning arrangements were spelled out in our wills and a testamentary trust that was created by that will. That's the way business is done in Georgia, since probate is cheap and fairly easy. All that changed when we relocated to California, a community-property state with court costs substantially higher than those in Georgia. Perhaps partly as a result, in California, like many other states, revocable living trusts have become a standard part of estate planning. Upon learning this, I realized that I should investigate them further. Gary agreed, so I got busy.

I quickly found that by setting up a revocable living trust, not only do Gary and I maintain complete control over our assets, but our kids could ultimately end up with a substantially larger inheritance. Stay with me, and you'll see how this works.

First, I have to transfer our assets into a trust. This means that instead of listing me or Gary as the owner of those assets, the bulk of them will be titled in the name of the trust. And honestly, aside from the hassle involved in all the paperwork, having our assets in or out of a trust makes no difference. Because we're the trustees of our own trust, we retain complete control of all the assets. When I die, my revocable trust becomes irrevocable and splits into two or three different parts.

This is how that part works: For starters, as I've already discussed, you and I and every other American are allowed a certain automatic exemption from estate taxes. In 2003 that amount is $1 million. (It increases after that; see Table 8.1.) Since I'm married, Gary is entitled to an unlimited marital deduction. So I could pass all my assets directly to him tax-free. If I do that, however, my children will have to pay estate taxes on the whole amount when Gary dies. So instead, on my death the amount of my exemption is rolled into what is called a *bypass trust* for our children. Why? If Gary instead got that $1 million personally, it would become part of his estate, which means that our kids would eventually have to pay estate taxes on it—somewhere in the range of 37% to 50% of its value. But by instead putting it into a bypass trust of which Gary is trustee, Gary can use as much of the money as he wants or needs to during his life. Upon his death, since that money isn't technically his, there's no tax to pay. It bypasses any and all taxes, which is how you can remember its name. In case that's a bit confusing, here's a diagram of how much estate tax would be due in 2002 or 2003 without (Figure 8.1) and then with (Figure 8.2) a bypass trust:

Figure 8.1
Estate Tax Due in 2004 without Bypass Trust

SCENARIO I

Combined marital assets of $3 million

Husband's share of assets $1,500,000

FIRST DEATH—HUSBAND DIES

He passes $1,500,00 to his wife,
using the unlimited marital deduction.
No estate tax.

Wife's net estate $3,000,000 ($1,500,000 from husband plus $1,500,000 of her own assets)

SECOND DEATH—WIFE DIES

Wife's net estate ($3,000,000)

Estate tax equals $705,000 due after credit of $555,800. Amount remaining for beneficiaries equals $1,295,000.

Estate tax accounts for 24%
of the couple's assets.

Figure 8.2
Estate Tax Due in 2004 with Bypass Trust

SCENARIO II

Combined marital assets of $3 million

Husband's share of assets
$1,250,000

FIRST DEATH—HUSBAND DIES

Husband passes $1,500,000
(amount equivalent to exemption)
to a nonspouse beneficiary
or to a bypass trust.
No estate tax.

Husband passes $0 to wife
No estate tax.

Bypass trust or nonspouse beneficiary $1,500,000	Wife's net estate $1,500,000 ($0 from husband *plus* $1,500,000 of her own assets)

SECOND DEATH—WIFE DIES

No estate tax.

Wife's net estate ($1,500,000).
No tax after $555,800 credit
cancels tax.

Estate tax equals $0. Total amount remaining for beneficiaries equals $3,000,000. ($1,500,000 from wife plus $1,500,000 from husband)

Estate tax equals $0 (compared with 24% of couple's assets
in Scenario I). Beneficiaries receive $705,000 more with
bypass trust in place.

Had Gary and I remained in Georgia, we could have made a similar arrangement. But since Georgia isn't a community-property state, we would have had to make sure that our assets were titled so that we could each fund a bypass trust on our own.

Now let's get back to trust alternatives. To review, a bypass trust is designed to capture whatever is exempt from tax. Once I've put the full $1 million that doesn't get taxed into a bypass trust, and if my half of our assets happen to be more than $1 million, I can put the rest in a *survivor's trust* for Gary. Since he and I are married, he won't have to pay tax on that money, no matter how much or how little he gets. The unlimited marital deduction is great if you've tied the knot. But it's also led to great inequities, since same-sex partners aren't allowed to marry and are therefore deprived of this considerable financial advantage. (Although you can still put as much as you want into a survivor's trust for someone who is not legally your spouse, it will be taxed.) Remember the story of the ninety-one-year-old bride?

Here's another issue that many families need to consider.

Let's say that I had children from a prior marriage. In this case, instead of leaving part of my assets in a survivor's trust (or in addition to a survivor's trust), I could put them in a *qualified terminable interest property trust,* otherwise known as a *QTIP.* During his lifetime, Gary would get any income produced by the money in the QTIP, as well as access to whatever funds he needed in an emergency. Upon his death, however, that money would go straight to whomever I had designated as beneficiaries. If I had children outside our marriage, this would be a terrific way to guarantee their inheritance without handicapping my husband. A QTIP is available only to married couples and can be a particularly useful tool for blended families.

Like so many others in this situation, I'd obviously need to talk to my spouse about wanting to protect those children from a former marriage. I would expect him to understand and support my desire to look out for my children. It is my belief that in estate planning as in life, you look after your loved ones—all your loved ones. It's that simple.

You may be wondering if a revocable living trust makes sense for couples whose assets fall under the estate tax exemption ($1 million in 2002). The best way to answer that question is to think of the value of a trust on an "age plus money" continuum. The higher your assets and the older you are (or the closer to death), the more value you will receive from setting up a revocable living trust. If you're eighty years old and have a $300,000 estate, you may want a revocable living trust to take care of your potential incapacity and to avoid probate—even though you won't incur estate taxes. If you're only forty years old with a $300,000 estate, a trust may not seem as important or worth the money. If you are unsure where you fit in, it is best to consult with an experienced estate-planning attorney.

Again, the whole point of having a trust (along with providing for your potential incapacity) is to avoid probate and minimize the tax hit to your estate, thereby maximizing the value of what you leave behind. But you won't avoid probate if you don't transfer assets into your trust once it's set up. Unless you retitle all your assets, you've basically paid a lot of money for a worthless document. The change of ownership doesn't really change a thing when it comes to how you'll live or conduct business. The money and property that you place in your trust remain yours to do with as you please as long as you're alive. But it will make all the difference in the world to those who survive you—provided you do it right. And the biggest mistake that people make is not changing over all those registrations, even after they've gone to the trouble to set everything else up perfectly. Remember the story of Marcus's dad earlier in this chapter?

HELP WITH THE TERMINOLOGY

Confused about all these terms and labels? Why wouldn't you be? "My kids aren't in here!" exclaimed my friend Anna after reading through the new estate plan she'd drawn up with the help of an attorney upon her remarriage. It turns out that in the estate-planning world, your children as well as your other descendants are collectively referred to as your "issue." Who knew?

If you think that's bad, you're going to love this next part: Estate-planning lawyers don't even agree on what a lot of the terms they use every day actually mean. They use different names for the same thing, and the same names for different things. A bypass trust, for example, is also known as a credit shelter trust. If you have a bypass trust and a survivor's trust, it'll often be referred to as an AB trust. But which is A and which is B? That depends on whom you talk to. At least most people agree that the C in an ABC trust is the QTIP.

To make sure everyone's on the same page when it comes time to talk about your estate plan, we prepared a glossary of terms, which appears in Appendix C.

Chuck's Two Cents: Deciding How Much to Leave Your Kids

Deciding how much to leave your kids is a real dilemma. On the one hand, the desire to help your kids never goes away, even when they're grown. Being able to offer financial help for graduate school or a first home is very rewarding. And when it comes to estate planning, it's tempting to leave them as well off as possible. On the other hand, you don't want an inheritance to rob your children of their incentive. You may want to provide for them so that they never have to worry about money, but with that comes the danger of taking away their initiative. I know that I personally want my children to experience the immense satisfaction that comes from hard work and making it on their own.

Of course, there is no easy answer. Your answer will depend on your circumstances and on your kids. To my mind, you need to try to find an amount that will be meaningful to your kids but that won't make a paycheck meaningless—an amount that will help them do something but that won't allow them to do nothing.

WHAT'S IN, WHAT'S OUT

In the end, you could argue that it all boils down to the details. Here's what typically should be included in your trust:

- Investment accounts
- Stocks
- Bonds
- Real estate
- Bank accounts
- Limited partnerships

. . . and what can't or shouldn't:

- Beneficiary accounts such as life insurance, annuities, and retirement accounts (the ownership of a retirement account cannot be legally transferred to a trust)
- Personal property such as jewelry, antiques, furniture, and cars

---

Making *Your* Plan

By now I hope you have a notion of how all this works. So now it's your turn. In this section, we'll walk you through the first steps of creating your own estate plan.

TAKING STOCK

The only way to make sure your wishes are clear to the attorney you appoint (and perhaps to other family members) is to explain them thoroughly and completely. This means you'll want to come to that initial appointment or meeting as prepared as possible, with a checklist in hand of all you need to cover. Don't assume that you'll remember everything off the top of your head. If you're like me, you always think of that one critical question you forgot to ask as you're driving home. Just as with a doctor's visit, it's best to come armed with a list of all questions you want to ask and issues you want to discuss.

When dealing with lawyers, this type of organization not only saves time, it saves money, as it cuts down on billable hours. And it's the only way I know to make sure you cover all your bases. So before you visit your attorney, do your homework. Make sure you're prepared with complete information about your family, a complete list of your assets and liabilities (see Worksheet 8.1), and details of how your property is titled and vested—for example, your 401(k) plan, the origins of your property (important for community-property states), and the details of any existing trusts. When you meet with your attorney, also bring copies of your deeds, your prenuptial agreement, documents for any trusts of which you're the beneficiary, and any partnership agreements. Before you get down to detailed planning, you also should have a general notion of where you want your assets to go.

Start by listing all your assets at their current market value (the price you could sell the asset for today, rather than the price you paid for it). This list should include your investment holdings, all your retirement plans, and the value of any life insurance policies in which you have incidence of ownership. Also include real estate and significant pieces of art or other collectibles. Be sure to note whether you own the property alone, or whether the title to that asset is held in joint tenancy, as community property, or in some other way. Also make a list of your personal effects such as cars, jewelry, and furniture. Finally, make a separate list of any potential future assets, such as an inheritance.

Next you'll want to calculate your liabilities: everything you owe, including the mortgage on your home(s), the total balance on your credit cards, and any other debt you might have.

To get a rough idea of the value of your estate, which can affect everything from how you set up your estate plan to your tax strategy, you can subtract what you owe (your total liabilities) from what you own (your total assets). This will give you an estimate of your net worth.

Worksheet 8.1
Estate-Planning Worksheet

Assets	Value	Liabilities	Value
Real Estate		Mortgages	
Home	$_____	Mortgage 1	$_____
Vacation/property	$_____	Mortgage 2	$_____
Rental property	$_____	Home equity line	$_____
Land	$_____		
Bank Accounts		Loans and Debts	
CDs	$_____	Credit card debt	$_____
Savings	$_____	Unsecured credit	$_____
Money market	$_____	Life insurance loan	$_____
Checking	$_____		
Retirement Accounts		Total Liabilities	$_____
IRA	$_____		
Roth IRA	$_____		
Keogh	$_____		
SEP	$_____		
401(k)	$_____	Net Taxable Estate	
Investment Accounts			
Stock brokerage	$_____	(Total Assets – Total Liabilities)	
Mutual funds	$_____		
Stocks in certificate form	$_____	$_____	
Bonds	$_____		
Annuities	$_____		
Money market	$_____		
Business Ownership Interest			
Sole proprietorship	$_____		
Partnership	$_____		
C corporation	$_____		
S corporation	$_____		
Limited liability company	$_____		
Personal Property			
Autos	$_____		
Home furnishings	$_____		
Jewelry	$_____		
Art	$_____		
Life Insurance Policies			
Term	$_____		
Group	$_____		
Whole	$_____		
Universal	$_____		
Survivorship	$_____		
Other	$_____		
Total Assets	$_____		

Last, you'll want to figure out in broad strokes where you want the money to go. Ask yourself whether you want to give your money to your family, your friends, or a specific charity. It's really that simple, although if you wish, you have lots of room to be creative. After all, this doesn't have to be an all-or-nothing decision. You can generously support your favorite charities (receiving some sizable tax benefits in the process) as well as create an inheritance for your loved ones.

CHOOSING AN ATTORNEY

Now it's time to find the best estate-planning attorney you can. Let me reiterate that it's a big mistake to try to draw up your own will and/or trust. For starters, despite the proliferation of estate-planning kits, this is not a case of one-size-fits-all. And even if you could find a boilerplate kit that fit all your needs, the whole business of estate taxation is so densely complex that plenty of accountants won't even touch it. It's no wonder then that those who try to go it alone tend to make really bad choices without even knowing it. "All too often people will find a clause that sounds neat, and they stick it in, and it may have horribly adverse tax consequences that they didn't think about or of which they are not aware," says estate-planning attorney and law professor Michael Ferguson.

Remember, you get what you pay for. When it comes to estate planning, your beneficiaries could end up with a whole lot of nothing (or at least a whole lot less than they would have) if you cut corners or pinch pennies. I can't say this too many times: A good attorney is absolutely critical.

WHAT'S THIS GOING TO COST?

Depending on where you live, a simple will might cost you $200 to $500 in attorney's fees. Setting up a revocable living trust can cost five to ten times more, depending on the complexity of your estate. Some attorneys charge by the hour, others on a fixed-fee basis. Since the former will probably have you sweating as you watch the minutes and hours tick by, the latter may be preferable, especially since you'll know exactly what it will cost you right from the start.

You can begin your search for an attorney by asking for a recommendation from a trusted friend. You might also want to check with the American College of Trust and Estate Counsel. Headquartered in Los Angeles, this nonprofit professional association has a membership of approximately twenty-seven hundred estate-planning specialists across the country, all of whom are selected on the basis of their professional reputation. Their public website, www.actec. org, includes a list of members and is a great way to find a reputable lawyer in your area. Many state bars certify estate-planning specialists and have websites that will identify them. The American Bar Association has a standing committee on specialization and a website with links to the state websites.

Once you've found an experienced attorney, make sure he or she is open to answering any and all questions in plain, simple English. Avoid anyone who seems too busy to bother or who indulges too freely in legal-speak that you can't understand. Finally, you'll want to find someone who's sympathetic and sensitive. While creating an estate plan won't be the easiest thing you'll ever do, your loved ones will probably have to speak to the very person you're selecting at one of the worst times of their lives: after you have died. If you don't think they'll be able to talk comfortably to the attorney you're considering during that most trying time, find someone else to write up your document.

PURELY PERSONAL

Once you've hammered out the costs, you need to deal with the really important stuff: how the people in your life fit into this equation—starting with your children.

Providing for your children. Designating a guardian for your minor children may be one of the toughest challenges you'll face in this whole process. One couple I know delayed signing their will for thirteen years because they couldn't come to an agreement on whether his family or hers would have custody of their children should they both die at the same time. Once the kids came of age and guardians were no longer an issue, they finalized the long-overdue document.

When Gary and I revamped our estate plan upon relocating to northern California, we experienced firsthand how difficult this decision is. We were fortunate to have several good choices for a guardian, but choosing among them seemed impossible. After many failed attempts at making a decision, we finally turned to our estate-planning attorney, who counseled us, "Don't worry about what your kids are going to need five or ten years down the line. Instead, think about which family is best suited to take care of them right now." He suggested that we ask ourselves the following:

- Does the prospective guardian share your values?
- How intimately does this person know you and your family?
- How many children does the prospective guardian already have? Would he or she be able to care for others?
- What if the unthinkable happened, and the guardian's spouse should die? Would he or she still be able to care for your children?
- Where does the guardian live? Do you want your children to be uprooted from their school and familiar environment? You may not mind moving a three-year-old across the country to live with your sister in New York, but you're sure not going to want to do that to somebody who's in junior high or high school and has an established network of friends. So your choice of guardian may change as your children age, or if circumstances change for the family you've selected.

With that, our perspective cleared, and this difficult decision proved much easier. In three or five years we'll revisit the question again to see if our decision still stands. And should something happen to change our minds in the meantime, we can always change our will.

Once you've selected who would take care of your children in the event of your death, you'll have to determine when they would best profit from receiving part or all of your estate. Once you're gone, your money can provide the kind of safety net you would have provided while alive. On the other hand, give them too much too early, and you risk taking away their incentive to perform or produce on their own. So this decision depends as much on your kids as it does on your own sense of what life has in store for them. Some people who feel that their kids are very mature stipulate that they can have the money at eighteen, but a more common age is thirty. Others delay it even further. One woman we know specified that her son couldn't get his inheritance until he was sixty-five! He was a spendthrift, and his mother knew he would need the money for his retirement. My favorite story involves the twice-divorced mother of a seven-year-old girl who, when asked by her estate-planning attorney when her daughter should get the money, promptly responded "half at thirty-five and half at forty-five." "Why those ages?" asked the attorney. "I want my daughter to have half for her first marriage and half for her second," the woman replied.

What you must consider next is difficult, if not unthinkable: whom you want to inherit your estate should your kids (or whomever else you've designated as your beneficiary) predecease you. Although this is highly unlikely, it is a contingency for which you should plan. If it were to happen, would you want your parents, your siblings, your friends, or the causes you care about to inherit your estate?

Attorneys-in-fact. As we've already indicated, you should appoint the people you know best as your attorneys-in-fact both for your finances and for your health care. While the court will appoint someone (known as a conservator) for you if you've neglected to do it yourself, those proceedings are time-consuming, and worse yet, you'll have no say in who holds your life—or life savings—in his or her hands.

If you have a revocable living trust, your successor trustee will take responsibility for your assets. But it can still be useful or necessary to have an attorney-in-fact who can transact business outside of the trust (for example, for your retirement account, bank account, Social Security payments, health insurance claims, and the like). The trustee of your trust will have no legal authority over these assets.

Executor and trustee. You also need to choose an *executor* (or *personal representative,* as it's called in several states) for your will, and a *trustee* if you have a trust. These offices entail significant responsibilities, so you'll want to make sure the individuals you approach understand exactly what's involved before they say yes. You'll also want to feel very confident that they can and will handle the responsibility well.

The executor of a will has two primary tasks—plus a lot of miscellaneous chores. The hardest, by far, involves closing up someone's house after he or she dies. Not only is the job physically demanding, it's emotionally wrenching. Second, he or she needs to hire a competent attorney to handle the legal details according to the deceased's wishes. In addition, the executor needs to compile all the assets, pay any bills, and oversee the distribution of assets. Either way, an executor with financial savvy can make a world of difference.

A trustee's job involves all that and more. It doesn't stop with the distribution of assets—it involves managing the assets on an ongoing basis and balancing the needs of the current beneficiaries with the needs of future beneficiaries. The job lasts as long as the trust does—which potentially makes it a lifelong obligation.

That's why many people prefer corporate trustees whose business it is to manage trusts. Although this works well in many cases, there are potential problems. For example, you can't designate a particular individual when opting for a corporate trustee; you have to designate a firm. Down the road, should your heirs feel that your estate is being mismanaged, it may be difficult for them to make a change since your trust will have automatically become irrevocable upon your death. It is also possible that with all the business mergers and acquisitions, the company whose trustee department you choose today may someday get swallowed up by another corporation.

One solution is to designate an individual trustee (again, a financially savvy one if possible) from your personal circle, then give that person the authority and the means to hire a financial advisor (who can be replaced if need be) to manage your estate. So whom should you choose as trustee? Frequently choosing one of your children or some other beneficiary is the best idea. This person will have everything to gain by handling your affairs as efficiently (both in terms of time and money) as possible. If you have more than one child, naming them all trustees can invite trouble. By the time they're adults, they often have different lives and needs, which can open the door to conflict. There may also be rifts between siblings that can further complicate things. You'll also want to designate first and second alternate trustees, should the original trustee die or become unable to perform the task.

To minimize hard feelings or misunderstandings, spell out the compensation for both the executor and trustee in your will and/or trust. The onetime fee for an executor is usually in the range of 2% to 3% of the estate. The annual fee for an institutional trustee is about 0.75% to 1.5% of the estate and approximately 0.25% to 0.75% for an individual, depending on the size of the estate.

FILE THIS!

Whoever you choose as executor or trustee will need to know where all your paperwork is. You're going to want to make sure the papers are safe and kept together in one place, preferably in a fireproof box at home or in a safe-deposit box at a bank. If you opt for the latter, your executor or one of your beneficiaries should have a key and be listed as a signer on the box. Otherwise, there will be no way of getting your papers after you die.

You'll want to assemble the following documents:

• Your will
• Any trusts
• An updated list of your assets
• A letter that spells out who gets your personal effects: your jewelry, valuable furniture, books, china, artwork, and so on
  • Insurance policies
  • Powers of attorney
  • Real estate deeds
• Partnerships or interests in limited liability companies (LLCs)
  • Titles to everything else you own, such as your car
  • Auto registrations
  • Patents, trademarks, or other royalty or rental income
  • Stock certificates
  • Savings bonds
  • Loan documents
  • Bank account numbers
  • Military discharge papers for veterans' benefits
  • Citizenship papers/birth and marriage certificates
  • Social Security information

Note: Should you opt to keep your papers in a safe-deposit box, be aware that if the fees are not paid for two years in a row—either before or after your death—the box can be drilled open and all property removed by the bank. Any assets will go to the state.

Your four-legged friend. Last (but perhaps not least), there's your trustworthy furry friend. All too often people neglect to provide for their pets, assuming that family members or friends will take them. But if you don't talk to those people and work it out beforehand, your beloved buddy could well end up in an animal shelter. Should your human loved ones be unwilling or unable to care for your pets, in some states you can set up a trust for the care of your pet. Alternatively, you can find an animal protection program like the SPCA that, for a specified sum payable upon your death, will either take care of your animal for the rest of its life or find it a new home. To learn what's available in your community, check with your vet, the local chapter of the Humane Society, the SPCA, or other nonprofit humane shelters in your area.

The Right Stuff

You've done it! Even if you haven't lifted a finger yet, simply taking the steps to understand this whole business is a major achievement. The rest simply involves implementing your plan. This is also the time to talk about your decisions with your beneficiaries and key family members once you've gotten them down on paper. In short, you'll want to explain the terms of your will and/or trust. In doing this, you can also share your hopes, your values, and your love for them. In addition, you can help protect them against any disconcerting surprises later on should your plan differ from what they might expect. If you're leaving a child with special needs more than you're leaving his siblings, in order to cover the cost of care, talking about that will help them understand your reasoning and help prevent resentment. Finally, by sharing your own plans, you can help encourage your loved ones to make theirs.

My colleague's father, RT, did exactly that with his adult children and their spouses. Calling a family meeting, he took one couple at a time into his home office and explained the estate-planning decisions that he and his wife had made. He didn't get into the details of who would be left what, and he never mentioned any dollar figures. Instead, he focused on strategy. For example, he would say: "We're going to set aside this percentage to be placed in a trust fund for your children [his grandchildren]." Then he would explain the tax advantages of doing it that way. He even drew a little flowchart, with a picture of a house that said "Mom and Dad" at the top of a page and different arrows showing where the money would flow and why.

His goal? To demystify his estate plan and to show his children and their spouses how they could potentially handle their own estate planning. That was nine years ago. Since then he's amended his estate plan as needed to take advantage of changes in the estate tax law, periodically updating his adult children. "He doesn't tell you what you should do at all," says his daughter Susan. "He just explains what he's done and why."

RT had never been particularly financially minded. So why was he so diligent about his own estate planning and about helping his offspring handle theirs? In the mid-1980s, RT's mother-in-law realized that she needed help protecting the Pennsylvania farm that had been in her family for sixty years. She didn't want it to be sold off to developers after her death. Since her husband and eldest son had passed away, she turned to RT—the oldest male in the family. Although RT wasn't particularly savvy about finances or estate planning, he helped his mother-in-law identify both how she wanted the land preserved and the steps she needed to take (including hiring an estate-planning attorney).

Realizing that his own mother also owned a family farm that would be passed down upon her death, RT next turned his attention to her. "You'll do what's best," she responded. "You kids know what I want." But in fact her heirs didn't know; the issue had never been discussed. And to complicate things, they all had their own ideas about how the farm should be treated.

RT's mother knew that she wanted the farm to remain intact, but she hadn't spoken up—or even thought about how she could make that happen. Getting her to address the matter wasn't easy. Although she was remarkably peaceful about the notion of her own passing, she was a very private individual and felt uncomfortable discussing her estate plan. For her, it was easier to face death than to talk about money.

Fortunately, RT was able to convince his mother that she wouldn't have to reveal any details to her children. She would, however, have to come to terms with how she wanted to protect the farm, develop a legally viable plan, and make her wishes clear. In addition, with advance planning she could reduce the taxes on her estate. With her son's support and the advice of an estate-planning attorney, she arranged to have the farm donated to a conservancy, thereby protecting the land. She also spelled out that a specific portion of the land could be sold for development. In this way she protected her land, provided for her children, and avoided a lot of potential conflict.

DON'T TOUCH THAT!

Your children, even grown ones, may be quite resistant to talking to you about your estate plans. In many cases, the idea of your passing away bothers them more than it bothers you. In addition, you may not realize how much of an emotional cost is inherent in inheriting money. Some people feel guilty about the windfall, others undeserving.

Because of this, you can do as much damage by insisting kids discuss something they don't want to discuss as you can by not discussing it at all. When you find your moment, however, bringing up the subject in terms of your dreams for them—and the kind of lives they see for themselves—focuses attention where it belongs: on life rather than death.

On the flip side, inheritance is not something to be wielded as a threat, something that can be taken away if your heirs don't behave the way you want them to. Estate planning, in the truest sense, is a way to extend a helping hand beyond the grave—to give assistance, to preserve your life's work, and where it's needed, to protect people from themselves. It's best to look at your estate planning and what you pass along as a token of love and esteem. You should feel free to convey your visions to your heirs, but only after you've heard and accepted the visions they have for themselves.

Things Change

People freeze when they think about estate planning. Sensing that they have a single shot to make plans that will last forever, they become immobilized. Unless you're setting up an irrevocable trust, however, that's simply not true. Indeed, not only will you get the chance to make any changes you want or need, you should also plan to revisit your will or trust every three to five years, or whenever you make some major change such as:

- Marriage
- Divorce
- Birth of a child or grandchild
- Loss of a spouse (or death of any other known beneficiary)
- Loss of a parent (or someone else who has depended on you financially)
- Moving to another state (since laws vary from state to state)

You'll also need to reconsider your estate plan whenever tax law changes in a major way, which tends to happen about every ten or so years. Your attorney or accountant will stay current with all changes, and you will certainly hear about major changes to the tax laws in the news.

Because most of us can expect major changes in our lives, when you are drafting a will or a revocable or irrevocable trust, you want your attorney to build in as much flexibility as possible. For example, instead of giving a precise dollar figure for your bypass trust, your attorney can stipulate "the maximum allowable by law." Also, if you have a pour-over will, it will cover any newly acquired assets.

EARLY-BIRD ALERT

If your revocable living trust (or will with testamentary trust) was drafted before 1990, you should probably have an estate-planning attorney review it. In the last ten years or so, as attorneys have had more experience with the way revocable living trusts work when people die, they've found ways to fine-tune the language and make the documents much more flexible.

Perhaps even more significant are changes to tax law. As an extreme example, if the language in your trust puts your entire personal exemption in a bypass trust for your children, you could be unwittingly depriving your spouse of any inheritance at all. Let's say that your estate is equal to $2 million. When you wrote your trust in 1995, you stipulated that your children would receive the "maximum exemption" amount. Back then this was $600,000, leaving $1,400,000 for your spouse. In 2004, however, the exemption moved to $1.5 million, so in that year your spouse would receive only $500,000. In 2006 he or she would get nothing. And in 2010, when there will be no tax (and therefore no exemption), your entire estate would go to your spouse, with your children receiving nothing. In other words, with tax law in such a state of flux, you could get caught on either side.

Why Wait?

We want to close this discussion with one last notion. Instead of waiting until you die, you can give a portion of your assets to your family and friends while you're still alive and actually see what a difference you're making. As we've already said, you can give up to $11,000 a year to whomever (and however many people) you want, free of tax. These under-$11,000 annual donations aren't counted against either your lifetime gift exclusion or your estate-tax exclusion. Neither are any payments for someone's education or medical expenses, as long as you send the money straight to the institution rather than to the individual accruing the bills.

One caveat: Gifting doesn't get the stepped-up basis benefit that accompanies your death. Remember that if you will someone $10,000 worth of stock, even if you paid just $100 for it, your heir will not have to pay capital gains tax on that stock. He or she will be able to use the readjusted cost basis and pay capital gains tax only on any gain that is earned after he or she owns the stock. Not so with gifting. If you give someone $10,000 worth of stock that you paid $100 for, he or she will have to pay a capital gains tax on the $9,900 you made on the stock. So it may be better to give them cash.

The important thing is to consider giving now if you're in the financial position to do so, which is exactly what one former army war nurse in her eighties did. After consulting with an estate-planning attorney with her nieces at her side, she realized that she would probably never go through all her money while she was alive, and that she'd rather start doling it out now. So in addition to setting up a special needs trust for a nephew with a disability, she's begun giving each of her nieces and nephews $10,000 a year. Avoiding some taxes and seeing her money's impact doubles her pleasure.

CUSTODIAL ACCOUNTS

A custodial account is simply an account that is set up and managed by an adult for the benefit of a minor. Because custodial accounts are governed by either the Uniform Transfers to Minors Act or the Uniform Gifts to Minors Act (depending on your state), they do not require special legal documents. This can make them a simple and inexpensive way to remove assets from your taxable estate and at the same time provide for the young people you care about most.

Before you plunge ahead, though, realize that if the donor of the gift is the custodian (for example, if you gift assets to your child and you are also the custodian for their account), the IRS generally maintains that the value of the custodial account is part of your estate. On the other hand, if your parents (your child's grandparents) gift money to your child and you are the custodian of the account, that money is removed from your parents' estate. As an aside, one of the reasons that the new 529 college savings accounts (which we discuss in detail in Chapter 6) are so attractive is that even though you stay in control of the assets, they are removed from your estate.

Another potential drawback of a custodial account is that the gift is irrevocable and becomes the child's sole property when he or she reaches the age of majority. As the custodian of your child's or grandchild's account, you manage the assets until that time. Once he or she turns either eighteen or twenty-one, however, you are required by law to turn the assets over to the child, at which point you can only hope that he or she will manage and spend the money responsibly. For more details about custodial accounts, as well as a discussion of other education accounts, see Chapter 6.

CHARITABLE GIVING

In addition to giving money to those who are close to you while you're still alive, you may want to help finance those causes close to your heart. The simplest way to do this is to make an outright gift. Provided that your charity is IRS-approved, you can give as much as you want without incurring estate taxes. Not only are the assets removed from your taxable estate, but the gift can also create a deduction for your current-year income taxes.

Besides an outright gift, you can also set up a charitable trust as part of your estate. There are a couple of different ways to go here, both of which provide distinct benefits not only to the charity but also to your estate.

First, you can set up what is known as a *charitable remainder trust*. In this type of trust you will receive income from the trust based on IRS formulas for a specified amount of time. An alternative is to establish a *charitable lead trust*, which in some ways is the mirror image of the charitable remainder trust. In this case, your charity will receive income from the assets you've donated for a specified amount of time, after which time the assets go to your named beneficiaries.

You should consult with your estate-planning attorney about the tax consequences and other relevant issues before making a decision about which trust to use. Each of them is a fine way to give to charities.

Something to Talk About

• *What legacy do you hope to leave for your children and others?*

• *Do you have a will? If not, do you really want your assets to be distributed according to your state's intestate laws?*

• *Do you or your parents need a trust, or is a will sufficient?*

• *How can you talk to your parents to make sure their estate is in order?*

• *If you have established a trust, have all your assets been properly signed over to it?*

• *Have you done what you can to avoid probate and unnecessary estate taxes?*

• *If you have minor children, have you appointed a guardian for them?*

• *Whom do you want to designate as your executor, trustee, and attorney-in-fact?*

• *How do recent changes in tax law affect you or the rest of your family? Do you need to update your trust or will?*

• *What dreams do your adult children harbor? How could an inheritance help them realize those dreams?*

• *Could your children become financially dependent or devoid of their own ambition if you left them money? How can you make sure that doesn't happen?*

• *At what point will your kids be responsible enough to manage an inheritance on their own?*

• *Are there special people in your life you would like to support with a monetary gift?*

• Do you want to pass on a portion of your wealth now or all of it when you die?

• Do you have a favorite charity you'd like to support, now or later?

• Are you so successful that your parents should consider leaving your share of their inheritance to your siblings or other family members instead?

• How can you encourage all your family and friends to discuss and draw up their own estate plans if they keep putting it off?

9

Expect the Unexpected
(and Protect Your Finances)

All families face unanticipated upheavals—everything from illness and job setbacks to death and divorce. Consider, for a moment, that the average age of widowhood in the United States is fifty-six years old. The country's divorce rate continues to top 50%. As we entered an economic recession in 2001, more than a million workers were suddenly laid off, and small businesses across the country were forced to shut their doors.

When it comes to dealing with the unexpected, my family is no exception. I was nine years old when my parents divorced. Of course at that age I had no way of knowing about the financial implications of divorce. But one thing I learned is that life doesn't always go the way you would like it to.

In 2001 my father-in-law, Edwin, died unexpectedly. Although Gary's mother and her three sons miss Ed tremendously, this closely knit family had the benefit of being prepared—at least financially. Ed's estate plan was in order, he had taken out proper insurance, and he had set up their portfolio to provide adequate income. So in many ways we were as prepared as a family can be. Certainly nothing can spare a family from the emotional trauma of losing a loved one, but as we pulled together after Ed's death, we learned first-hand the benefit of advance preparation.

Being prepared for the unexpected means several things. As we've stressed earlier in this book, part of your safety net involves having enough liquid assets to cover at least two to six months of living expenses. Another crucial component involves being adequately insured. In this chapter we discuss health, life, long-term care, and disability insurance and help you determine how much coverage you should have. If you're already up to speed, you may want to skim or even skip over this basic information, but we'll also address the less obvious kind of protection that money can't buy: educating yourself about your family's finances and talking openly with the rest of your family members so that you know that everyone else is prepared as well. From the dissolution of a marriage to (ironically enough) a financial windfall, unless you've taken the appropriate steps, you may find yourself vulnerable. Ditto if you focus exclusively on building your wealth but neglect to insure that wealth against unanticipated events.

If you're like most of us, you don't want to think about this sub-

FULL PROTECTION

Although we don't cover homeowner's or auto insurance in this book, both are essential parts of your complete insurance package. Another important but frequently overlooked type of insurance is an *umbrella policy* that extends your liability protection beyond the coverage provided by your other policies. If you're in a car accident or someone slips and falls on your property, this extremely inexpensive coverage could save your day—and your nest egg. Where to buy coverage? In general, it's best to go to the same company that provides your homeowner's insurance. That way you can be sure that the coverage will dovetail with what you already have.

ject because it's just so unpleasant. Unfortunately, though, that denial can cost—emotionally and financially. Remember, by definition, unexpected things happen out of the blue. Clearly, we can't control the future, and we can't protect ourselves against all eventualities, but we can take the necessary steps to be as prepared as possible. By making sure that all those "what if" and "just in case" arrangements are in place, you, your spouse, and your parents can give yourselves the peace of mind that comes from knowing that you're in the best possible position to accept life as it comes.

To Your Good Health!

Paying for insurance each month can seem like a complete waste—until you need it. Then the word *godsend* comes to mind. In this time of escalating health care costs, however, too many families are literally "just one serious illness away from financial collapse," says Harvard law professor Elizabeth Warren, advisor to the National Bankruptcy Review Commission and one of the authors of a 2001 study published in *Norton's Bankruptcy Advisor*. "The difference between what we saw forty years ago and what we see today is that forty years ago, when families were hit by a modest medical problem, they still had flexibility in their budget. Today, families are carrying so much more consumer debt that even a modest medical bill can put them over the edge financially, and they end up in collapse." Indeed, the study found that illness is a factor in nearly half of this country's more than one million yearly bankruptcies.

Surprisingly, these bankruptcy filings involve not people who lack health insurance but rather middle-class families with inadequate coverage. So to start, I'm going to ask you just one question: Is your policy—as well as that of your adult children or parents—up to snuff? With costs ranging from $13,500 for a week's hospital stay to $8,500 a month for rehabilitation, an illness or accident could end up swamping your whole family's future, turning hard luck and hard times into a full-fledged personal and financial disaster.

Ask any health care professional around—from a surgeon to a physical therapist—and he or she will likely tell you that the health care they can provide is increasingly being dictated by bean-counters instead of medical personnel (or even medical necessity). So it's critical to have as many beans in your pocket as possible—and the right beans at that.

Whether you're buying health insurance for the first time or are simply reexamining your policy to make sure it will get the job done, it's worth reviewing a few basics.

HEALTH INSURANCE: A BRIEF PRIMER

Health insurance plans come in a variety of shapes and sizes. Before exploring the specifics of each, however, you first have to discuss whether you and/or your loved ones prefer managed care (for which you'll pay less money in return for fewer choices) or a fee-for-service policy (in which you'll pay more for the right to see the health care professional or doctor you want). In a sense, it's a little like buying a car. Before you can debate the merits of a sedan versus a sports car, you must determine whether you're looking for fuel economy or power. Once you've made the overarching decision of managed care versus a fee-for-service policy, your search automatically narrows.

Managed care—usually the most affordable kind of medical insurance and the kind offered by most employers—basically provides you with a group of doctors affiliated with a few specified hospitals. Within this basic construct, you have a few alternatives.

• HMOs—short for health maintenance organizations—cut costs (theirs and yours) by funneling all care through primary care physicians who, in addition to overseeing your health, act as gate-keepers to the pricier specialists. Without your primary care doctor's authorization, either you don't get that specialized treatment or you pay for it yourself. This requirement, along with the often-large numbers of members and brief office visits, can make you feel like you're part of the assembly line process in Charlie Chaplin's

Modern Times. The upside: lower premiums (the cost of the insurance), small copays (the amount you pay each time you receive care—usually $5 to $15) instead of deductibles (the amount you would have to pay before your insurance paid benefits), often better preventive care, and frequently less paperwork.

• POSs—short for point-of-service HMOs—allow you to venture outside the HMO network for specialized care without prior authorization from your primary care physician. While this rapidly growing type of insurance doesn't cover the entire cost, a POS will cover a percentage—usually from 50% to 80%—of the cost it deems usual and customary. (I'll talk about this last sticking point in the section on fee-for-service policies.)

• PPOs—short for preferred provider organizations—permit you to use their network of doctors or hospitals or anyone else you choose without a referral. If you use their doctors, they reimburse more of the expenses than if you go out of network. Either way, you're going to pay a higher premium for the right to choose.

Fee-for-service policies, typically not available through group plans, allow you to go to whatever hospital you like and see the primary care physician or specialist of choice whenever you like. You pay for this privilege, however. Monthly premiums are higher, and the insurance pays benefits only once you've met your yearly deductible. Then it pays for 70% to 80%—not of the bill, mind you, but of the amount the insurance company deems reasonable (or to use their term, "usual and customary").

So what's usual and customary? That's the catch. (Anyone not in an HMO, or whose entire family including parents isn't part of an HMO, needs to listen up!) Let's say you have $1,200 in doctor bills after a minor car accident. For argument's sake, let's assume you've already paid $300 toward your $500 deductible that year. You figure that you'll have to put out another $200 to reach the deductible, plus 20%—or $200—of the remaining doctor's bill ($1,200 minus $200 equals $1,000; 20% of $1,000 is $200). But wait! Even though you live in San Francisco or New York, where costs are considerably higher than they are in other parts of the country, your insurance company has decided that the "reasonable" cost of the care you received is $500 less than what you spent—that is, it's worth only $700. In this case, instead of getting reimbursed for 80% of $1,200, you'll get 80% of $700 ($560), after you've paid your entire deductible. In this example you'll collect only the difference between $560 and $200, or $360! You're out of pocket for $840, or more than two-thirds of the bill.

NO LAPSES

Leaving a job? Take your health insurance with you, at least until you can arrange for other coverage, either through your new company or through an individual plan. Legislation enacted in 1986 and commonly referred to as COBRA (Consolidated Omnibus Budget Reconciliation Act) can help make sure you don't wind up without health insurance coverage for even a day. But don't let this lull you into a false sense of security. You will be covered, but it's pricey—so pricey that many who've lost their jobs can't afford it. In any case, you should start looking for a new health insurance policy just as soon as you can. Unless Social Security considers you to be disabled, the maximum continuation coverage under COBRA is eighteen months.

WHERE MEDICARE AND MEDIGAP COME IN

If you or your parents are sixty-five or older (or if you're disabled and unable to work), Medicare—federally funded health insurance—is available. Indeed, anyone receiving Social Security is automatically sent a Medicare card when they turn sixty-five. Anyone not receiving Social Security should apply for Medicare three months before their sixty-fifth birthday to make sure they don't miss the enrollment period.

Medicare comes in two distinct parts:

• Part A covers hospitalization up to sixty days per benefit period once you've met the deductible. It is free to anyone who has forty or more quarters of Medicare-covered employment. (In 2002 you'll have to pay a monthly premium ranging from $175 to $319 if you or your spouse haven't met this requirement.) Sounds pretty good, right? Well, yes—and no. The deductible can be pretty steep ($812 in 2002). Should you wind up in the hospital for more than sixty days, you'll have to pay $203 a day for the next month, and double that for the following two. After 150 days it's all on you. And the deductible isn't just a once-a-year expense. If you're hospitalized seventeen times, you'll have to pay seventeen deductibles.

• Part B is the medical insurance component. Premiums of about $50 a month are subtracted from your Social Security (or railroad retirement or civil service retirement) check. Or you'll receive a bill for your premium every three months, if you don't happen to get any of these payments. The annual deductible is just $100. After that, you pay 20% of your medical bills from doctor fees to diagnostic tests. They pay the rest.

So far so good. But Medicare doesn't cover everything by a long shot. Preventive care (including routine physical exams), dental care, eyeglasses, hearing aids, and prescriptions are not covered. Those costs can mount up, as can that 20% you're responsible for. Also, if your doctor doesn't assign a particular service to Medicare, you may have to pay the entire charge.

Enter Medigap, insurance sold privately that's designed to bridge the gap between your expenses and what Medicare covers. How much you pay depends on how comprehensive you want that supplemental insurance to be. Remember that shopping for a Medigap plan is just like shopping for any other insurance plan—you need to make sure you're buying from a top-rated company that will deliver exactly what you need. So don't miss the next section on finding the right plan for you. Also, you'll want to make sure that you're not doubling up on coverage, and that you have the right to renew.

Although not available in all communities, Medicare + Choice plans could also be worth checking out. These are usually HMOs that operate under the Medicare umbrella. As with any other managed care program, your monthly premium covers all expenses as long as you remain within the system. Since you're not responsible for a percentage of the expense, the need for Medigap disappears.

FIGHTING FOR REIMBURSEMENT

If Medicare should deny you or a loved one treatment, or reimburse you less than you think you deserve, don't just sit and take it. Ask to see a review of your claim, then appeal the decision. And don't let a third party tell you that Medicare won't cover something either. Insist that the provider submit the claim regardless. If Medicare does turn you down, you know what to do—appeal the decision. You have a 70% chance of achieving at least partial success, according to the Centers for Medicare and Medicaid Services (CMS), the institution that manages Medicare. You can find more information at www.hcfa.gov or by calling 1-800-MEDICARE (1-800-633-4227).

Indeed, I would argue that these days you should always stand up and fight for what you think is right when it comes to health care. The squeaky wheel is usually the one that gets the oil, while all too often the quiet ones just go flat.

Chuck's Two Cents: On Being Adequately Insured

Insurance is a hot topic these days. As a result of the huge changes in the health care industry, we as individuals are required to know more about health insurance than previous generations ever did. Disability insurance is becoming more and more common, and long-term-care insurance, something a lot of people hadn't even heard of twenty years ago, is now used more than any other kind of insurance. Around a third of those who carry it end up needing it, a compelling argument for considering it.

All that attention and hype can make you feel as though you should be signing up for every kind of insurance available. Fear plays a role, too; your imagination can kick in and start coming up with all kinds of dire scenarios that cause you to want to max out on every type of insurance available.

If you begin to feel that pressure, I urge you to step back and look at things objectively. It's true that a wise insurance plan can give you and your family some peace of mind, but the important thing is to be adequately insured, not overly so. Don't let your emotions cause you to go overboard. At the same time, this is not a time to put your head in the sand. Being inadequately insured can undermine even the smartest and most careful and thorough financial planning.

The best advice I can give you is to be thorough in your research and analysis. You don't need every kind of insurance out there, and I urge you to look at each type in an objective manner. Only some research and analysis will tell you if you need it.

Once you decide what types of insurance make sense for you, you should also look closely at the providers you're considering and make sure they have solid track records and good ratings. When looking at policies, look at group rates first and do some comparison-shopping, making sure that the policies you compare offer the same coverage. Because rates and policies vary tremendously, I think you're wise to get quotes from three or four companies.

CHOOSING THE RIGHT PLAN

Once you've determined which type of medical insurance works best for your life and budget, you need to ask the next big question: How much coverage is enough? Amazingly, a $1 million lifetime cap (meaning the policy will cover a maximum total of $1 million in medical bills over your lifetime) is the absolute minimum. Though I hope you never come close to using that full amount, I do need to warn you that a chronic or terminal illness, or a disabling accident, could make that number woefully inadequate.

Of course in that unfortunate case, there's always Medicaid, the federally funded medical insurance. The rules for Medicaid, a government-sponsored safety net for low-income families or for those whose assets have been consumed by medical expenses, are complicated and vary state-by-state. But as Virginia Morris points out in her book *How to Care for Aging Parents,* many people qualify for Medicaid long before they think they do. If you or your parents are even nearing this point, I recommend that you pick up a copy of Morris's terrific resource or borrow it from the library. It will give you much food for thought as well as discussion.

When you're comparing health insurance plans, make sure you're comparing apples to apples. Things to think about include:

• The premium—the amount you pay to cover you and your family, whether you're paying the full amount yourself or just the portion your employer doesn't.

• The deductible—how much you'll have to pay out of pocket each year before the policy starts to pay benefits. HMOs notwithstanding (since they usually don't have deductibles and are usually the least expensive), in general the higher the deductible, the lower the premium.

• The copayment—the dollar amount you pay for any medical service, whether for a doctor's visit, a hospital stay, or a prescription.

• The annual cap—the maximum out-of-pocket amount you'll ever have to pay in a given calendar year.

• The lifetime cap—the maximum amount the insurance company will pay for your medical expenses over your lifetime. Although rare, a few policies have no lifetime cap at all, which can be a huge benefit. Of course, you'll likely have to pay more for this benefit.

• Annual limits for specific services like dentistry and mental health.

• What's not covered at all.

• Restrictions, including preexisting condition exclusions. Make sure you know what your policy's restrictions are and how long they will last.

If you and your spouse both have health insurance plans through work, remember that you can combine them. Perhaps one plan has better health insurance, and the other has a better dental plan. When Anna and Josh married, they opted to go with his medical plan simply because the premiums were lower. Though they still have the least-expensive deal in town, the questionable care they've received is prompting them to switch. Saving money is great until it starts to interfere with your greatest asset of all: your health. Also, since most company plans let you change your coverage once a year, make it a habit to review your selection each year as your needs—and those of your family—change.

VITAL SIGNINGS

In Chapter 8 we talked about signing a *durable power of attorney,* a document that authorizes whomever you choose to use your assets to pay for your care in the event of a debilitating accident or illness. We also discussed signing a *durable power of attorney for health care,* which grants a person the right to make medical decisions on your behalf. These documents are both critical when it comes to ensuring that you're taken care of in the manner you'd like, with your wishes honored until the end. If you haven't made the time to draw up and sign those documents yet, don't put it off another day. There's simply too much at stake.

The easiest way I've found to check out health care plans is to log on to the National Committee for Quality Assurance's website at www.healthchoices.org. While you won't find rate information, you will find an evaluation of your current health insurance company, as well as ratings of all the health care insurers in your area. Their Health Plan Report Card gives grades of one to four stars in five separate areas:

• Access and Service—Quality of care and customer service (including following up on grievances). Appeals and health plan denials are also evaluated.

• Qualified Providers—Credentials of the plan's doctors (including any sanctions of malpractice suits against them), as well as how satisfied members are with their physicians.

- Staying Healthy—Preventive care services, including tests and screenings.
- Getting Better—Clinical performance, including the use of new medical procedures and up-to-date drugs and devices.
- Living with Illness—Programs and care that can help people manage chronic illness.

Once you've determined which insurance companies meet your standards, you can evaluate whether they meet your needs in terms of what they offer in their plans, whether your doctors and hospitals are included, and any and all annual costs, deductibles, and copayments. You can even print out a worksheet from the site to help you keep all this information straight.

REMEMBER THAT YOU MUST FILE TO COLLECT

Too many people never get reimbursed for medical expenses simply because they neglect to fill out the claim forms. Though they're not usually terribly confusing, these forms often end up in that pile of to-do chores that never stops growing. And that's when you, your family, and your parents are healthy. Once you start including hospital bills, your pile of yet-to-be-submitted health insurance claims could take over your desk! Fear not, however. If you find yourself unwilling or unable to face the dreaded medical paperwork pile, you can hire an insurance claims agent (also known as a medical billing agent, public health adjuster, or medical insurance consultant) to do the work for you. You'll have to pay, of course, usually either by the hour (from $25 to $55) or by percentage (10% to 15% of whatever's reimbursed). But since so many people never file the claim at all, that's a whole lot better than nothing.

Life Goes On

Now that you know you can handle any medical expenses that may come your way, it's time to make sure that your family will be cared for in the event of your death. I realize that many of you may be tempted to avoid this step. The irony inherent in all insurance is that you're spending money on something you hope you'll never use. And perhaps this is never truer than it is with life insurance. But don't let yourself stay on that path of denial too long. Life insurance is an essential part of protecting the people you care about. It can provide a safety net exactly at the time they need it most. If it is neglected, the results can be devastating.

My colleague Nancy recalls that when her dad died of cancer, her mom was left with three kids not far from college age and a huge mortgage. "We had never prepared for anything like that," Nancy says. The family hadn't managed to save much, and there was almost no life insurance to fall back on. Instead of simply being able to mourn the loss of her husband, Nancy's mother was forced to confront the seemingly impossible task of providing for her family by herself. "It was a really hard, scary time," says Nancy.

The frightening statistic is that Nancy's family is in good company. In fact, most Americans—60%—either have no life insurance at all or are underinsured. If you fall into one of these categories, we encourage you to reevaluate your situation now. In this section we'll help you determine not only whether you need insurance but also what type is most appropriate, how much you need, and how to find the best policy.

WHO NEEDS IT?

Years ago people bought life insurance as a way to cover their burial costs. As time passed, it became a stopgap measure to cover their dependents until they could get back on their feet. Today most people use life insurance as a way to see that their loved ones will be able to maintain their quality of life for years to come.

Given this interpretation, ask yourself if your life insurance needs—which change as your life circumstances change—have been satisfactorily met. If you're single with no children and no one else to support, you probably don't need life insurance at all. At the other extreme, couples with substantial assets and no dependents may not need it either; in effect they can afford to self-insure. But for the vast majority of people who fall in between, life insurance is essential.

If you have children, you need to have enough life insurance to cover their expenses until they are old enough to support themselves. Depending on your children's ages, this could be up to eighteen years of income (or more). You may also need to carry life insurance even if you don't have children or your children are grown. Do you support your parents? Does your spouse or significant other depend on your income? How well would they live if you were no longer there to provide for them? The answer, in many cases, is not well.

Remember, too, that you don't just want to insure the working spouse, especially if you have children. If your partner cares for your children or has other household responsibilities, you'll need to be sure you can cover those expenses.

WHAT YOU NEED TO KNOW ABOUT LIFE INSURANCE

There are two basic types of life insurance: *term* and *cash value* (otherwise known as *permanent* life insurance). We'll discuss term life insurance—the most straightforward of the two—first. Not only is it the easiest to understand, but it is also by far the least expensive and the best choice for most people. In fact, with improved mortality rates and greater competition, term insurance rates have plummeted in the last few years.

Term life insurance. Term insurance is pure insurance. You buy a specific amount of coverage for a specified length of time up to a maximum age. (Since term policies don't typically allow you to insure past age eighty, a fifty-year-old could technically buy a thirty-year policy, but a fifty-one-year-old couldn't.) In general, the premiums are guaranteed by the insurance company and can't be raised during the term you select (which can be five, ten, fifteen, twenty, twenty-five, or thirty years at the most). Make sure, though, that the guarantee holds for the full term; some policies offer long terms—say twenty years—but guarantee the rates for only part of the time.

For example, let's say you buy a twenty-year $750,000 policy. Should you die during that time, even if it's nineteen years and 364 days into your policy, your beneficiary gets $750,000. Should you die twenty years and one day later, however, your beneficiary gets nothing.

You could renew your policy, of course, but here's the potential rub. If you wait until those twenty years are almost over before renewing, your rates will rise considerably, since you're now that much older (assuming poor health doesn't make you ineligible). Even if you renew ten years down the line, you'll suffer a significant rate increase. Fortunately, there's a very simple way around this problem. If instead of buying a twenty-year policy, you buy a thirty-year policy, you can always stop paying the premiums when you feel that you no longer need the coverage. But because you've locked in your rate, your overall cost will be lower.

Cash value, or permanent life insurance. Cash value insurance is another animal altogether. The premiums are much higher than those for term insurance because you're providing insurability for your lifetime, and instead of buying pure insurance, you're buying an investment as well. Of course this could be a sound choice if the investment does well. But for most people the usual lackluster returns don't justify the higher premiums and extra costs.

Before we get into the details, let's first run through how a cash value policy works. Unlike term life insurance, there's no expiration date on a cash value policy. As long as you pay your premiums, you should be covered. In addition to lifelong coverage (hence *permanent*), these policies offer a savings component (hence *cash value*). A sliding percentage of each premium you pay is set aside—more at first, and less as you age—and the actual cost of the policy rises. The insurance company usually invests that money, which you can then make withdrawals from or borrow against as it grows tax-deferred. Should you cancel your coverage, you may be able to receive a portion—or even all—of your policy's cash value.

The problem with all this? In a word: cost. A $1 million, twenty-year term policy might cost a healthy forty-year-old man about $850 a year. A cash value policy, on the other hand, might cost that same forty-year-old two to four times that much depending on the type of policy he chooses. If he invests the annual difference in a no-load mutual fund and earns an 8% annual rate of return, he would likely wind up with a lot more money than he would have with the cash value policy.

But before we dismiss cash value policies altogether, we should acknowledge that they can make sense in certain circumstances. One way to think about this is that term insurance offers the best low-cost protection for a limited time (say, until your children graduate from college or until your mortgage is paid off). But if you're looking for longer-term coverage needs (especially if you have reason to fear that your health could deteriorate), it's possible that the permanent nature of the coverage could justify the extra cost. In addition, a cash value policy could have a place in your estate plan—for example, if you wanted to set up an insurance trust to pay for estate taxes or other debts. Or if you have a child or other dependent whom you believe will never be able to financially take care of him or herself, a cash value policy can provide an extra layer of protection. "The more complicated your financial situation, the more complicated your estate-planning needs will be, which leads to a more sophisticated insurance solution," says one Schwab insurance expert.

Now that we've covered the basics, let's run through four of the most common types of cash value policies. The major difference among most of them is how your cash value is invested. We won't review all of the permutations, but the following will introduce you to your basic choices. For many people, the fourth type, *universal variable life insurance,* may be the best choice as it offers fixed coverage, the insured gets to direct the investments, and the contract has the most flexibility.

• *Whole life insurance* invests your funds in fixed-rate securities like bonds. You and your family have no say in how or where the money is invested. Although the rates are not guaranteed, they tend to range from 1% to 5%. At those rates, you're either losing ground or barely staying level, when it comes to inflation.

• *Variable life insurance* allows you to choose how your cash value is invested from the investment choices (including stocks and bonds) available in the particular policy you choose. Historically, these returns have soundly beaten earnings derived from whole life insurance policies. With those higher returns, however, comes the higher risk inherent in equity investing.

• *Universal life insurance* invests the cash portion of your premium in fixed-rate accounts. Once again, you don't participate in the decision of where your money is invested. You do, however, have some control over when it's invested, since you can usually raise or lower the amount of the premium you pay (and therefore determine how much money is diverted into the savings component of your policy) once a year. When the rates are low, you will probably decide to contribute less than when the rates are higher. Most universal life policies also offer loan provisions, which allow you to borrow your cash value. Since it is a loan, the gains are not taxed as long as your policy remains in force.

• *Universal variable life insurance* gives you investment control, allowing you to determine whether you want a conservative portfolio with little associated risk or an aggressive portfolio that could potentially yield higher returns (and bigger losses as well). Like universal life, you can stop, raise, or lower your premiums annually, and you can borrow your cash value.

CAUTIONARY NOTE

If anyone ever tries to sell you on the idea of investing in whole life insurance products instead of a retirement vehicle like a 401(k) plan, just say no. Though whole life makes sense for certain people, it's never a substitute for one of the viable retirement vehicles discussed in Chapter 7.

In short, stick with term coverage for your family if you need life insurance to protect them, and stick with your retirement plans for your retirement.

HOW MUCH WILL YOU NEED?

Now we're getting down to the crux of the whole issue: exactly how much life insurance you need to provide for your loved ones. Although there are no hard-and-fast rules that will give you the answer, there are a few ways to determine the amount.

The simplest (and least accurate) method is to "ballpark" the number. An industry standard advocates six to twelve times your income. Now that's a pretty big range. Whether you opt for the low or the high end of that estimate will depend on how many dependents and financial obligations you have, along with any special needs.

As an alternative, you can buy enough coverage so that the annual investment return from the insurance proceeds will have a good chance of replacing your income. For example, if your family needs to replace an income of $50,000 a year, and you believe that you can earn an 8% average annual return, you would need to purchase $625,000 of coverage ($625,000 times 0.08 equals $50,000). This would allow you to spend that $50,000 of income a year without eroding any of the principal. Of course, you also have to factor in inflation, as well as the possibility that you might not receive that 8% return.

But wouldn't it be a lot more comforting to take the guesswork out of all this? Worksheet 9.1 can provide you with a more customized approach that balances your specific expenses and goals against your assets. (You can also log on to www.schwab.com/insurance to calculate your needs online.)

It's also important to reevaluate your needs periodically. Speaking very broadly, chances are that you will require more coverage when you're younger, and less when you have other assets to help shoulder the load. When your family is young, you're more likely to have a high mortgage, education costs, and other expenses associated with raising a family. Once your kids are grown, these expenses may well decrease, and your need for life insurance may decline as well.

SIGN ME UP

The good news is that signing up for life insurance is fairly painless. If your employer offers a group life insurance plan, that's likely the

Worksheet 9.1
Estimating Your Life Insurance Needs

Immediate Cash Needs at Death	Self/Spouse
Cost to Settle Your Estate: Estimate court costs, legal and accounting fees, final expenses, and other miscellaneous costs necessary to settle your estate. For a rough figure, allow 5% of the value of your estate.	_____
Personal/Business Debt: Include all current liabilities, such as credit cards, loans, credit lines, etc.	+ _____
Real Estate Loans: Include the amount of any loan secured by real estate, such as first or second mortgages, equity lines, contracts for deed, etc.	+ _____
Income and Estate Taxes: Estimate any unpaid personal, business, or estate taxes.	+ _____
Subtotal: Immediate Cash Needs at Death	= _____ (1)

Future Cash Needs	Self/Spouse
Family Income Fund: Estimate funds needed to generate income to cover daily expenses for your family. Often figured at 6 times annual gross income.	_____
Education Fund: Amount needed for children's college education.	+ _____
Spousal Retirement Fund: Funds needed to supplement your spouse's retirement income (optional).	+ _____
Other: Supplemental funds for dependents with special needs; charitable causes; business and estate needs.	+ _____
Subtotal: Future Cash Needs	= _____ (2)
Total Cash Needs (1 + 2):	_____ (A)

What You Have Now	Self/Spouse
Cash and Savings: All money in checking and savings accounts, money market accounts, certificates of deposit, and Social Security benefits.	_____
Lump Sum Employee Benefits: The amount your beneficiaries will receive from pension plans, 401(k) plans, or other employer-sponsored benefit programs.	+ _____
Investments: Stocks, bonds, IRA accounts, etc.	+ _____
Other Assets: Estimate the value from selling your collectibles, artwork, etc. Do not include equity in the family home unless it would be sold.	+ _____
Existing Policies:	+ _____
Total Assets:	= _____ (B)
Total Life Insurance Coverage Needed:	
Total Cash Needs Minus Total Assets:	_____
	(A minus B)

easiest way to get automatic coverage at a competitive rate. Chances are good, though, that the basic coverage won't be sufficient, in which case you can buy supplemental coverage either through your employer or on your own. If you're considering more coverage than the basic amount your employer provides, you may want to shop outside to lock in insurance at your current age. That way, if you change employers or retire early, you won't lose your coverage. Also, at some ages supplemental insurance can be cheaper to buy on your own.

Once you're out in the marketplace, an underwriter will review your current state of health, past medical history, and life expectancy. If you're young and healthy, your premiums will probably come in on the low side—unless, of course, you're a professional stuntperson or race-car driver, in which case all bets are probably off.

These medical reviews are always part of the application process for term and cash value insurance. In almost all cases, a medical exam is included, and a medical professional will usually come to your home or office at no cost to you and do the kinds of basics you're probably used to (height, weight, blood pressure, pulse, and so on). You'll typically also have to provide blood and urine samples.

NAMING NAMES

Don't overlook the important business of assigning backup beneficiaries to your life insurance policies. Let's say you want to name your spouse as the primary beneficiary. Not to be morbid, but if he or she dies with you in a car accident, your children (assuming you have any) would be your secondary beneficiaries. Should you all go together, you'd probably want to have named a final beneficiary (such as your grandchild, sibling, niece, nephew, or close friend). Without that safeguard, the life insurance payout becomes part of your probate estate and is subject to all the expenses and delays we discussed in Chapter 8.

Aside from paying the bills, that's all there is to it. Of course, this latter point is significant, because the last thing you want to do is allow your policy to lapse because of missed payments. Setting up a payment plan where the premium is automatically deducted from your checking account can prevent this costly oversight.

GET WHAT'S COMING TO YOU

In most cases you're not going to get a thing unless you file a claim. That's not a big deal, assuming you can find a copy of the policy. One phone call and a little paperwork, and you're done. Remember that this can be emotional since it includes filling out and signing proof-of-death forms and attaching a certified copy of the policy-holder's death certificate.

On the other hand, if you're not sure about the policy or its coverage, you'll have to do a little detective work. The American Council of Life Insurers suggests the following:

• Check the deceased's papers and address and telephone books to look for life insurance policies and the names of insurance agents.

• Contact every insurance company with which the deceased had a policy, even if you're not sure it is still in force.

• Check with the employee benefits office at the deceased's latest and previous places of employment or with the union welfare office.

• Check the deceased's bankbooks and canceled checks for the last few years to see if any checks were written to pay life insurance premiums.

• Check the deceased's mail for a year after death for premium notices, which are usually sent annually.

• Review the deceased's income tax returns for the past two years. Look for interest income from and interest expenses paid to life insurance companies.

FINDING THE BEST RATE

It's finally time to go shopping—comparison-shopping, that is. You may find plenty of agents wanting to sell you unnecessary—and unnecessarily expensive—policies. So as usual, it pays to do a little digging.

These days researching life insurance rates is as easy as logging onto a website. For example, www.schwab.com/insurance provides term insurance rates. Other informative sites include the Insurance Information Institute's www.iii.org, San Francisco's Consumer Action's www.consumer-action.org, and the Federal Consumer Information Center's www.pueblo.gsa.gov.

When buying any kind of insurance, you want to be sure to buy from a company that you believe is financially sound and that will be around and able to pay when and if it's time to collect. It won't do you any good at all to find the lowest premium from a company that can't deliver when it counts. Thanks to the Internet, you can find company ratings at www.ambest.com.

You also want to make sure that you're comparing apples to apples. That's not always easy, due to similar-sounding terminology that really isn't similar at all. Let's say you're shopping for a twenty-year term policy. You can find policies with twenty-year true guarantees (your premium is locked in so it doesn't change a nickel for that entire twenty years) or twenty-year guarantees where your premium is locked in only for the first few years. Though the latter are often less expensive in the beginning, you have no way of knowing how high those premiums could ultimately go. I suggest that you go for the sure thing, even if it costs a bit more. More than likely, you'll come out way ahead in the end.

UPGRADING TO A LESS EXPENSIVE POLICY

Even if you just bought your term life insurance policy five to ten years ago, rates have dropped so much in the last couple of years that you could potentially buy twice the insurance you now have for the same price. Of course, age and health considerations enter into the equation. Still, a quick check could save—or buy—you a bundle, especially if your policy is ten years old or more.

Long Day's Journey into Night

Congratulations—you now have your health and life insurance taken care of. But unfortunately, that's not quite enough. When my friend's mother, Lee, got sick in Italy, her health insurance not only covered the month of intensive care abroad, it paid for bringing her home—including an ambulance ride on both ends, two ER nurses flown out from the United States, and ten seats on the plane to accommodate a stretcher, the two nurses, and her spouse.

Ironically, once Lee was back on U.S. soil and the emergency had passed, she was not so fortunate. Although her health insurance policy did provide for limited physical, occupational, and speech therapy services, it didn't cover the round-the-clock care that Lee required. What Lee needed, but didn't have, was *long-term care insurance.*

Long-term care insurance is set up to provide benefits when you're unable to perform certain "activities of daily living," such as bathing, dressing, or eating, for an extended period of time. Policies can cover medical care as well as support services—in either a hospital, an assisted living facility, or your own home. It's designed to pick up where private health insurance or Medicare leaves off, and as Lee's family found out, it can play a pivotal role in a patient's recovery.

Like Lee, 86% of Americans don't have long-term health care insurance—despite the fact that people age sixty-five or older have a 40% lifetime risk of entering a nursing home and needing the coverage. What this obvious discrepancy tells us is that the life savings of millions of Americans are in jeopardy of being eroded in a few years or less. The flip side is that if these same individuals did obtain long-term care coverage, the *total* cost of all their premiums would be significantly less than the cost of a single year in a nursing home.

WHO NEEDS LONG-TERM COVERAGE?

As with all insurance, the need for long-term care insurance falls onto a continuum. If you qualify for Medicaid, it will cover nursing care. At the other extreme, if you have considerable assets and can afford to pay $50,000 to $100,000 a year for nursing care, you may not need extra insurance. Long-term care insurance is for the group in the middle.

As you make your decision, consider the following facts provided by the National Center for Assisted Living:

• In 2002, the national average cost for one month in a nursing home was more than $4,600, or over $55,000 a year. Your actual cost could be twice as high, depending on where you live. It is also likely to rise, perhaps faster than inflation.

• In 2002, the national median cost for assisted living was between $2,000 and $2,500 a month.

• Medicare does not cover extended nursing home stays. Medigap's nursing home benefits end after a hundred days.

• Medicare will cover in-home care only under very strict circumstances. Medigap does not cover in-home care.

• One-third of those who have long-term care insurance eventually use it.

SPARE YOURSELF AND YOUR SAVINGS

Given what you now know, it's time to start planning—not only for your own care but for your parents' care as well. Because many of us eventually will pitch in and help pay for our parents' medical expenses, helping them buy long-term care insurance can help spare your own savings as well as theirs.

Studies show that not only have most of us not discussed our potential long-term health needs, we haven't even thought them through. That's ironic, since according to Dr. Muriel Gillick, physician-in-chief at Hebrew Rehabilitation Center in Boston and author of *Lifelines: Living Longer, Growing Frail, Taking Heart* (W. W. Norton & Co., 2000), 95% of the people surveyed say they want advanced medical planning. "What's keeping them from doing it is that no one brings it up," she says.

We avoid the subject for the same reasons we avoid talking about estate planning or life insurance or anything else that has to do with illness or death, whether ours or that of our loved ones. The fear of either or both makes it easier to deny, deny, deny—until reality hits us in the face.

The time to talk about—and invest in—long-term care insurance is well before you or your loved ones need it. That's because the choices for you and your parents become increasingly limited (and increasingly expensive) as time goes on. Indeed, waiting too long can mean that you forfeit the chance for insurance altogether. Shortly after being diagnosed with ALS, the disabling and degenerative disease commonly known as Lou Gehrig's disease, my colleague's seventy-six-year-old dad asked his son if he should get a long-term care policy. "It's too late," Joe was forced to explain. "I sure wish I would have talked to my dad about long-term care insurance when he still could have qualified," admits Joe.

The best time to buy long-term care insurance may be when you're in your mid- to late-fifties and are still healthy. This way you not only limit your risk of being declined but you can lock in lower premiums than those that will be available to you if you wait another ten to twenty years. For example, a policy that costs you $800 a year today at age fifty-five could cost you double that if you wait until you're sixty-five, and double or triple that if you wait until you're seventy. On the other hand, if you buy a policy when you're still young, you may be paying for many extra years of coverage. Clearly there are no easy answers.

These days an increasing number of adult children are considering purchasing long-term care insurance for their aging parents as a way to protect their inheritances or their own nest eggs. "My dad has figured out that if he gets sick, I can just sell the property he owns, invest the money, and then use the interest to pay for his nursing home costs," says a friend of mine. "But that assumes that his property value will hold and that interest rates will be high enough to get the necessary annual income. That also means that I'd be having to contend with all that just as he falls ill—an emotionally wrenching time better spent at his bedside. I'd sure feel a lot more comfortable if he had a long-term care policy."

CHOOSING THE RIGHT POLICY

When looking for a policy, you first need to determine the appropriate level of coverage. This will vary not only from state to state but from city to city and especially from an urban to a rural community. If the nursing homes in your area run closer to $100,000 a year than $50,000, you'll need more coverage rather than less. Ditto for the rates that health care aides and nurse's assistants receive for home care.

Once you've approximated what that yearly cost would be today, you'll have to factor in inflation. If you're buying a $100-per-day benefit that you won't use for twenty years, you'll need to adjust that figure for inflation. Even better, you can include an inflation-protection factor in your policy. This will increase your premium but ensure that your daily benefit keeps up with the rising cost of long-term care.

You'll also want to be certain that your nursing home costs cover the length of time you may need them. While many nursing home stays are short, the average stay is roughly two and a half years, according to AARP's Independent Living division. So you'll want to err on the safe side and buy at least three years' worth of coverage. If you can afford it, you may want to play it really safe and opt for a longer maximum benefit period or even a lifetime guarantee. This is particularly true for those of you concerned about the likelihood of long-term illness.

Also check that the policy covers both nursing home and in-home care. In short, you want your benefits to apply wherever you're being cared for, whether you or your parents wind up in a nursing home, an assisted-living facility, an adult day care center, or your own residence. Most people want to remain at home as long as possible, so make sure you have that choice.

Finally, make certain that your premium rate is guaranteed (or at least capped at a certain amount). Nightmare stories of initially low rates being hiked beyond affordability abound. You also need to determine that the company you're considering has an excellent rating. In addition, you may want to check with your state's insurance commissioner to see if the company has had past complaints. Since you won't be using this insurance for many years, you want to be reasonably sure that your company is still in business when you need it. And before you write that check, ask your insurance agent to provide you with a record of the rate increases implemented in the past. You don't want to get priced out of this insurance just when you actually might need it.

YOU DON'T HAVE TO GO IT ALONE

As anyone who has been in this situation can attest, caring for an elderly loved one who is ill can be a frightening and lonely endeavor. If you're feeling overwhelmed and confused by what you should do, an elder care consultant can help you figure out how your loved one's needs have changed, what you need to do, and how to do it. They also have information about the abundant resources that are available. The National Institutes of Health's Work and Family Life Center can provide referrals. You can reach the Elder/Adult Dependent Care Referral Service by calling the NIH Work and Family Life Center at 1-301-435-1619 or TTY 1-301-480-0690.

Chuck's Two Cents: Helping Your Parents— It Really Does Pay to Talk

One of the surprise gifts of my adult life has been the joy of being able to help my parents in their later years, and I suspect I'm far from alone here. Society is changing at a fast pace. A few generations ago aging parents moved in with their adult kids. These days that's getting pretty rare—but while our parents may not need to move in with us, they may still need our help. In fact, I'd go so far as to estimate that between one-half and two-thirds of those reading this book will have parents who could use some type of assistance. Once you recognize the need, I also encourage you to be sensitive to your parents' feelings. Offering help without taking away inde-

pendence or hurting someone's dignity can be tricky business. But it can be done, and the rewards can be great.

There are different kinds of help. First there's real financial help; maybe your parents could use a little extra monthly income to make them more comfortable. There's also emotional support and advice, particularly after the death of a spouse. The survivor often needs some coaching and encouragement to keep things going and to make all the decisions she or he is faced with. You may want to make sure your parents' estate plan is current in terms of changing tax laws and inflation. My dad was an estate lawyer, but he wasn't vigilant about his own estate plan. When he died, the numbers in his will had not been adjusted for inflation. Everything had been done twenty years earlier and never revisited.

Every family is different, and you'll know best what your parents need. It will depend on their personalities and their financial situation, on their mental health and physical well-being. It's possible that one of the best things you can do is simply start the conversation. I speak from experience here. Years ago, once I no longer had to worry about simply making ends meet, I was able to relieve my parents of some of their financial stress by asking my dad if I could help support my dependent sister. He allowed me to take over that responsibility, and it opened a door for us. After all those years of silence about money, we were finally able to discuss everything from where my parents wanted to live once they were no longer fully able to care for themselves to how I could help supplement their income.

After my dad died, my mom wound up needing nursing care and housekeeping assistance. Realizing that she could no longer handle her accounts, I took over her check-writing and banking. I'm very grateful I was able to help them; being able to do so was a true gift. And I never would have known what they'd needed if I hadn't broached the subject.

In Case of Disability

Nobody plans to become incapacitated or disabled. We hope to live full, productive lives and to eventually pass away at a ripe old age, doing what we most love. But life has a way of surprising us. According to the National Association of Insurance Commissioners, if you're between the ages of thirty-five and sixty-five, you have a 30% likelihood of facing a period of ninety days or longer during which you won't be able to work. Think about that. How long could *you* survive without a paycheck?

Enter disability insurance, which is designed to protect one of your most valuable assets—your earning power—from the impact of a disabling accident or illness. When combined with health, life, and long-term care insurance, disability insurance can help provide you and your family with the peace of mind we keep talking about. If you become disabled, a variety of plans (workers' compensation, Social Security, veterans' benefits) may help but likely won't be sufficient. Disability insurance is one of the best ways to make sure that your disability, no matter how severe, doesn't turn into a full-fledged financial disaster.

WHAT TO LOOK FOR IN A PLAN

When you're shopping for a disability insurance policy, you'll want one that:

• Replaces a significant portion of your monthly income (the ceiling is generally 60%) during the length of a disability.

• Pays tax-free benefits. (Note, though, that this applies only if you've paid the premium yourself on an after-tax basis; you will have to pay tax on all benefits paid through employer-paid policies.)

• Is portable, which means that you can keep the coverage if you change jobs—for the duration of the policy.

• Waives its premiums while you're on disability. If it isn't part of your basic policy, you can purchase this *waiver of premium,* as it's called, separately.

• Provides retraining to help you recover your ability to earn income and return to a full and independent lifestyle.

• Provides "same-occupation" coverage. Some policies won't consider you disabled if you can hold down any job at all. So, for example, if a surgeon who has lost the use of his or her hands doesn't have *same occupation* (or "own-occ") coverage, he or she could be deemed able to work as a telemarketer and denied benefits.

But if you're not a specialist and would be willing to work in some other capacity, you might consider insuring your income rather than your profession. This more affordable alternative provides you with the full amount of the benefit your policy specifies should you not be able to work at all. If you can work part-time only or are forced to take lower-paying employment, it should make up the difference between those reduced earnings and the monthly amount for which you're insured.

There are a number of other alternatives to consider, so you'll want to talk with an insurance specialist before making any final decisions. That doesn't mean, however, that you can't get started on your own.

HOW AND HOW MUCH?

The group coverage provided by your employer is often the least expensive coverage available. If you're not covered at work, or if you're inadequately covered, disability policies are also available to most working individuals at reasonable rates. Trade and professional associations often offer discounted disability coverage, so check those first. If you don't belong to any, this may very well be the time to join.

As a rule, individual coverage will prove both more comprehensive and more expensive. A woman in her thirties could easily pay $28 to $90 a month for a disability policy with a ninety-day waiting period worth $2,500 a month—depending on how long the benefit pays out. In her forties she could expect to pay $45 to $120. A thirty-year-old man could pay $10 to $60 per month and a forty-year-old man could pay $17 to $90 per month for similar coverage. (Because women tend to submit more claims than men, their premiums typically run about 30% higher.)

Just as with life insurance, you'll want to opt for a company that has a solid track record, since none of this will do you any good if you buy from a company that goes out of business, or cancels the disability portion of its business, before you need it. Currently the industry leader, by far, is UnumProvident. That makes things pretty simple. On the other hand, it also limits comparison-shopping possibilities. Still, prices can vary quite a bit, so it definitely pays to shop around.

How much disability coverage is enough? Consider:

• How much income you'd need to replace if you were disabled for a sustained period—say six months. Would 50% of your salary be sufficient? If so, your work policy coupled with Social Security, company disability benefits, or your spouse's income may be adequate. If not, you may be able to supplement that policy through either the same company or another vendor.

INSURANCE YOU DON'T NEED

It seems like every time you turn around, somebody's trying to force more insurance on you—often insurance you don't need. The following fall into the *don't-bother* category:

• Life insurance for your young children. They don't have dependents, which is what life insurance is for.

• Mortgage life insurance. It's too expensive for what it provides. You can get the same coverage for a lot less with term life insurance.

• Credit card life insurance. Ditto.

• Flight life insurance. If you have life insurance, you're already covered.

• Rental car insurance. If you have an auto policy, you most likely don't need this if you're traveling within the United States. But if you're traveling abroad, it may be a good idea, as your personal policy generally doesn't cover you in foreign countries. In either case, check your policies for details and limitations. The same goes for credit cards that offer insurance protection as long as you pay for the rental car with their card.

• How long you'd be able to cover your living expenses before your benefits began. Would it be 30 days? 120 days? The longer the waiting period before your benefits start, the lower the cost of your annual premium.

If you can afford it, buy a policy that will provide benefits until you're sixty-five. That will cost more, but it will also protect you better than a policy that lapses after paying you only two to three years' worth of income.

Come What May

So far we've been talking about insurance you can buy to protect your assets. But we also need to discuss the kind of no-cost insurance that can protect you if you're forced to face the loss of your spouse through either divorce or death.

Of course no one is ever fully prepared for a marriage to collapse. Even under the best circumstances, a divorce can be an overwhelming process that leaves one physically and emotionally exhausted. And while the stress and pain inherent in the end of a marriage can be excruciating, the grief of having a spouse or partner die—whether the death is sudden and unexpected or the result of a lengthy illness—is almost always devastating.

Why bring up all this heartbreak in a book about family money? Because financial burdens make both death and divorce all that much harder, and confusion about financial affairs during these trying times is all too common.

With one out of every two new marriages in the United States today ending in divorce, it's clear that good preparation is crucial. Nine months into her marriage to Dave, my friend Diane, then age thirty, quit her accounting job to help out with the family retail business and care for their newborn son. In an effort to reduce the Social Security tax, her husband suggested that he take a raise rather than pay her independently. She agreed. By their first wedding anniversary, however, Diane had realized the precarious position in which she had placed herself. "I had a mortgage, a child, no job, and no direct ownership in either of our two shops," she says. When she asked her husband to invest in a life insurance policy, he balked, assuring her that his parents would always take care of her and the child. Diane's insistence finally won out, however, and Dave purchased a $500,000 insurance policy of which she was the beneficiary. Though it had been an ordeal, "that satisfied me," she says. It shouldn't have.

Though Dave had married a woman whose professional life involved dealing with other people's money, he gave her little of her own. "Oh, if you need money, just ask me for it," he would say breezily when she brought up the topic. By definition that put her in an unequal position in the relationship, but she was reluctant to engage in another battle like the one over the life insurance. Still, as all the family assets—including their home—remained titled in Dave's name alone, she continued to worry. "Well, it's all half yours legally anyway," her husband would answer. "It really doesn't matter."

It did. When Diane and Dave's marriage ended five years later, Diane was faced with the even greater challenge of demonstrating her rights to a portion of the couple's assets. After two years in court, Diane and Dave finally reached a fair settlement. She's grateful but chagrined that she didn't look out for herself in the first place. "I'm not at the top of the tree when it comes to intellect, but I'm not at the bottom either," she says. "It's amazing to me how little women know about the basics of divorce upon entering marriage—even bright, educated ones."

The loss of a spouse can bring the same potentially ruinous financial consequences and can prove overwhelming in the best circumstances. My colleague Louise's family is a case in point. Her father not only provided for his wife, he supplied her with everything she needed to know in the event of his demise—down to the location of the power of attorney document she'd need in order to handle certain financial transactions. But even with all that planning and all those step-by-step instructions, taking over as head of the financial household proved downright daunting. There was still a lot to learn, a lot to understand, and a lot to handle.

PREPARATION IS YOUR BEST PROTECTION

In short, you simply can't run the risk of neglecting your finances or your financial education, whether you're in the first blush of love, happily married after many years, wading through the aftermath of a split with your mate, or trying to survive the death of your spouse. Why? Because both divorce and the loss of a spouse can leave you financially strapped (if not insolvent) unless you've taken certain precautions before and after the fact and invested in a little personal insurance to help see you through.

When it comes to keeping your head even though you've lost your heart, I often think of one of the Schwab TV commercials in which the former duchess of York, Sarah Ferguson, is telling one of her daughters a bedtime story about the knight who's going to fall in love with her, marry her, and give her a wonderful life. Just in case that doesn't work out, Fergie adds, her daughter will need to understand "the difference between a P/E ratio and a dividend yield, a growth versus a value strategy . . ." In short, she'll need to learn to take care of herself.

That's right. We *all* need to know how to fend for ourselves. We would like to think that a sense of fairness will always prevail in divorce as well as in the rest of life, but of course this isn't always the case. The only way to protect yourself is to be aware from the beginning. It doesn't matter if you're a man or a woman, married or living together—every adult should take care of the following to assert his or her financial independence:

- Establish your own line of credit and your own checking account.
- Make sure you know where your bank and brokerage accounts are located and who handles them.
- Have a working knowledge of investments in general, and complete familiarity with your family's assets.
- Take steps to prepare for your own retirement, including putting money aside on a regular basis.
- Make sure that any property that is rightfully yours is titled in your name.

• Establish a relationship with your family financial advisor even if you're not the primary money person.

On Your Own

I sincerely hope that you never need the following advice. But once again, statistics (and undoubtedly your own friends' and family's experiences) tell us you might.

In case of divorce: Despite emotional pain so intense that you may have trouble even contemplating the future, you need to protect yourself by taking some immediate steps and then thinking about what you'll need for the long term. Even if you feel undeserving, ask yourself if your spouse could have achieved what he or she did without your support. Quickly signing away your rights to assets or custody, for example, is almost always a bitterly regretted mistake.

Self-protection, however, doesn't necessarily need to come at your ex's expense. Though anger may cloud your better judgment initially, a fair distribution of assets on both sides will make both parties feel better about the arrangements in the long run. It will also facilitate any necessary postdivorce communication, including that involving children.

Here's what you'll need to do to protect yourself:

• Close your joint checking and savings accounts. Check with your attorney and banker about taking out half of the money from a joint account and putting it in your own account.

• Ask your attorney about placing the assets from a closed account in an escrow account until your divorce settlement is complete.

• Once you have your own line of credit in place, close your old joint credit card and charge accounts. Date the letters, and clearly state that you're not responsible for new charges. Keep copies of all correspondence.

• Freeze the assets in all joint brokerage accounts. Immediately notify your investment advisor in writing that you are separated, and ask that no transactions be made without your approval.

• Carefully consider how all of your marital assets will be split. Make sure that your spouse's pension and retirement accounts are included in your settlement agreement.

If your spouse has died: The last thing on your mind when your mate dies is dealing with anything but your grief. While that can't be helped, you *can* enlist loved ones to help you handle the unavoidable financial matters that surface almost immediately. In all likelihood they'll be incredibly relieved to have a concrete way to help. It may even prove a channel for their own grief. Either on your own or preferably with the assistance of your family, you'll need to:

• Locate the will, as well as any trust documents and letters of instruction, and make sure that anyone who needs a copy—including the estate's executor and your attorney—has one.

• As probate estates and trusts are separate legal entities from both the deceased individual and his or her beneficiaries, you will need to apply for a new tax ID number for these entities to make sure they are properly reported and accounted for.

• File for life insurance benefits with insurance companies, the employee benefits department of your spouse's employer, and others as appropriate.

• Apply for Social Security benefits that you and your minor children might be entitled to. You'll need proof of death from the funeral home or a death certificate; Social Security numbers for yourself, the deceased, and his or her dependent children; your birth and marriage certificates; your divorce papers if you're applying as a surviving divorced spouse; and the deceased's most recent federal tax return.

• Contact your banks and credit card issuers to change your joint loans, cards, and accounts to your name only. If you have been using your spouse's credit cards, or a supplementary card to his or her account, you'll need to begin to establish a personal line of credit.

Additional steps if you've lost a spouse to either death or divorce . . .

• Before you make any financial decisions, take your time and evaluate your situation carefully.

• Look before you leap when well-intentioned friends and family start offering financial advice.

• Watch out for unscrupulous brokers and financial advisors ready to make money off of your misfortunes.

In addition, you'll want to:

• Establish or rebuild a financial safety net equal to at least two to six months of living expenses.

• Revisit your investment portfolio to make sure your asset allocation is still appropriate for your goals and time horizon. Consider consolidating your accounts if that will help you stay on top of things.

• Determine your immediate goals, and reexamine your longer-term goals. When you're concerned about basic survival, this may seem frivolous and unrealistic. Still, it's important to reaffirm life—yours and your family's—at this trying time.

DON'T SWEEP IT UNDER THE RUG

If you've lost your spouse to death or divorce, you probably feel like you're barely holding on. Still, you can't underestimate or avoid dealing with what your young kids might be going through as well. In most cases, emotional distress is compounded by a heavy dose of fear. *How is the family going to pay the bills now? What is life going to look like for us, for me, and/or my siblings? Will things be okay? Am I still loved?* When parents don't address these issues, kids may assume the worst. Being kids, however, they don't tell you that, probably because they don't realize it themselves. It's up to you to break that silence.

• Reassess your retirement plan. Just because you're on your own doesn't mean that you lose your ability to create a meaningful future.

• Explore your career choices. A new job can open up new possibilities—on the professional and financial fronts as well as the personal, emotional, and social ones. When making a move, negotiate for the best benefits you can get—including a top-notch retirement plan and solid health, disability, and life insurance plans.

• Make sure not to lose sight of yourself and your needs in the rush to care for your family.

Fortunes and Misfortunes

Let's imagine for a minute that you've come into some money. Maybe you've received a large divorce settlement. Perhaps your lottery ticket paid off. Or, to steal a line from the movie *The Secret to My Success,* maybe you made your money the old-fashioned way— and inherited it. Well, good for you.

Whether you've hit the jackpot or are still waiting for that lucky strike, knowing what to expect and how to handle it will help you see that the money works for you today, tomorrow, and in the years to come. All too often, though, that pot of money disappears much too fast. Remember Lauren from Chapter 2, who struggled with debt before she managed to switch gears from spending to saving for her retirement? In the beginning she simply wasn't prepared to handle assets as large as her divorce settlement. And as it turns out, that's par for the course. Most windfalls evaporate almost as quickly as they appear.

Emotions aside, it's often the pressure of spending and handling a large sum of money that is problematic. Of course, if these recipients had talked out their goals with their family and friends, learned the ABCs of finances and investing, and agreed on how to manage and talk about money as a couple and as a family—in short, if they had done what you have—this unexpected money could produce far less strain and far greater gains.

Chuck's Two Cents: Investing a Lump Sum

Receiving a lump sum is certainly cause for celebration, but it's also cause for caution, and a time to do some careful planning about how to invest it. If you find yourself in this situation, keep the following points in mind:

• First, pay your taxes, if there are any. Generally speaking, money received as part of a divorce settlement is not taxable, and money received in an inheritance has already been taxed. Money from a retirement plan is taxable, which is why people often choose to roll it over into an IRA, where it won't be taxed until you withdraw it. As always, ignoring the tax implications can be a big mistake, so you should speak to a qualified tax advisor.

• Second, look at how this sum affects your overall financial picture. Take a look at your entire portfolio, and review your asset allocation. Is this a large enough amount that you'll want to do some rebalancing? A lump sum may give you the money you need to add to the investment class you want to increase.

• Third, take your time, especially if you're in the middle of difficult personal circumstances; for example, if you've just received an inheritance from a loved one. For now, just make sure the money's working for you—in a money market account, for example. Once you've decided how to invest the money, you don't have to do it all at once. You may want to invest it a little at a time, perhaps 10% a month over the course of ten months to a year. Or maybe you want to invest it over a longer period of time—three years or so. (I say three years because that's generally how long economic cycles last; by investing over that period of time, you'd typically hit the highs as well as the lows.)

• Fourth, if in doubt, get some professional advice from your family lawyer or accountant or financial advisor. If you don't have an advisor, get some personal recommendations, and take some time to interview a few candidates and find the right person. And remember, be sure you get expert, objective advice, with no conflict of interest.

• Finally, be on your guard. Sad to say, there are plenty of people ready and willing to take advantage of the new recipient of a good-

sized chunk of cash. Some watch the obituaries and prey on surviv-
ing spouses. Others go after lottery winners. Be careful about whose
advice you take and whom you hire to help you out, especially if the
market's doing well. In that kind of environment, you may find a lot
of people vying for your attention—and your money.

Certainly a properly handled windfall can be a true bonanza, helping you and your family to realize all those dreams you've been talking about since you started reading this book. And even if your
windfall hasn't arrived, figuring out what you'd do with it is a terrific way to kick-start a family conversation and gives you a chance
to revisit almost every facet of your family's financial dealings. So
go to it. And remember—it pays to talk!

Something to Talk About

• *Does your family health history put you at greater risk? How*
does that affect your insurance needs?

• *Is your health insurance—or your parents'—as comprehen-*
sive as necessary? Would a serious illness break you financially? Is
your policy best suited to your needs?

• *Have you and your spouse each signed a durable power of*
attorney for finances and a durable power of attorney for health
care? Have your adult children? Your parents?

• *Do you have adequate life insurance? Does your spouse?*
Your parents?

• *Do you know how and where you each want to be cared for,*
should you become seriously ill? Have you shared your desires
regarding long-term health care planning and advance directives
with your spouse and your children? Have you checked with your
parents about their wishes?

• *Have you and your siblings formulated a long-term care plan*
for your parents?

• *Could you pay for long-term care requirements if one of your*
family members needed it?

• *What are your choices if either one of you—or your par-*
ents—could no longer live independently?

• *Do you need disability insurance? Do your parents or your adult children?*

• *Are you financially prepared for a divorce? For the loss of your spouse?*

• *Do you know where the family records are located?*

• *How would you handle a windfall?*

Epilogue

Passing It On

It is our hope that this book has not only helped you and your family understand and take control of your finances but that it has also shown you the benefits of ongoing, honest discussions. Hopefully you have invested in your personal dreams, your children, and your retirement; made sure that your parents and their futures are adequately provided for; created an insurance safety net to protect yourself and your family against any downturns; and drawn up an estate plan to ensure your legacy.

Now there is one other area we would like you to explore. Having learned how to take care of yourself and your family, you may be in a position to reach out and take care of others. You may do so not only by sharing your money and your time but by passing on your knowledge.

Not long ago *Newsweek* published a wonderful first-person essay by a doctor who recalled his father's nightly dinnertime question. "What have you done for someone today?" he would ask each of his children, thereby stressing not only that such altruism was important but that such acts were part of the daily business of living. Like this doctor's father, we encourage you to think of charitable giving, volunteerism, and educating your peers and associates about money and investing as an integral part of your life.

Remember those family conversations about the dreams that drive your financial plan? The same sorts of discussions can guide your charitable giving. Then you were planning your future and your family's. Now just let yourself imagine how you can improve the lives of others.

Even before you calculate how much you can afford, ask yourself what you want your money to accomplish. Your answers will reflect what's important to you, and those values will dictate where—as well as how much—you give. Once you've decided that, check to see if your employer has a matching program; clearly your dollar will go a lot further with this supplement.

Don't forget to discuss your contributions with your children. If you plant the seed early, there's a much better chance that giving will be a part of their future. Since kids learn best through experience, you'll want to do more than talk (although that's certainly a great start). For example, you can set a family philanthropic goal and then engage in a series of family fund-raising activities. You might even place money in a charitable trust and involve your children in how the money is distributed. At the very least, ask your kids (no matter how old they are) to identify those causes they want to support, and get them to donate even a small amount on a regular basis. Like saving and investing, charitable giving should become a habit rather than an occasional inspiration.

Philanthropy, however, is not limited to giving dollars and cents. The sharing of one's time, energy, and passion can leave an equally enduring mark on the world. And you'll likely find that volunteerism brings you far more than you give: an increase in your sense of personal value and strength that results from contributing and feeling needed, as well as the perspective on life that comes from getting outside of yourself.

Change happens one person—and one family—at a time. To make sure that your family becomes involved, you'll want to include every member in your discussions about where to devote your efforts, and you'll want to encourage your children to become involved in their own volunteering activities. You can make volunteering a family affair by finding a cause in which you can all participate together. If you can't find such an organized effort in your area, start your own. That's what one group in California did. Now, once a year they gather to complete a new project. They've repaired, painted, and landscaped schools; cleaned and replanted parks and neighborhoods; and fixed up old homes and community centers. That kind of labor not only makes a difference in the lives of others, it cements humanitarian values while engaging in a process that will bond your family even more tightly.

Of course, giving—whether of time or money—relies on having achieved enough financial security to indulge in worrying about someone outside your immediate family. In addition, we encourage you to share your wealth of knowledge with others—to take the lead in passing on what you know about money and investing with your friends, your colleagues and neighbors, and all those around you—in effect, to establish a legacy of a different kind. Help others to make financial dialogue a priority, so that they too can achieve financial independence and freedom of choice.

In short, kick money out of the closet each and every time you can. In so doing, you not only help cultivate a new generation of confident investors, you also start a secondary chain of events. Taking care of yourself financially gives you the option to feed your soul by taking care of those around you. Sharing your know-how not only allows others to better their lot in life, it gives them the choice to reach out and touch those around them as well—by giving their time, money, and knowledge.

And that's quite an impact.

Appendix A

Getting Organized

The quickest way to stop feeling overwhelmed by your paperwork, no matter how daunting it may seem right now, is to sort it out into categories that make sense to you. As you go along, make sure you note any files that seem skimpy or downright empty. If you've got little to nothing in the insurance or retirement folder, that should trigger a discussion about attending to this obvious omission.

Whether you store all this paperwork in a file cabinet or in a series of marked boxes or labeled accordion files, here are the major category headings and the files that go under (or into) them:

Bank Accounts
- Checking
- Savings

(Keep account statements for three years. Hold on to canceled checks for tax-deductible items for seven years.)

Investments
- Taxable accounts
- Children's accounts

(Hold on to annual statements and trade confirmations, so you'll know how much you actually paid for the stock when it comes time to figure out your cost basis.)

Retirement
• Brokerage accounts *(your 401(k), 403(b), IRA, SEP-IRA, Keogh, etc.)*
• Pension fund
• Social Security

Home Sweet Home
• Title or deed to your home
• Final settlement statement *(You'll need this paper, which you received upon the close of escrow, should you decide to sell.)*
• Mortgage payments
• Home improvement receipts *(Those will eventually be added to the value of your home.)*
• Lease *(if you rent instead of own)*
• Security deposit receipt
• Rent payment receipts or canceled checks

Insurance
• Health insurance policy
• Life insurance policy
• Disability insurance policy
• Long-term care policy
• Car insurance policy
• Homeowner's/renter's insurance policy
• Umbrella insurance policy
• Any other insurance policy you might have

Taxes
• Current year's tax return
• Last three years' tax returns, along with backup receipts *(Although you don't need to keep your backup material more than three years,*

you should hold on to your tax returns for seven. To be on the safe side, and to make things easy on yourself, you might consider simply stashing the return, along with the corresponding backup, for years four, five, six, and seven, in deep storage.)

Debt
- Credit card statements
- Car loan statements and paperwork
- College loan statements
- Personal loan papers

Wills and Trusts
- A current copy of your will
- A current copy of your living trust
- Durable powers of attorney for finances and health care

(Include contact information or a business card for the attorney who drafted any of these legal documents.)

Personal
- Birth certificate
- Marriage certificate
- Passport
- Prenup
- Divorce decree

Appendix B

Bibliography

Adams, Jane. *I'm Still Your Mother: How to Get Along with Your Grown-Up Children for the Rest of Your Life*. New York: Delta Trade Paperbacks, 1994.

Belsky, Gary, and Thomas Gilovich. *Why Smart People Make Big Money Mistakes*. New York: Simon & Schuster, 1999.

Collins, Victoria, Ph.D., CFP. *Best Intentions: Ensuring That Your Estate Plan Delivers Both Wealth and Wisdom*. Chicago, Ill.: Dearborn, 2002.

Ealy, Dr. C. Diane, and Dr. Kay Lesh. *Our Money Ourselves: Redesigning Your Relationship to Money*. New York: American Management Association, 1998.

Estess, Patricia Schiff. *Money Advice for Your Successful Remarriage: Handling Delicate Financial Issues with Love and Understanding*. Cincinnati, Ohio: Betterway Books, 1996.

Estess, Patricia Schiff, and Irving Barocas. *Kids, Money and Values*. Cincinnati, Ohio: Betterway Books, 1994.

Gillick, Dr. Muriel. *Lifelines: Living Longer, Growing Frail, Taking Heart*. New York: W. W. Norton & Co., 2000.

Glink, Ilyce. *100 Questions Every First-Time Home Buyer Should Ask*. New York: Times Books, 2000.

Godfrey, Neale S. *Ultimate Kids' Money Book*. New York: Simon & Schuster Books for Young Readers, 1998.

Kaplan, Ben. *How to Go to College Almost for Free*. New York: HarperCollins, 2001.

Mellan, Olivia. *Money Harmony: Resolving Money Conflicts in Your Life and Relationships*. New York: Walker & Co., 1995.

Mellan, Olivia, and Sherry Christie. *Overcoming Overspending: A Winning Plan for Spenders and Their Partners*. New York: Walker & Co., 1995.

————. *Money Shy to Money Sure: A Woman's Road Map to Financial Well-Being*. New York: Walker & Co., 2001.

Millman, Marcia. *Warm Hearts and Cold Cash: The Intimate Dynamics of Families and Money*. New York: Free Press, 1991.

Morris, Virginia. *How to Care for Aging Parents*. New York: Workman, 1996.

Otfinoski, Steve. *The Kids' Guide to Money: Earning It, Saving It, Spending It, Growing It, Sharing It*. New York: Scholastic, 1996.

Pearl, Jayne A. *Kids and Money: Giving Them the Savvy to Succeed Financially*. Princeton, N.J.: Bloomberg Press, 1999.

Richards, Susan C., CFP. *Protect Your Parents and Their Financial Health . . . Talk with Them Before It's Too Late*. Chicago, Ill.: Dearborn Financial Publishing, 1999.

Schwab, Charles R. *You're Fifty—Now What? Investing for the Second Half of Your Life*. New York: Three Rivers Press, 2002.

Smith, J. Walker, and Ann Clurman. *Rocking the Ages: The Yankelovich Report on Generational Marketing*. New York: HarperBusiness, 1997.

Tannen, Deborah. *I Only Say This Because I Love You: How the Way We Talk Can Make or Break Family Relationships Throughout Our Lives*. New York: Random House, 2001.

————. *You Just Don't Understand: Women and Men in Conversation*. New York: Quill, 2001.

Appendix C

Glossary of Investing Terms

actively managed fund. A mutual fund in which individual stocks, bonds, and/or cash-equivalent investments are bought and sold based on research or other criteria used by fund managers. Actively managed mutual funds generally try to outperform the market.

administrator. A person named by the court to represent a deceased person's estate when there is no will, or the will did not name an executor, or the executor named in the will is unavailable or declines to serve. Also called a *personal representative*.

alternative minimum tax (AMT). A tax system devised to ensure that at least a minimum amount of tax is paid by high-income individuals and corporations.

annual report. A financial statement issued each year by a corporation or mutual fund. It lists assets, liabilities, and earnings, as well as some historical information. Each of the company's shareholders receives a copy of the annual report.

asset. A property that has monetary value, including personal assets (e.g., house, car, jewelry) and financial assets, such as savings and investments.

asset allocation. The process of dividing your money among the three types of asset classes: stocks, bonds, and cash-equivalents. You decide on this division based on your tolerance for risk and your time horizon.

asset class. One of the three major types of investments: stocks, bonds, and cash-equivalents.

attorney-in-fact. The person legally designated to act on your behalf through a *power of attorney* document.

back-end load. A sales charge on a mutual fund that is applied when you sell shares of the fund (as opposed to a *front-end load,* applied when you buy shares).

balanced fund. A mutual fund that attempts to produce the highest return, consistent with a low-risk investment strategy, from a mix of stocks, bonds, and cash-equivalents.

bear market. A declining market in which prices are falling for a sustained period of time.

beneficiary. The person or organization designated to receive the funds or other property from a trust, insurance policy, or retirement account.

blue chip stock. Generally speaking, the stock of a large, well-established company. Blue chip stocks typically offer less risk because of their solid track records.

bond. A type of investment that is similar to an IOU from a corporation or a municipal or federal government. You loan the borrower some money, and in return it promises to repay the full amount on a specific date and pay you interest in the meantime.

bond fund. A mutual fund that includes only bonds—typically corporate, municipal, or U.S. government bonds.

bond maturity. The lifetime of a bond, concluding when the final payment of that obligation is due.

bull market. A market in which prices rise for a sustained period of time.

bypass trust. A trust that is set up to bypass the surviving spouse's estate, thereby allowing full use of the applicable exemption amount for both spouses. Also known as a *credit shelter trust.*

capital gain. The profit you receive when you sell an investment for more than you paid for it. Capital gains are taxable income and must be reported to the IRS on your tax return.

capital gains distribution. A payment you receive when your mutual fund makes a profit by selling some of the securities in its portfolio. Capital gains distributions are usually made annually, often at the end of the calendar year.

capitalization. See *market capitalization.*

cash-equivalent. An investment that can easily be converted into cash, such as a *money market mutual fund* or a *Treasury bill.*

certificate of deposit (CD). An investment made with a financial institution in which a specified amount of money is deposited for a specific period of time, at a preset, fixed interest rate.

certified financial planner (CFP). A professional planner who has met the Certified Financial Planner Board of Standards' requirements in education, experience, and ethical conduct; passed a ten-hour comprehensive examination in investment, tax, estate, retirement, and insurance planning; and agreed to follow a code of ethics.

certified public accountant (CPA). A professional who specializes in accounting. He or she may also have earned a personal financial specialist, or PFS, designation from the American Institute of Certified Public Accountants.

charitable trust. A trust that you set up for a qualified charity so that you can leave all or part of your estate to that charity or nonprofit organization. A charitable trust can be a *living trust* or a *testamentary trust.* A charitable trust allows you to retain some interest in the asset in the form of either the income stream or the principal. You receive a tax benefit for the portion of the donated gift, allowing you to maximize the tax advantages of your giving.

chartered financial analyst (CFA). A financial analyst who has met certain standards of experience, knowledge, and conduct as determined by the Institute of Chartered Financial Analysts. The successful candidate must pass three examinations covering economics, security analysis, portfolio management, financial accounting, and standards of conduct.

common stock. Securities that represent an ownership interest in a company (as opposed to *preferred stock,* in which stockholders usually receive preferential treatment).

community property. A form of ownership between a husband and wife, available in Arizona, California, Idaho, New Mexico, Nevada, Texas, Washington, and Wisconsin. Laws vary from state to state, but the basic rule is that all property earned or acquired by each spouse during marriage (except for gifts or inheritances received by either spouse as his or her separate property) is treated as owned one-half by each spouse.

compounding. The growth that results from investment income being reinvested. Compound growth has a snowball effect because both the original investment and the income from that investment are invested.

concentrated equity position. Holding a large amount of one company's stock in your portfolio. A concentrated equity position is often due to company stock options, but it can also be the result of inherited stock or holding too much company stock in a 401(k) plan.

conservator. An individual appointed by the court to administer the affairs of an incapacitated adult.

Core & Explore™. Schwab's investment philosophy that strives to minimize a stock portfolio's risk of lagging the market, while increasing its probability of outperforming it. The C&E portfolio seeks to capture the benefits of holding a diversified Core of U.S. companies while retaining the potential of beating the market with high-quality, more specialized Explore holdings.

cost basis. The price you paid for an investment, as opposed to its current market value.

Coverdell education savings account (ESA). A tax-deferred account established to help pay the higher education expenses of a child, grandchild, or other designated beneficiary who is a minor.

credit shelter trust. See *bypass trust.*

death tax. Tax imposed on the property of a person who has died. Federal death taxes are generally called *estate taxes;* state death taxes are frequently called *inheritance taxes.*

defined benefit plan. An employer-sponsored retirement plan in which your employer alone funds your retirement plan and to which you don't contribute. These plans are open only to "vested" employees—those who have been employed for a certain time, typically between five and ten years. The amount you receive when you retire is calculated according to a formula that considers your salary and the length of your employment.

defined contribution plan. An employer-sponsored retirement plan in which you, your employer, or both of you contribute to your retirement account. Unlike defined benefit plans, these plans allow you, the employee, to have some say in how and where your money is invested. In some cases, the employee is responsible for all of those decisions. Defined contribution plans are very popular and include *401(k)s, 403(b)s,* and *ESOPs,* to name a few. You do not have to be vested to benefit from the plan.

designated beneficiary plan (pay-on-death account, transfer-on-death account, Totten trust). A plan that allows you to choose your beneficiaries and specify what percentage of your account assets will be left to each one. Assets passed in this way will avoid the probate process.

disability insurance. Insurance that replaces your income in the event an illness or injury prevents you from working.

diversification. Lowering risk potential by spreading money across and within different asset classes such as stocks, bonds, and cash-equivalents.

dividend. The part of the income earned by a company issuing stock that is distributed to shareholders. You can specify that your dividends be reinvested to buy more shares, or that they be paid to you in cash.

dollar-cost averaging. Investing the same dollar amount in the same securities at regular, scheduled intervals over the long term, with the aim of stabilizing your returns.

domestic stock mutual fund. A mutual fund that invests primarily in stocks issued by U.S. companies. These funds are classified according to size (*large cap, mid cap,* and *small cap*) and style (*growth* and *value*).

Dow Jones Industrial Average (DJIA or "the Dow"). A measure of the performance of a collection of thirty "blue chips"—primarily industrial stocks considered leaders in the market.

durable power of attorney. A power of attorney that remains in effect even if the person who has created it becomes incapacitated.

earnings. A company's net income or profit, usually quoted in millions of dollars.

earnings per share (EPS). A company's total earnings for a period (its net income minus preferred dividends), divided by the number of common shares outstanding.

equity. Another name for *stock,* representing ownership of a corporation.

ESOP (employee stock ownership plan). A company retirement plan that invests in and pays benefits in the form of company stock instead of cash.

estate plan. A document that establishes who will receive your property and possessions after your death. Its most common tools are wills and trusts.

estate tax. A transfer tax imposed on the value of property left at death; often called an *inheritance tax* or *death tax.*

executor. The person or institution named in a will who is responsible for the management of the assets and the ultimate transfer of the property; commonly referred to as a *personal representative.*

exemption amount. The amount of a person's assets that can be transferred free of tax, either during lifetime or at death.

expense ratio. For mutual funds, the percentage of a fund's average net assets that are used to pay fund expenses. This percentage accounts for management fees, administrative fees, and any *12b-1 fees.*

FDIC (Federal Deposit Insurance Corporation). A U.S. government agency that insures for up to $100,000 cash deposits (including certificates of deposit) that have been placed in member institutions.

fee-based management. A form of financial management in which the manager's fee is based on a percentage of assets under management, usually around 1% or 2%.

fixed-income investment. An investment that is similar to an IOU for borrowed money. Most such investments produce a steady stream of income in the form of interest payments. The borrower, called the *issuer,* can be a government—municipal, state, or federal—a corporation, or a bank or savings and loan.

foreign funds. A mutual fund that invests in developed markets outside the United States.

Form ADV. The standard form used by investment advisors to register and update registrations with the *SEC* and the jurisdictions that require advisors to register. The form is also used to comply with SEC Rule 206(4)-4, which obligates investment advisors to disclose material financial and disciplinary information to clients.

401(k) plan. A *defined contribution plan* in which your employer takes money directly from your salary and places it in a tax-deferred retirement account, which means that you don't pay taxes on this money until you retire or withdraw it. The decision about how and where the money is invested is usually yours. Employers often match your contributions, sometimes as high as dollar for dollar up to a certain percentage.

403(b) plan. Basically the equivalent of a *401(k) plan* in the world of charitable and nonprofit organizations, including educational institutions. Your contribution is deducted directly from your salary before taxes, and your employer can contribute.

front-end load. A sales charge on a mutual fund that is applied when you buy shares of the fund (as opposed to a *back-end load,* applied when you sell shares).

gift tax. A tax imposed on a transfer of property by gift during the donor's lifetime.

gift tax exclusion. A provision in federal law that permits you to make tax-free gifts of up to $11,000 (as of 2002) per individual each year. Married couples may jointly give tax-free gifts of up to double that amount.

grantor. See *trustor.*

growth and income fund. A mutual fund that seeks both capital appreciation (growth) and current income. Investments are selected based both on their appreciation potential and on their ability to pay dividends.

growth fund. A stock mutual fund that seeks long-term capital appreciation. Growth funds generally buy common stocks of companies that advisors believe have long-term growth potential.

growth stock. The stock of a company that has previously seen rapid growth in revenue or earnings and is expected to see similar growth beyond the short term. Generally speaking, growth stocks pay relatively low dividends and sell at a relatively high price, considering their earnings and book value.

guardian. The person who is legally responsible for the care and well-being of a minor (or in some states, of an incapacitated adult). Appointed by a court, the guardian is under court supervision.

index. A composite of companies that measures changes in market behavior. Well-known market indexes include the S&P 500 Index, the Dow Jones Industrial Average, and the Nasdaq Composite Index.

index fund. A mutual fund that seeks to track the performance of a market *index,* such as the S&P 500 Index, by investing in the stocks or other securities that make up that index.

inflation. An increase in the cost of living, measured as a percentage and classified according to its severity. Mild inflation occurs when the price level—an average of all prices—rises from 2% to 4%. Moderate inflation is an inflation rate of 5% to 9%. Severe inflation (or "double-digit" inflation) is inflation that threatens a country's economy, in which money loses its value and people turn to barter rather than relying on currency.

inheritance tax. State death taxes imposed on the property received by inheritance.

international stock fund. A mutual fund that invests in securities outside the United States. International stock funds include global funds, which invest in securities issued throughout the world (including the United States), and foreign funds, which invest in developed markets exclusively outside the United States.

inter vivos trust. See *living trust.*

intestate. Having made no valid will.

IRA (individual retirement account). A self-funded retirement plan (a plan that you, not your employer, establish and fund) that provides tax benefits. There are several different types of IRAs: *traditional IRA, rollover IRA, Roth IRA,* and *SEP-IRA.*

irrevocable trust. A legal agreement that is permanent and cannot be revoked or changed.

issue. In estate-planning language, your descendants: children, grandchildren, and so on.

issuer. The corporation, municipality, or government agency that issues a bond or security.

joint tenancy with right of survivorship. A form of joint ownership in which two or more individuals own an interest in the same property. At the death of one individual, ownership of the decedent's share transfers equally to the surviving owners. Assets transferred in this way avoid probate.

Keogh plan. An employer-sponsored retirement plan for a partnership (or for a sole proprietorship for self-employed people). A Keogh requires significantly more paperwork than an IRA, and it's more complex to understand and manage.

laddering. A strategy in which you buy bonds (or Treasury notes) with increasing maturities that are staggered so that the interest gives you a steady stream of income.

large-cap stock. The stock of a company whose median market capitalization is in the top 5% of the largest domestic companies. A large-cap mutual fund is a mutual fund that invests only in large-cap stocks.

life insurance trust. An irrevocable trust that is generally established for the purpose of excluding life insurance proceeds from the estate of the insured and the spouse of the insured for death tax purposes.

limited power of attorney. A legal document in which an investor gives a third party, usually an investment manager or financial institution, the authority to trade on his or her behalf but limits the ability to transfer assets out of the investment account.

liquid investment. An investment that can be easily converted to cash.

living trust. A trust that is set up while a person is alive. Also known as an *inter vivos trust,* it can be revocable or irrevocable.

living will. A document in which a person states that they do not want to have their life prolonged by technical assistance.

load. A commission or sales fee charged on a mutual fund. A mutual fund without a load is a *no-load fund.*

long-term care insurance. Insurance that covers some or all of the expenses a person incurs as a result of required long-term care.

lump-sum distribution. An amount of money received (say, from a pension plan or divorce) all at once rather than in periodic payments.

market capitalization. The total value of a company's stock, as calculated by multiplying the number of outstanding shares by the price per share.

maturity date. In a fixed-income investment, the specified date at which the issuer promises to repay the money it has borrowed.

Medicare. Federally funded health insurance available to all people over age 65 and to younger people with disabilities or other medical conditions.

Medigap. An insurance plan designed to supplement Medicare. These plans are sold by private insurance companies (not by the government), and they cover some of the things that Medicare doesn't.

mid-cap stock. The stock of a company whose market capitalization falls between *large cap* (top 5%) and *small cap* (bottom 80%).

money market mutual fund. A mutual fund that invests solely in securities that can easily be turned into cash, such as *Treasury bills, certificates of deposit (CD),* and short-term loans. Money market funds are designed to maintain a stable $1 share value, but there is no assurance that they will be able to do that.

municipal bond (or "muni"). A debt security issued by a state or local government or one of its agencies. Munis typically pay interest at a fixed rate twice a year, and the issuer promises to return the principal at maturity. In general, interest paid on municipal bonds is exempt from federal taxes.

mutual fund. A type of investment that pools the money of many investors to buy various securities, including stocks, bonds, and/or cash-equivalents. Mutual funds can offer diversification and professional management within a single investment.

Nasdaq. Acronym for the National Association of Securities Dealers Automated Quotation System.

net asset value (NAV). The market value of a single share of a mutual fund. It is calculated at the end of each business day by adding up the value of all the securities in the fund's portfolio, subtracting expenses, and dividing the sum by the number of shares outstanding. Mutual funds are traded based on their NAVs. Funds with an offer price identical to the NAV are either *no-load,* or they are *load* funds carrying a contingent deferred sales charge.

net profit. The remaining profit on an investment once you've deducted all expenses.

net worth. The value of your estate, which you calculate by subtracting what you owe (your liabilities) from what you own (your assets). Your net worth is your estate's taxable value.

no-load fund. A mutual fund that does not carry a sales charge or commission. The initials NL in the offer price column of a mutual fund table mean that the fund is no-load, so you can buy and sell its shares at the price listed in the NAV (net asset value) column.

operating expense ratio (OER). A mutual fund's annual expenses (operating expenses, management fees, and *12b-1 fees,* if any) expressed as a percentage of the fund's average net assets. These expenses are deducted before calculating the fund's NAV.

operating expenses. Costs incurred by a mutual fund in its day-to-day operations. Every fund is subject to some degree of operating expenses, which usually include management fees, annual fees, administrative costs, and maintenance fees.

own occupation coverage. In disability insurance, a choice that specifies that you will be paid if you can't do the work you currently do, not just any work.

P/E ratio (price/earnings ratio). A measurement that represents the relationship between the price of a company's stock and its earnings for the past year. To get a company's P/E, divide its current price by its *earnings per share (EPS)* for the past year.

personal representative. See *executor.*

portfolio. The combined stock, bond, and cash-equivalent investments held by an individual investor, a mutual fund, or a financial institution.

portfolio manager. The person in charge of managing a mutual fund's holdings.

pour-over will. A will that is used in conjunction with a revocable living trust to "pour over" any assets that are not transferred to the trust prior to the trustor's death.

preferred stock. A class of stock that has a claim on the company's earnings before payment is made on the common stock if the company declares a dividend.

principal. Funds put up by an investor to purchase a security. For bond investing, the principal is the face amount of a bond. For example, the principal amount of a $10,000 bond is $10,000.

probate. A court process that validates a person's will and oversees the distribution of assets subject to the terms of the will.

prospectus. A legal document that describes a mutual fund and offers its shares for sale. It contains information required by the *SEC* and state securities regulators, including the fund's investment objectives and policies, investment restrictions, fees and expenses, and how shares can be bought and sold. Every mutual fund is required to publish a prospectus and provide it to investors free of charge.

qualified domestic trust (QDOT). A trust used to postpone estate taxes when one spouse leaves property to a noncitizen spouse.

qualified terminable interest property (QTIP) trust. A marital trust with property left for the use of the surviving spouse as life beneficiary.

registered representative. An employee or partner in a brokerage firm who is registered to handle customer accounts. A registered representative must pass an examination administered by the National Association of Securities Dealers (NASD).

reinvest. To use dividends from an investment to buy more shares of that investment.

REIT (real estate investment trust). A company that purchases and manages real estate or real estate loans, using money invested by its shareholders.

retirement plan distribution. A withdrawal of funds from a retirement plan.

revocable trust. A trust plan that gives the trustor the power to alter the trust terms or revoke the trust.

rollover IRA. A transfer of assets from a qualified plan to an IRA without tax. If you change jobs, retire, or get a divorce settlement that includes a distribution from a company retirement plan, you can "roll it over" into an IRA to preserve your capital and keep its tax-deferred status.

Roth IRA. A tax-deferred retirement plan to which your contributions are not deductible, but if you meet certain qualifications, your withdrawals—including interest—are without tax.

SEC. The Securities and Exchange Commission.

securities. Stocks that signify ownership interest in a company, or bonds that indicate a credit relationship with a borrower, such as a company or government agency. Some other types of securities are options, warrants, and mutual funds.

SEP-IRA (Simplified Employee Pension—Individual Retirement Account). An alternative pension for those who are self-employed or who own a small business with employees.

settlor. See *trustor.*

share. A unit of ownership in company stock or in a mutual fund investment.

small-cap stock. The stock of a company with a relatively small total market value, meaning a median market capitalization in the lower 80% of the largest domestic companies.

Standard & Poor's 500 (S&P 500) Index. A well-known capitalization-weighted index consisting of five hundred of the most widely traded U.S. companies that are listed on the New York Stock Exchange (NYSE) or the American Stock Exchange (AMEX).

stock. An investment that represents a share of equity ownership in a company.

STRIP (separate trading of registered interest and principal) security. A Treasury *zero-coupon bond,* which doesn't pay interest until maturity. You purchase STRIPs from a brokerage firm.

successor trustee. A trustee who takes over when the current trustee resigns, becomes incapacitated, or dies.

tenancy-in-common. A form of joint ownership in which two or more persons own interest in the same property. At the death of a tenant-in-common, ownership transfers to that person's designated beneficiaries or heirs, not to the other joint owners.

term life insurance. A type of life insurance that is in effect for a specified period, usually a five-, ten-, fifteen-, or thirty-year term.

testamentary trust. A trust that becomes effective at your death through the probate of your will.

traditional IRA. An IRA to which you can contribute up to $3,000 a year if you qualify, which you do if you or your spouse is employed.

Married couples that file jointly may contribute up to $3,000 to each spouse's IRA for a total of $6,000 annually, even if one is a nonworking spouse, provided combined contributions do not exceed combined compensation. That money then grows tax-deferred until you withdraw it, which you can do without penalty after the age of 59½. You have complete control over what you invest your money in.

Treasury; Treasury bill (T-bill), note, or bond. Securities issued by the U.S. government. T-bills are short-term obligations that mature in one year or less; Treasury notes mature between one and ten years; Treasury bonds are long-term (ten- to thirty-year) obligations.

trust. A legal arrangement in which one person (the *trustor*) transfers legal title to property to a trust and names a fiduciary (the *trustee*) to manage the property for the benefit of a person or institution (the *beneficiary*).

trustee. The person or institution (corporate trustee) who manages a trust and trust property according to the instructions in the trust agreement and any applicable laws.

trustor. The individual who establishes a trust; also referred to as the *settlor* or the *grantor*.

12b-1 fee. An annual fee assessed by some mutual funds to cover the costs of marketing and distribution, as a percentage of the fund's total assets. For a fund to be considered no-load, its 12b-1 fee must be 0.25% or lower.

unlimited marital deduction. A gift and estate tax deduction that is available for transfers between spouses, either during lifetime or at death; under federal law there is a complete interspousal exemption.

value fund. A mutual fund that invests in companies whose assets are considered undervalued or in companies that have turnaround opportunities, with lower P/E ratios.

volatility. The magnitude and frequency of changes in securities' values. The more volatile an investment, the higher its risk and return potential.

will. A legally binding document directing the disposition of one's property, which is not operative until death and can be revoked up to the time of death, or until there is a loss of mental capacity to make a valid will.

zero-coupon bond ("zero"). A bond that does not pay interest until maturity. A zero is sold at a discount from its face value, and its value increases as it nears maturity. Your return comes from the appreciation. There are three types of zeros: corporate, municipal, and Treasury.

Index

ABOUT THE AUTHORS

Carrie Schwab-Pomerantz is the president of the Charles Schwab Corporation Foundation. She founded and now spearheads Schwab's Women's Investing Network, the company's initiative designed to educate and inspire women investors across America. A registered stockbroker for the last two decades, she graduated from the University of California, Berkeley, with a bachelor's degree in political science, and later earned an M.B.A. from George Washington University. She serves on the American Red Cross's advisory council of executives and also as an advisory board member for Cool Girls, Inc., an Atlanta-based mentoring and after-school program for low-income girls. She and her husband, journalist and author Gary M. Pomerantz, live near San Francisco with their three children.

Charles R. Schwab is the founder, chairman of the board, and co-CEO of the Charles Schwab Corporation, which is one of the nation's largest financial services firms (www.schwab.com). He is a member of the board of trustees of Stanford University, where he earned his B.A. in economics and his M.B.A. from the Graduate School of Business. Author of the bestselling *Charles Schwab's Guide to Financial Independence* and *You're Fifty—Now What?,* he is also the founder and chairman of the Schwab Foundation for Learning, a nonprofit agency providing support and guidance for parents of children with learning difficulties, as well as chairman of All Kinds of Minds Institute, a nonprofit institute dedicated to the understanding of differences in learning. He is the father of five children and lives with his wife, Helen, in the San Francisco Bay area.

Also by Charles R. Schwab:

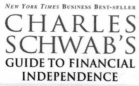

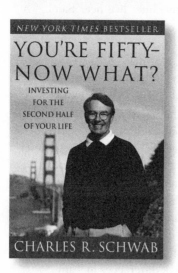

NEW YORK TIMES BESTSELLER

CHARLES SCHWAB'S GUIDE TO FINANCIAL INDEPENDENCE
0-609-80272-0
$12.00 paperback

Do you know where you want your investments to take you but not how to get there? This book is the answer. It's like having the founder of a $350 billion brokerage firm sit at your kitchen table and distill his 40-plus years of wisdom in a one-on-one session with you.

YOU'RE FIFTY—NOW WHAT?
0-609-80870-2
$14.00 paperback

If you are among the millions of Americans who recently have turned fifty or will soon, this is the book for you. *In You're Fifty—Now What?*, one of the most trusted and respected names in the financial services field offers you valuable advice for retiring with the money you'll need to have the kind of life you want.

THREE RIVERS PRESS • NEW YORK